BUSINESS

Robert W. Bignold

BUSINESS BY THE SPIRIT
Copyright © 2008 Robert W. Bignold
First Edition Printing 2016
Second Edition Printing 2019

All rights reserved. This book is protected by the copyright laws of the United States of America. No part of this publication may be reproduced, stored in a retrieval system, or transmitted in any form or by any means, (electronic, photocopy, recording) without the prior written permission of the Estate of Robert W. Bignold.

The use of short quotations or occasional page copying for personal or group study is permitted and encouraged. Permission will be granted upon request.

ISBN: 9781793820839

For worldwide distribution, printed in the U.S.A.

BUSINESS BY THE SPIRIT
Copyrighted © 2008 Robert W. Bignold
Unless otherwise noted, all Scripture quotations are from the Spirit Filled Life Bible, New King James Version, Copyright © 1991 by Thomas Nelson, Inc.

Second Edition *Business by The Spirit*
Edited by: Robin R. Robbins
RRR Consulting & Publishing
www.robinrobbins.com

Please note that our publishing style capitalizes certain pronouns referring to the Father, Son, And Holy Spirit, He, Him, the Word, the Cross, and may differ from other publisher's styles and new Bible translations. To standardize Scripture content, all that have been used were directly taken from biblegateway.com Scriptures quoted and the translation or version are identified by acronym as follows:

Scripture quotations noted, NLT are from the Holy Bible, New Living Translation, Copyright © 1996 by Tyndale Charitable Trust.

Scripture quotations noted, MSG are from The Message, Copyright © 1993, 1994, 1995, 1996, 2000, 2001, 2002, by Eugene H. Peterson.

Scripture quotations noted, TLB are from the Living Bible copyright © 1971 by Tyndale House Publishers.

Scriptures quotations noted, AMP are from the Amplified Bible, Copyright © 1954, 1958, 1962, 1964, 1965, 1987 by the Lockman Foundation.

Table of Contents

About The Author Robert W. Bignold	6
Introduction To Business By The Spirit	8
Introduction To Part I: Getting Started In The Spirit	16
Chapter 1: Learning Spiritual Principles In The College Of Hard Knocks	19
Chapter 2: When You Experience A Setback, Don't Blame God	30
Chapter 3: Disciplining Your Mind And Body For Success	38
Chapter 4: The Secular World Uses Biblical Principles To Succeed	46
Chapter 5: Overcoming Fear	54
Chapter 6: Beware Of New Age Mind Science Teaching	72
Introduction To Part II: Understanding The World We Live In	80
Chapter 7: The Issues Of Life	82
Chapter 8: The Purpose Of Prosperity	99
Chapter 9: Understanding The World We Live In	105
Chapter 10: Abraham's Blessings Are Yours	121
Introduction To Part III: Understanding The Laws Of The Kingdom	137
Chapter 11: Our Lives Are Governed By Laws	139
Chapter 12: The Law Of Success	143
Chapter 13: The Law Of Seedtime And Harvest	147
Chapter 14: The Law Of Giving And Receiving	154
Chapter 15: The Law Of Love	165
Chapter 16: The Law Of Faith	177
Chapter 17: Hope Is A Partner To Your Faith	193
Introduction To Part IV: Doing Business By The Spirit	200
Chapter 18: Fighting The Good Fight Of Faith	204
Your Confession Must Be Consistant	210
Chapter 19: Spiritual Authority In The Area Of Finances	213
Chapter 20: Activating The Angels	226
Chapter 21: Business As The Spirit Wills	236
Chapter 22: Hearing The Holy Spirit In Business	250
Introduction To Part V: Developing Wisdom For Wealth	264
Chapter 23: Know The Condition Of Your Finances	266
Chapter 24: Getting Started Right In Life And Business	283
Chapter 25: Investing For A Bountiful Harvest	298
Introduction To Part VI: Life's Most Important Issue Life After Death	322
Chapter 26: Dealing With The Most Important Issue Of Life	325
I Remember Bob	338
Letter To The Fellowship: Barbara Bignold	338
Words From The Lord In July 2016	342

About the Author Robert W. Bignold

Robert W. Bignold was the Owner and President of the *"ORB Organization"* a successful Seattle Based Architectural, Planning and Engineering firm, from 1967 until he sold the firm in 2006. He continued working as a consultant to his former company, where he acted as the design manager on a $120 million dollar project they were designing for the Corps of Engineers in Fairbanks, Alaska. He was also the owner of Renton West, Inc., a real estate investment firm.

Mr. Bignold graduated from Washington State University with a Bachelor of Science degree in Architectural Engineering. Following graduation from the University, he was commissioned an officer in the U.S. Army and served two years with the 76th Engineering Construction Battalion in the Nation of Korea. Mr. Bignold rose to the rank of captain before leaving the Army for civilian life.

He was a former International Director of Full Gospel Business Men's Fellowship International and served as National President of the Full Gospel Business Men's Fellowship in America until his passing.

Robert was a dynamic teacher, speaker, and writer whose goal was to mentor young businessmen and women, sharing the spiritual business principles he had learned during his thirty years of experience as a Christian businessman, as well as helping them to travel regularly to various nations of the world ministering in the Word and the Spirit. In past several years, Bob taught *Business by the Spirit* in the nations of Russia, Uganda, Nigeria, Guatemala, Costa Rica, Japan, Taiwan, Canada, and the United States. He also spoke in churches and business groups in England, Wales, and Germany. Bob believed that the marketplace is full of men and women who have the gifts of God within them but don't recognize their gifts, including those who recognize their gifts but are often hindered from using them because of the ecclesiastical mentality of the western church.

Bob's goal was to help those individuals find their gifts, train them to apply the spiritual business and ministry principles he had learned, and to release their gifts and change the world they live in. It was his desire that every man and woman of God learn how to live a successful life through the application of the Word and the Spirit in their lives.

INTRODUCTION TO BUSINESS BY THE SPIRIT

"... If you have faith as a mustard seed, you will say to this mountain, 'Move from here to there,' and it will move; and nothing will be impossible to you" (Matthew 17:20).

Think about the above statement for a moment! Jesus said, "If you have faith as small as a mustard seed nothing will be impossible to you!" Faith is the only way that you and I can receive anything from God, except through a manifestation of the *gifts of the Spirit*. Faith will work for you anytime, but the gifts of the Spirit operate only as the Spirit wills, not according to your wishes or your desires. In the above scripture we are talking about the "God kind of faith"--the kind that God gives to believers when they are born again (Romans 12:3). Understanding the "God kind of faith" and how to develop it, should become the most important quest of any businessperson desiring assistance from the Creator.

FAITH IS OFTEN CONSIDERED ONLY IN A RELIGIOUS CONTEXT

Faith is often thought of only in a religious context, but there is a natural human faith which is available to anyone desiring to achieve success in life. Faith is simply the ability to see something presently not yet visible, as clearly as if it were already visible and available for our use. "Now faith is the substance of things hoped for, the evidence of things not seen" (Hebrews 11:1). Another translation says, "What is faith? Faith gives substance to our hope" The free enterprise system is built upon faith; anyone who wishes to participate in that system has to be willing to work first and then 'hope' for a reward. Nothing is assured, as every task we undertake contains risk.

Successful people working in the free enterprise system must have faith that they will succeed; even those who are not believers exercise faith - faith in the system and in their ability to succeed in that system. How much more should believers have faith in their ability to succeed when they have the Creator of the universe backing them?

EVERY SUCCESSFUL BUSINESSMAN EXERCISES FAITH

In order to function effectively in the business world, one must exercise faith! A home builder exercises faith when he builds and markets a home. First, he must find a suitable piece of property, and then he must obtain government permission to sub-divide and develop the property. Next, he must build roads, install water, sewer, power, natural gas and make a myriad of other improvements before he can even start building a home. Then he must obtain a design for the home, order the materials and engage a number of different sub-contractors in order to properly complete the construction of his homes. He might work for months or even years before he is able to sell a single house. And then again he might not sell his homes for the price he needs to make a profit.

THE WORLD REWARDS THOSE WHO SEE WITH THE EYES OF FAITH

The world in which we live is designed in such a way that the ability to see things that are not yet visible as clearly as if they were visible and available for our use is rewarded. Over the years I have applied the "Spiritual Law" described in Matthew 17:20 to move seemingly impossible mountains that had arisen in my business. But because of my lack of understanding, I did not make this and other spiritual principles a part of my daily business life until very late in my business career. You see, I generally viewed these spiritual principles as life preservers which were available to help in the crisis situations that develop in life and business. It was only in the last few years of my business career that I understood that these principles were meant to become a way of life; they were to become a routine part of our daily business activities. I hope that by sharing my spiritual journey that you will be able to avoid some of the spiritual missteps which I have taken.

THE PURPOSE OF GODLY PROSPERITY IS TO EXPAND THE KINGDOM

The primary purpose for God prospering you is world evangelism; it is to fulfill the great commission. If you will learn to follow His Spirit, He will make you wealthy. God is not opposed to you being wealthy; instead He is opposed you being covetous. The Apostle Paul states that if we give bountifully, as we purpose in our heart, and not grudgingly or of necessity, then God is able to make all grace (the entire corporate power of heaven) abound toward us, so that we will always have enough to meet every need. He is able to make us rich in every way, so that we can be generous on every occasion. If you are willing and obedient, the Holy Spirit will lead *you*. He will expand your resources, and multiply your finances so that together with Him you can increase His kingdom on the earth. And one more thing--when God makes you wealthy, praise Him for it, but be careful to separate who you are from what you own. The eyes of the Lord go throughout the earth to find an obedient individual through whom He can funnel the silver and gold to advance His kingdom.

Some teach that we can use faith to produce whatever we need or want in life; all one needs to do is give into the offering plate, name the things for which we are believing (cars, house, boats, etc.), exercise our faith, and watch these things manifest in the physical world. This is not the biblical prosperity message; it is a hyper-prosperity gospel based on greed and selfish indulgence, taught by the new age and mind science religions. Unfortunately, some of these same teachings have found their way into the Christian church. Beware of such teaching; it distorts the biblical faith message and the New Testament prosperity principles.

GOD NEVER CHANGES!

The God of the twenty-first century is the same God that commanded Moses to part the Red Sea by stretching out his rod over the sea (Exodus 14:15-31). He is the same God that caused the walls of Jericho to collapse when Joshua and the Israelites acted in faith on God's word (Joshua 6:1-27). He is the same God that gave Jehoshaphat a dramatic victory against the combined power of three enemy nations--a victory against overwhelming odds, a victory he won without even drawing a sword. Jehoshaphat won the battle the same way we all do, by acting in faith. You see, he told his people, "Believe in the Lord your God, and you shall be established; believe His prophets, and you shall prosper" (2 Chronicles 20:1-30).

God says, "For I am the Lord; I do not change" (Malachi 3:6). He is the same God to you and me as he was to Moses, Joshua, Jehoshaphat, and a host of other men of faith that God has used throughout history to accomplish great physical feats of victory. You may be thinking that God selected these men and granted them victory because they were special; you may have thought that God blessed them because they were saints, men who had never messed up. No, the overwhelming majority of these biblical heroes were men like you and me! They were ordinary men, ranchers, fishermen, businessmen, military men, tax collectors and government leaders. Even more, most of these biblical heroes continued to work in their secular professions while they performed their work for the Lord.

THE OLD TESTAMENT HEROS OF FAITH SPENT TIME WITH GOD

The thing which set these men apart from their peers was that they spent time with God, meditating on his word, seeking to know His will. Moses spent forty days on the mountain receiving the Law of God (Exodus 24:1-18,). Joshua meditated upon the Word of God day and night, and did all that it required of him, and by doing so he made himself successful (Joshua 1:8-9). Jehoshaphat taught the Word of God to the people and brought reform to the nation of Judah (2 Chronicles 17:1-10). And when he was attacked by three godless kings, he humbled himself before the Lord, and his faith in God's Word defeated his enemies without his ever having to fight a battle. If you are not spending time in prayer and meditation in God's Word, you have no right to ask Him for help. Jesus said, "My people know My voice."

BUT THEY WERE HUMAN; THEY MADE MISTAKES

But all of these men were human; they made mistakes. Moses failed to speak to the rock to bring forth water as God had commanded him, and his disbelief prevented him from entering the promised land (Numbers 20:7-12). Joshua failed to seek the counsel of the Lord concerning the people of Gibeon

(Joshua 9:8-16), and his disobedience eventually brought disaster upon the Israelites (2 Samuel 21:1-6). Jehoshaphat allied himself with a wicked king, and his disobedience caused God to rebuke him (2 Chronicles 19: 1-3).

THE IMPORTANCE OF THE MANUFACTURER'S HANDBOOK

When we purchase a new piece of equipment for our business, we expect the firm that designed and manufactured the equipment to provide us with operating instructions, a manufacturer's handbook to familiarize us, and guide us in the operation of the equipment. Such a handbook describes the piece of equipment, gives the purpose of the equipment, and explains how to keep the equipment functioning properly as well as trouble shoot common problems that develop with the equipment. When serious problems occur not covered in the handbook's troubleshooting guide, it is often necessary that we consult directly with the manufacturer, but we need the handbook in order to obtain the phone number or address of the manufacturer. If the equipment were quite complex, it might even be necessary to have the manufacturer's representative instruct us in the use and care of the equipment. Most successful businessmen would never attempt to operate a new piece of equipment without first studying the manufacturer's handbook.

OUR MANUFACTURER'S HANDBOOK IS THE BIBLE!

Perhaps because I think with the systematic, structured mind of an engineer, the existence of the Bible seemed logical to me. If there is a God who dwells in a spiritual unseen world, who created something as vast and complex as our physical universe, and who made a physical being as intricate as a human being, surely he would give us a set of operating instructions to explain how His creation works, a Manufacturer's Handbook so to speak.

After I was born again, my engineering mind reasoned that if I wanted to determine the Manufacturer's plan and purpose for my life, I needed to study the Manufacturer's Handbook, or if you prefer the Creator's Handbook, the Bible. I found that in His handbook, God had provided a description of mankind, His purpose for mankind, and how to keep mankind operating properly. He also gave us pointers on how to trouble shoot common problems that develop in our lives, and when serious problems develop the Creator's Handbook tells us how to make contact with the Creator, our heavenly Father. The Creator's Handbook not only gives purpose and direction to our personal life, but to our business life as well. It instructs and guides us as to how to live a happy, healthy, prosperous life. I refer to the Bible as the Creator's Handbook often in this book because I want you to change the way you think about the Bible. I want you to begin to think of it as having been authored by our creator, the only being who is capable of guiding us to a proper understanding of our lives and the physical and spiritual worlds in which we live. When the Creator's Handbook teaches a principle that contradicts what you perceive with your physical senses, learn to accept and believe the Creator's Handbook.

THE CREATOR'S HANDBOOK IS LIKE A GOLD MINE

The handbook provided by the manufacturer of a new piece of equipment is written in the common language of our day, and it includes illustrations and photographs that make it easy to understand. On the other hand, some forty different "men of God," wrote the Bible as the Spirit of God inspired them. Furthermore, it was written over a period of approximately sixteen hundred years. The Bible manuscripts that we study today are translations of the original Hebrew and Greek texts. Since God knew the Bible would be used over a period of thousands of years, He had to describe the various human characteristics, and life and business principles, in a language that would transcend time. The Bible, therefore, is like a goldmine through which we have to dig to get to the gold. One of our problems is that Christians in general and Christian businesspeople specifically spend very little time digging for the "gold."

GOD WANTS TO BLESS HIS PEOPLE

God wants to make His people rich, and He promised that He would add no sorrow to their riches (Proverbs 10:22), but in order for Him to fulfill his promise to you and me, we like the biblical heroes of old, must spend time with God. We must meditate on his word day and night, and we must act on His word in faith. Therefore, it behooves every Christian businessperson to make the development of faith in the integrity of God's Word, their highest priority. This is the goal of this book: to share with you the secret things of the kingdom of God. They are not secrets because they are hidden; they are secrets because they are spiritually discerned.

INTRODUCTION TO PART I: GETTING STARTED IN THE SPIRIT

Doing "business by the Spirit" requires us to reprogram our minds, as one's mind is the doorway to his spirit and to the development of the God kind of faith—the kind of faith which is required to live a successful, prosperous and fulfilled Christian life. The Apostle Paul said it this way, "...let God transform you into a new person by changing the way you think." (Romans 12:2b NLT). God has given us His word to get our thinking straightened out.

The Creator's Handbook reveals a fascinating truth concerning the makeup of man that is unacceptable to the secular atheist world. It reveals that you and I are not physical beings; we are "eternal spirits" who have a soul (a mind, will and emotions) and live in a physical body. It further reveals that within the spirit of man dwells a spiritual sense, which lies largely dormant in most men and women. It is through this spiritual sense of faith that we contact the Creator and enlist His help in leading successful, fulfilled lives. By faith we see things that do not yet exist as clearly as if they **did** exist.

When you were born again, the Spirit of God moved into your spirit, and your "spirit man" (the real you) became a new creation, a new person who has a desire to believe God's Word and obey His voice; but your mind and your body did not change. Your mind was trained by your body's senses; it is carnal, it is body-ruled, it only believes what it sees, hears, feels, tastes and smells; and it is at odds with God's Word. As long as your thinking is at odds with God's Word, your believing will also be at odds with His Word, and it will cause you to speak negative, doubt-filled words, which will prevent you from receiving the promises of God.

In the opening chapters of this book, I share some of the difficulties which I and other business people experienced in transitioning from doing business according to worldly principles to doing business according to spiritual principles. We compare biblical success principles with secular success principles; and we emphasize the absolute necessity of disciplining your body and retraining your mind in order to purge your soul of the fear and negative emotions which are the primary cause of under achievement and failure in life. We also point out that God has given us absolute control over only **one** thing - our will - and we must exercise our will if we are to be successful in life. We must take control of our thoughts, and reprogram our minds with the Word of God so that we think like God thinks. He always believes victory and success, and so should you!

Since the new age human potential teachers have had so much to say concerning the power of the mind, many Christians have been reluctant to say or teach anything that deals with the mind, for fear of being associated with these mind science religions. But the Word of God has a great deal to say about the mind and its relationship to the body and spirit, and therefore we should not neglect its instruction on this very important subject.

I have also considered it necessary to include an entire chapter dealing with new age, success motivation books and seminars that accompany many secular business training courses. I have even observed these same books being sold by some Christian book sellers. Many immature Christians have also become innocently involved in reading these books and attending these seminars, thinking that they are Christian-based because they quote principals from the Christian - Judeo Bible, but unfortunately they generally mix these Christian principles with those of Buddhism, Hinduism, and other religious doctrines.

CHAPTER 1

CHAPTER 1
LEARNING SPIRITUAL PRINCIPLES IN THE COLLEGE OF HARD KNOCKS

"Beloved, I pray that you may prosper in all things and be in health, just as your soul prospers" (3 John 1:2).

GETTING STARTED IN BUSINESS

Starting a new business is challenging even in good economic times, but it was particularly difficult in the Pacific Northwest in the late sixties and early seventies. I went into business with two partners in the late 1960's. Just as we were getting the business on its feet, the area's largest employer, The Boeing Company, implemented a massive staff reduction, which plunged the Seattle area into a major recession. I recall a large billboard on the I-5 corridor just outside of the city which proclaimed, "The last person out of town turn off the lights." Times were tough, and I became consumed with the task of making my company successful. It seemed that I was traveling continually, attempting to obtain the new sales required to expand the company and keep our staff busy. Recently my sister gave me a *Seattle Times* newspaper article concerning my company that she had saved for thirty-seven years. The caption on the article declared "Some Make It Despite the Times." The article, dated November 23, 1971, by *Seattle Times* business columnist Boyd Burchard, reported that despite Seattle's difficult economic times, my company had not only survived, but had increased its sales by some seven hundred percent. Reading that article brought back memories of the difficulties we faced, as well as the long hours and hard work it took to overcome them and make the company successful.

BECOMING SPIRITUALLY MINDED

A little over three years later in the early part of 1975, I met Barbara, a lady who would later become my wife. She had grown up in a Christian family, and several years before we met, rededicated her life to Jesus Christ. When Barbara talked about the Lord, it reminded me of my mother, a born-again Christian who used to take me to church when I was a boy. About a year after we met, Barbara and I were married. When we returned from our honeymoon, I noticed a book entitled *Power and Praise* which had been left on our living room table by my new Methodist mother-in-law. As a result of reading that book for several months, faith developed in my heart, and I asked Jesus Christ to become my Lord and my Savior.

I continued to read the book, which discussed the baptism in the Holy Spirit for another seven months. One evening I also asked Jesus to baptize me in the Holy Spirit, an experience which radically changed my life. Several months later at my urging, Barbara also asked for and received the baptism in the Holy Spirit. At the time these changes were occurring in our lives, we were attending a mainline denominational church, and while there were no doubt people in that church who were born again and baptized in the Holy Spirit, none of them had ever talked to Barbara and me about either experience. Other than the fellow who wrote the book, we knew of no one else who had received the Baptism in the Spirit.

But several weeks later we heard about the Full Gospel Business Men's Fellowship, a group of successful business men who also believed in the gifts of the Holy Spirit. After making several inquiries we found that they met monthly in a prestigious downtown Seattle hotel. We began attending their meetings and found them to be exciting and alive; they were nothing like the typical church services that we were used to. There were no rituals, no religious doctrines—just men sharing their experiences of God. These men were so excited as they shared what God had done in their lives, not five years ago, not ten years ago, but just the previous week. They talked about a living God; some told how He had healed them, and others explained how He had blessed their business. Hearing how God was helping these men in their businesses got my attention; it had never occurred to me that God would help anyone be successful in business. I wanted to hear more; I could hardly wait until the next meeting!

DON'T BE INTIMIDATED

Shortly after we attended our first meeting of the Full Gospel Business Men's Fellowship, the chapter President Don Ostrom announced that the chapter was planning a mission's trip (they called them airlifts) to Europe in the fall of the year. He asked those who would like to go on that airlift to raise their hand, and I immediately raised mine. Then he asked those who wanted to go, but didn't have the finances, to stand while he prayed that God would provide the funds they required. Since money was no problem to me, I didn't stand; but inwardly I envied them because they had to exercise their faith to see God's provision. Several months after I made the decision to go on the airlift, several large projects which our firm was working on were delayed, and a month later we lost a large project which I had counted on to keep our people busy. For three months before the airlift, our firm was losing money. Since I usually brought in most of the new sales at that time, I was intimidated by the situation. I felt a lot of pressure to stay home, and try to obtain the necessary sales. But I had promised the Lord that I would go to

Europe, and I felt it important that I keep my promise to Him. At the time I left for Europe, we had people sitting around the office on make-work projects; my head was telling me I was crazy to go off to Europe when we needed new sales. But a week later when I called my office from Europe, I discovered that four sizable projects had been funded and our clients wanted us to get started with the design work immediately. I was so encouraged.

Several months after returning from Europe I was invited by a friend to a small Lutheran church near my home; a man from Texas, with a prophetic gift was speaking. Near the end of the meeting he paused and called me to the front of the room. He laid his hand on my head and began to prophesy. This was one of the first times I had experienced anything like this. He said *"My son, My son, you shall walk in the way of the Lord and you shall see things that many have seen, but they have turned aside under their devious ways. They have turned their backs on the ways of faith. They have been intimidated and have been pleasers of men, but you have said in your soul and in your spirit 'I shall walk with the Lord; I shall walk in the ways of my God.' Therefore saith God, I have given you a heart of Timothy, one that shall follow, and be instructed, and in due season shall find great and faithful works before thee."*

Then the Lord spoke through this man and named a number of things that He would accomplish in my life because I had refused to be intimidated. Now thirty years later, I realize that nearly all of the things which he prophesized have come to pass in my life. That prophetic word taught me that when you or I step out in faith and do something for God, the devil will often attempt to intimidate us. He will try to make us believe that we don't have enough faith, that God didn't hear our prayer, or that there is no God. He will do everything he can to prevent us from standing in faith on the Word of God. The devil will try to get us to abandon the work of God and take care of our own needs; and if we listen to his intimidating thoughts, he will soundly defeat us.

AS A YOUNG CHRISTIAN I HAD A RATHER UP AND DOWN EXPERIENCE

After I was born again and baptized in the Holy Spirit, it seemed that my spiritual eyes were opened. A few months earlier I wasn't even sure there **was** a God, but now I had an insatiable desire to spend time with Him and to learn more about Him. I still went into my office; I still managed my business, but it was no longer the primary focus of my life. Now I spent my evenings and free time reading the Bible and other spiritual books, and I had a hunger to learn all I could about the Lord and the Christian life. It was so exciting just to know that God was alive and find out that He loved me and wanted to bless me. However, I didn't understand how to receive those blessings, and, consequently, in the first several years as a Christian, I had a rather "up and down" spiritual experience. I didn't understand what faith was; I thought it was a mental activity. I would pray and ask God to help me win a certain project or to increase my company's profits; but when problems developed, and negative, defeating thoughts began to bombard my mind, I reasoned that I must not have faith. I became discouraged—I was fighting the fight of faith in my head, instead of in my heart and my mouth.

THE FIRST MAJOR FINANCIAL CRISIS

It was during a major financial crisis in my business life (over a period of three years my company had lost two thirds of our net worth), that I was forced to exercise the law of faith described in Mark 11:23. As a result of my applying that principle, God turned my business around and the following year we sold six times the amount of work which we had sold in any previous year. Within eighteen months, we gained back everything we had lost in the three years that we were in the financial test. As a result of that crisis I learned a very valuable spiritual principle, and over the years I have learned a number of other similar principles. The purpose of this book is to share these principles with you and other Christian business people, in hopes that it will prevent them from making the same mistakes I made.

LEARNING TO WALK BY FAITH

In the fall of 1984, some eight years after I first became a Christian, I sensed the Lord ask me to start chapters of the Full Gospel Business Men in the nation of Japan. I was the president of the Greater Seattle Chapter of the FGBM at the time; therefore, I asked Paul Crawford, a friend of mine who was going to be in the Orient in March of 1985, to return by way of Japan and make some contacts among Christian businessmen in that nation. Then in June of 1985 Paul and I toured Japan together. Finally, in October of the same year, we took a larger group of men and women from America and Canada to Japan, and began to organize Christian businessmen's chapters in that nation. At that time, I had never really considered what starting a Christian businessmen's organization in a nation like Japan meant in the economy of God, or the challenge it posed to the demonic rulers that had held sway over that nation for more than five thousand years. I was simply doing what I sensed God had told me to do.

Shortly after going to Japan, my business started experiencing some difficult financial problems. In 1986, we lost forty-five percent of our net worth. I really didn't make a connection between my efforts to establish a fellowship in Japan with my business problems; I just thought that we had a bad year and that it would get better the next year. But in 1987, it didn't get better; it got worse as we lost another twenty percent of our net worth. The next year (1988), my business continued to stagger along; we could barely make our payroll. Then in May of 1988, a man gave me a book entitled *War on the Saints*. As I read that book, I began to understand that my business problems were directly related to my doing God's work in Japan; but I still didn't know how to correct the problem.

IT TAKES MORE THAN PRAYER TO GAIN THE VICTORY

Now don't think I hadn't prayed about the problem; I prayed every day! I would wake up in the middle of the night and pray—in fact, I had been praying and asking God to help me for some two and a half years, but it takes more than prayer to get the job done. It takes *believing prayer*. And I, like many of you, didn't know how to pray believing prayer. But one thing I knew, something had to change or my company was going to go bankrupt. And another thing I knew, I was the one who had to change. Always remember this: God never changes (Malachi 3:6). If prayer isn't working, it's because you're not praying right; and it is you and not God who will have to change.

In the midst of my troubles, I decided to set aside some time to seek God for an answer. In fact, I sought him intensely for several days. Then the Lord began to speak to me about Mark 11:23: "For assuredly, I say to you, whoever says to this mountain, 'Be removed and be cast into the sea,' and does not doubt in his heart, but believes that those things he says will be done, he will have whatever he says." Now I was not ignorant of that scripture. I had heard men teach that what you believe in your heart and confess with your mouth would come to pass in your life, but on the other hand I had heard other men teach against that principle. They said believing that what you confess would come to pass was foolishness. Since I didn't know which group was right, I thought that I would just ignore that scripture. But you cannot ignore the word of God, particularly Mark 11:23. Like all spiritual laws, it will work in your life, either positively or negatively, whether or not you believe it. You may have said *"I don't believe that God will help me in my business,"* then you will have what you say—God will not help you in your business. You may have said *"nothing seems to go right in my life."* If you believe that in your heart and confess it with your mouth, then nothing will go right in your life. Mark 11:23 will work for you either positively or negatively whether you agree with it or not; it is a spiritual Law. "Death and life are in the power of the tongue, And those who love it will eat its fruit" (Proverbs 18:21).

BUT I DIDN'T KNOW THAT MARK 11:23 WOULD WORK FOR ME

Please understand that in 1988, when I began to seek God's wisdom concerning my business problems, I didn't know that Mark 11:23 would work for me. I had prayed and asked God to give us favor with our clients. I had asked God to help me in my business, but I had not yet acted on my conviction that God would help me. By this time, I had been a Christian for over ten years but I didn't understand that for God's Word to work, it had to be in my heart and in my mouth. I had experienced financial tests before, but now I was up against a bigger devil. Those principalities and powers that had ruled over the businessmen of Japan decided to teach me a lesson. They didn't like the prospect of Japanese businesspeople finding out about the love of Jesus. And God knew that I needed to grow in the principles of the Kingdom of God if I was to survive this financial attack on my business.

You see, in most instances the only way we can act on our faith is by speaking it. The Apostle Paul says "...take up the whole armor of God, that you may be able to withstand in the evil day, and having done all, to stand" (Ephesians 6:13). The evil day that Paul was talking about is the day that the devil comes to attack your family or your business, and one of those pieces of armor that Paul was talking about is the sword of the Spirit, which is the Word of God. That's why it is so important that we establish faith in our hearts by meditating upon the "Word of God." Remember, Mark 11:23 tells us, "If he believes that those things that he says will be done, he will have whatever he **says**."

I BEGAN TO SPEAK GOD'S WORD

In June of 1988, I began to act on Mark 11:23. I began to make what God's Word says about me and my business a part of my daily confession—a confession I repeated over and over every time I thought about my business: "*My business is prosperous and successful. I have given and it will be given unto me, good measure, pressed down, shaken together and running over; men will give unto me*" (based on Luke 6:38). "*I have given cheerfully; therefore God will make all grace abound toward me. The entire corporate power of heaven will be available to make sure that I will always have enough for every good work*" (based on 2 Corinthians 9:6-8). "*Devil you are a liar! The Word of God is truth absolute truth, and it will come to pass in my life.*" That is the way I confessed God's Word concerning my business. Over and over, every time I thought about my business problems, I would confess what God's Word said about those problems. When I would drive by a potential customer, I would say, *"In the name of Jesus, I command you to send prosperous work to the ORB Organization (my company's name)."* And the devil would come and sit on my shoulder and say, *"You are broke, flat out broke. How are you going to make your payroll next week?"* But I would reply, *"Devil, you are a liar! The Word of God is truth, absolute truth, and God will provide the money to pay my employees next week and the week after that and the week after that."*

THEN SUDDENLY THE ANSWER CAME!!!

You may ask, *How long did you confess the word of God before things changed, Bob?* I confessed the Word of God for nine long, hard months before I saw any change in the physical world. There were times when I wanted to give up; there were times when the devil would come and mock me for believing that confessing the Word of God with my mouth would change things. But I just kept on believing God and confessing His Word over my businesses. Then in February of 1989, our company was awarded the largest contract that we had ever received. And in quick succession, we were awarded a number of other contracts. In fact in 1989, we were awarded six times the amount of work we had been awarded in any previous year. Within eighteen months we had earned back everything that we had lost during the three years we were in the test.

When I first started to confess God's Word over my business, I really didn't believe that Word in my heart, and the adverse circumstances that had been pummeling my mind made it difficult for me to develop faith in my heart.

But gradually as I continued to confess God's Word, faith became **established** in my heart, and that faith caused my business to turn around. The battle had been long and hard. I had struggled with the financial problem for two and one half years before I understood Mark 11:23 would work for me, and then I had confessed God's word over the problem for nine long hard months before the victory was won. To tell you the truth, when the victory came I was emotionally exhausted; I remember praying *"Lord allow me a period of rest before the next big battle."*

After this experience I knew that Mark 11:23 would produce victory, but in my mind I classified the confession of God's Word as something we do when we get into a problem. I did not yet understand that when we meditate on God's Word day and night, we make ourselves successful. Like many of you, when the pressure was off, I neglected the confession of God's word.

CHAPTER 2
WHEN YOU EXPERIENCE A SETBACK, DON'T BLAME GOD

"Through wisdom a house is built, and by understanding it is established; by knowledge the rooms are filled with all precious and pleasant riches" (Proverbs 24: 3&4).
"A good name is to be chosen rather than great riches, Loving favor rather than silver and gold." (Proverbs 22:1).

THE MAN WHO REFUSED TO GIVE UP

Dave Soleim, a homebuilder friend of mine, became a born-again Christian when he was in his late thirties. At the time he became a Christian, he had been in the homebuilding business for a number of years, but he knew very little about the Bible or the Christian life. But he was excited about his new relationship with Jesus Christ. Dave was a generous man, and he naturally wanted to see the kingdom of God expand. Therefore, when he heard teaching concerning the law of giving and receiving, and heard other Christian business men testify as to how God had blessed them as they gave freely to the Lord's work, he also became a liberal giver. Although Dave hadn't spent that much time studying the Word of God, he began to hear a voice which he thought was God's, telling him to invest in a number of other businesses. In the next several years, in addition to his homebuilding business, Dave purchased an interest in six other businesses—businesses in which he had little or no experience: a car leasing agency, a land development company, a real estate company, a fishing boat company, a company that manufactured household games, and a sales and marketing company. Believing he was being directed by God, Dave made many of these decisions, contrary to the advice and judgment of his wife Jackie. One day God sent a mature Christian man to speak to Dave; he told Dave that it was not the voice of God he had been hearing, but of an evil, deceiving spirit that was misleading him and attempting destroy his Christian walk. Then he told Dave to burn the instructions he had received, and counseled him concerning the importance of testing every voice by the Word of God. He further counseled him that when making major business decisions, he and his wife should be in agreement.

Dave became involved in these multiple business activities in the volatile latter years of the 1970's, at a time when inflation in America was raging out of control. By the early 1980's, home mortgage interest rates had risen to eighteen percent, spelling disaster for his homebuilding business, and his home sales dropped to zero. Interest rates on his construction loans, the money he had borrowed from the bank to buy land and build houses, rose to twenty-four percent. At the same time, his ill-conceived investments in his other companies were also reeling under the burden of the high interest rates. Dave and his wife Jackie were in an impossible situation. They had a huge debt load, with seventy-five houses for sale in one area alone; their income was reduced to nothing. They owed the bankers more than twenty million dollars. Their friends and associates counseled bankruptcy, but Dave and his wife Jackie decided that they had to honor their debt. They did not want to give any reason for offense to their bankers and debtors by doing anything that would dishonor their Christian witness (2 Corinthians 6:3). Dave worked out a payment arrangement with his banker and other creditors that allowed him and his wife to reduce their debt to five hundred thousand dollars. It also allowed them, on a smaller scale, to continue building houses, and "tough it out" through the market downturn. After more than nine long, hard years of sacrifice and hard work, their debt was paid in full. As a witness to their Christian integrity, they still work with the same banker today.

While Dave was dealing with their business debt, Jackie was dealing with the creditors on the home front, threats of foreclosure on their home; just trying to find the money for food and clothing for their large family was a challenge. She would awaken in the middle of the night in a panic thinking, *What if we lose everything? How will we feed the children? What will become of us?* The spirit of fear moved in on Jackie's thought life like a dark thunder cloud. If her financial problems were not difficult enough, during this same period, Jackie's mother passed away, one of her best friends died of cancer, and her oldest daughter's fiancé was killed in a boating accident. Jackie wrestled with hopelessness and despair daily, her emotions in shambles.

At the time she was fighting to save their home from foreclosure, and just when it looked like they would lose it, a tax refund, or an unexpected insurance check would come along. However, what she had feared most finally happened—a sheriff's deputy nailed a foreclosure notice on the door of their home. Dave and Jackie lost their large home in an affluent neighborhood and were forced to move themselves and their children into a small house in the country. They sold what they could and cut back severely on living expenses. This couple who had always been givers now found themselves the recipients of their friends' charity, a bag of groceries on the porch, a twenty dollar bill on the kitchen counter—it all helped see them through this difficult period of their lives.

During this dark and bleak period, a group of twenty to thirty friends who met in their home each Friday for prayer and fellowship became a stabilizing force in their lives; and God's Word became the rock on which they stood. Jackie, thanking God for His Word, recalls: *"The 118th Psalm became my lifeline. I used it to compose a song and I sang it to myself daily. And it would lift my spirit and ward off the spirit depression that was constantly trying to gain entrance to my mind."*

THANK HEAVEN THEY DIDN'T BLAME GOD

During what were the most difficult years of their married life, Dave and Jackie continued to believe in God. They continued to attend their local church and to give what they could to the work of the Lord. They continued to grow in the knowledge of God and His Word. During the difficult, stress-filled years paying off their large debt—years when it would have been easy to doubt if there even was a God—the Lord encouraged Dave by speaking the following words into his heart: *"I have called you to be a homebuilder."* While they were living under enormous emotional and financial pressure, the type of pressure and stress that has caused many marriages to end in divorce, Dave and Jackie drew closer to God and closer to each other.

Today, this couple is still in the homebuilding business, and their company builds some two hundred homes a year and produces more than fifty million dollars in home sales annually. They are a godly couple who live and share their faith wherever they go. They continue to give liberally to their church and their Extended Hands Ministry gives annually to more than thirty Christian evangelistic and missionary works around the world.

Dave is the first to admit that, because of his inexperience in spiritual things, the voices he heard which led him to invest in so many different businesses were not the Spirit of God. When the financial problems began to consume their lives, thank heaven Dave and Jackie didn't blame God for their financial problems, and they didn't believe that they were so far in debt that God couldn't deliver them. Thank heaven they realized that "a good name is to be chosen rather than riches." Because their hearts were right, they have joined with other believers before them, who through faith and patience have inherited the promises that God made to Abraham (Hebrews 6:10-12).

LEARNING SPIRITUAL PRINCIPLES IS A PROCESS

When I first heard biblical teaching on "giving and receiving" and heard the testimonies of successful Christian businessmen whom God had blessed, I thought *"Bob, where have you been all these years? This sounds a lot easier than what you have been experiencing in your business; just give financially to the work of God and He will bless you."* But like my friend Dave I soon found out that there is more to obtaining the blessing of God than just giving to His work. Over the years I have observed a number of young Christian businessmen struggle in many of the same areas that Dave and I have. They have heard a message on "giving and receiving" and they reduced it to a man-centered law of cause and effect, a mere mathematical formula: *"If I pay my tithes and give offerings to the work of God, then He is obligated to bless me."*

Like Dave, by the time I became a Christian, I had already been in business for a number of years, so I generally knew how to operate in the world of buying and selling. But frankly for the first several years of my business life as a Christian, I knew very little about how to develop and exercise faith in God's promises. From time to time I would stumble on a biblical truth that would give me a small victory, but nothing that delivered the victory was promised in the scriptures. I would give to the work of God; I even went on a number of mission's trips to spread the Good News in other nations. I set goals for my business, and thought that I was exercising faith to bring those goals to pass; but when business and financial problems developed, what I thought was faith quickly dissipated and doubt and worry overtook me.

WE NEED TO CHANGE THE WAY WE THINK

The truth is that in the thirty years I have been a Christian, I have observed a number of Christians who have given tithes and offerings faithfully for years, but have never experienced anything extraordinary in their financial life. You may be wondering, *"How could that be, isn't God's word trustworthy?"* Yes, His Word is trustworthy, but immature Christians often do dumb things that prevent them from entering in to the full blessing that God intends for them. Most of the individuals who fail to prosper financially do so because they fail to change the way they think, the way they believe, and the way they talk.

We humans live in two worlds: a physical, temporal world and a spiritual, eternal world. Successful Christian businesspeople must operate in the physical world much like successful non-Christian businesspeople do; we need to make sales calls, produce a quality product or service, utilize efficient business and accounting systems, keep our eyes on the financial conditions that may affect our future business activities, and deal with the everyday problems that routinely develop in a business. If we want the blessing of God on our businesses, we also need to operate in an honest and ethical manner.

But we need to do more than just operate in an honest and ethical manner, as even non-Christians do that. We need to change the way we think; we need to understand what the Creator's Handbook has to say about the spiritual world, and how it relates to our lives and businesses. The first thing we need to understand is that Christ has redeemed us from the curse (poverty, sickness, and death) which came upon mankind when Adam sinned; and that He has made the blessings of Abraham (wealth, health, and eternal life) available to us through faith (Galatians 3:13&14). The second thing we need to recognize is that Satan is the god of this world and the world's financial system (2 Corinthians 4:4; Matthew 4:8-11), and he will try to prevent you as a Christian from receiving those blessings.

The most important thing for you to understand, however, is that Jesus Christ has already defeated the devil and won the victory (Colossians 2:13-15), but He has delegated the responsibility and the authority to enforce that victory to you and me (Luke 10:19). Jesus said to "do business until I return" (Luke 19:13). That means we are to enforce His victory by developing faith in His promises to prosper us, and then using that faith to stand against the forces of evil which are arrayed against us until His promises are manifest in the physical world—the world in which we need **His** prosperity (Ephesians 6:10-18).

It is very important for you to understand that doing "business by the Spirit" is a process; it is an adventure that requires you to discipline your body, and retrain your mind to think like God thinks. It requires you bring your soul and your spirit into agreement with the mind of God and with the spiritual laws that govern the universe. While I do not purport to have mastered all of His laws, or to even to have identified them all, it is my hope that the principles which I have learned and share with you in this book will help you avoid some of the pitfalls that Dave and I experienced in the early years of our Christian walk. It is my sincere desire that your application of these principles early in your Christian life will help you to advance more rapidly on the road to prosperity, and allow you to succeed in life far beyond what I have been able to accomplish.

CHAPTER 3
DISCIPLINING YOUR MIND AND BODY FOR SUCCESS

"Don't you realize that in a race everyone runs, but only one person gets the prize? So run to win! All athletes are disciplined in their training. They do it to win a prize that will fade away, but we do it for an eternal prize" (1 Corinthians 9:24-25 NLT).

In August of 2004 I arrived early for a doctor's appointment and thumbed through the August 9, 2004 issue of Time Magazine (1) which was lying on the waiting room table. An article entitled "Built for Speed by Alice Park" featuring American Olympic swimmer Michael Phelps caught my attention, and I began to read about him. In the U.S. Olympic trials held the previous month, Phelps had become the first swimmer to qualify for six individual events. (Phelps went on to win three gold and two bronze medals in the 2004 Athens's Olympics; and in Beijing in 2008, he did something no one else in the history of the Olympics has ever been able to do - he won an unprecedented eight gold Medals.)

In the article his coach Bob Bowman described Phelps as being "born to swim" - "blessed with a sinewy, whip-like body, a long torso and large hands and feet, plus a 6-ft.-7-in. arm span that extends 3 in. beyond his height (the usual ratio is 1 to 1). Phelps has as close to an ideal swimming body as you can get," (1). The article went on to say that Phelps would get up 6 a.m. every day and go into the pool, where he swam seven miles a day, 365 days a year. The author of the article, Alice Park, quoted Phelps as saying, "Christmas morning, I am at the pool." Phelps maintained that in order for him to be a champion, he had to change the way he swam every single stroke. Michael Phelps' coach called him "the motivation machine." (1) There are probably thousands of nineteen-year-olds that can match Phelps' physical qualifications, but none of them possess his desire to be a world champion. I was greatly impressed by the discipline and the motivation of this nineteen-year-old swimmer. He was willing to change, and he was willing to submit his mind and his body to a torturous daily discipline in order to win the Olympic gold, a prize that at best would be forgotten in a few years.

Several days after finishing the Phelps article I was sitting in a restaurant eating lunch when my thoughts returned to his story. I was thinking about the incredible discipline that Michael Phelps was willing to exercise to win the prize, when suddenly the Lord spoke the following words in my spirit: *"That's what you have been doing by meditating on My Word every day; you have trained your spirit to win."*

You see, since May of 2003, I have disciplined myself to spend an hour or more each day meditating on (thinking upon and confessing) God's Word. Every day I arise early and meditate on God's promises to prosper me, to heal me, to protect me, to guide me. I meditate on the authority over Satan that Jesus has delegated to me as a believer. I meditate on my rights and privileges as a citizen of the kingdom of God. When I first started this daily routine, I faced a major financial challenge in my business. (I discuss this challenge in detail in later in this book.) As I meditated on God's Word, my spirit began to grow stronger; and as faith in God's promises became established in my heart, that faith produced a fifty percent increase in sales over that of previous years, and it generated the highest annual profit that my company had ever experienced. Without realizing it I was training my spirit for the big event—not the Olympic trials like Michael Phelps, who competed for a temporal prize, but for an eternal prize. I am still amazed at the boldness that this daily meditation on the Word of God has produced in my spirit.

WE ARE TO DISCIPLINE OUR BODIES LIKE AN ATHLETE

"So I run straight to the goal with purpose in every step. I am not like a boxer who misses his punches. I discipline my body like an athlete, training it to do what it should. Otherwise, I fear that after preaching to others I myself might be disqualified" (1 Corinthians 9:26-27 NLT).

When you were born again, your spirit (your inner man) became a new creation and the old man passed away (2 Corinthians 5:17). But there was no change to your body or your mind; they remained in the same condition that they were before you accepted Christ. If your body craved rich, fattening foods before you were born again, it will still crave rich fattening foods after you were born again. If your body was involved in sensual sexual activity before you were born again, it will want to engage in sensual sexual activity after you were born again. Your body will have the same fleshly, carnal nature it had before you were born again, which is why Paul said, "…present your bodies as a living sacrifice, holy, acceptable to God…" (Romans 12:1).

Your born-again spirit, the inner man, is to discipline your body, take control over your body, and bring it into submission to the Word of God. In order for your spirit man to take control of your body, it needs the cooperation of your mind. But your mind is still in agreement with your body, because it was originally trained by the body's five physical senses.

OUR THOUGHTS DETERMINE OUR DESTINY

How well I remember a phrase from a secular success motivation book which I read some thirty-five years ago..." Thoughts are things and powerful things at that..." Yes, thoughts are powerful! Positive, faith-filled thoughts can put you ahead in life, while negative, fear-filled thoughts can hamper your success and even make you sick.

Your "spirit man" (the inner man) will translate into reality a thought driven by fear just as readily as a thought driven by faith. "For as a man thinks in his heart (his soul) so is he..." (Proverbs 23:7a). The Hebrew word **nepes,** translated *heart* in my Bible, is translated *psyche* in the Greek and should have been translated *soul* in the English. It refers to the mind, will, and emotions.

From the time you arise in the morning until the time that you fall asleep at night, your conscious mind is occupied with thought impulses. Your mind receives these thought impulses from four sources:

- ➢ First, these thought impulses—either positive or negative—come through stimuli received from the five senses, particularly the sense of sight and hearing.
- ➢ Second, you may receive thought impulses from the demon forces of darkness that sit on your shoulder and impress their negative and devilish thoughts on your mind.
- ➢ Third, the recall of your memories stored in your soul tends to strengthen the influence of thoughts upon your mind. When thought impulses from

various sources reach your conscious mind, they are sorted, filed, and recorded in your soul, similar to the way that a computer stores and retrieves information provided to it. When we wake in the night and think upon the negative things that have happened in our lives, those memories strengthen their hold on us.
- ➢ Fourth, if you are a born-again Christian, you may receive thoughts from the Spirit of God. The Spirit of God dwells in your spirit, and therefore His thoughts will rise up from within you. (Being able to hear the voice of God in business is so important that we will spend an entire chapter on the subject later in this book.)

Any thought that an individual allows to dominate his conscious mind will eventually find itself believed and acted upon by his spirit man. Through some powerful principles that God has not deemed necessary to divulge, the dominating thoughts of one's mind influence what they believe in their spirit.

The Manufacturer's Handbook says it this way, "... let God transform you into a new person by changing the way you think." (Romans 12:2b NLT). In another place it says that when you were born again your "inward man" (your spirit) delights to do the law of God, but your body is controlled by another law which wars against your mind and your spirit and keeps you in captivity to the law of sin (Romans 7:22-25). In these passages, Paul says that your spirit (your inner man), which is inhabited by the Spirit of God, wants to do what is right; but your mind, which has been programmed by the five senses, has a carnal (body-ruled) nature which tempts you to sin.

But Paul doesn't leave you without hope; he tells us that you can transform your mind, by changing the way you think by "... bringing every thought into captivity to the obedience of Christ" (2 Corinthians 10:3-5). (Christ **is** the Word of God.) Simply stated, we are to reprogram our thinking by meditating upon (thinking upon and confessing) the Word of God day and night until we think like Christ thinks.

"Man shall not live by bread alone, but by every word that that proceeds out of the mouth of God" (Matthew 4:4).

YOUR HEART- MOUTH AGREEMENT SHAPES YOUR LIFE

Earlier in this chapter I related how by meditating upon (thinking upon and confessing) the Word of God, I used the law of faith to change the condition of my business from near bankruptcy to prosperity. Like all spiritual laws, the law of faith will work either positively or negatively depending on the thoughts that we have allowed to dominate our conscious mind.

That is why the devil loves to play games with your mind and your emotions. He delights in filling your mind with lies, accusations and negative thoughts concerning your life, your family, and your business. He knows that if he can get you to meditate on his devilish, negative thoughts then eventually you will begin to believe them in your heart. And once you believe them in your heart, if he can coax you into confessing those negative thoughts from your mouth, they will come to pass in your life (Mark 11:23). But be encouraged, God has given mankind a will, and you have the ability to exercise your will to control your thoughts!

But tragically most men never exercise control over their thoughts or over their mouth, and in failing to do so they allow Satan and his devilish imps to control their lives. Many years ago I heard Kenneth Hagin, the founder of Rhema Bible Training Center, express this principle in the following words, and I have never forgotten them:

- The way you think...
- Determines what you believe in your heart (Proverbs 23:7a),
- Which determines the way you talk (Mathew 12:34b),
- Which determines what you have in life (Mark 11:23).
- Watch your thoughts; they become words

Recently I was in the reception area of a medical clinic and I noticed a decorative plaque hanging mentioned above from a secular viewpoint:

- Watch your words; they become actions
- Watch your actions; they become habits
- on the wall that reflects the same principles Watch your habits; they become character
- Watch your character; it becomes your destiny

WE ARE TO BE TRANSFORMED BY RENEWING OUR MIND

Paul entreats us to submit our body as a living sacrifice to God, and he encourages us to not be conformed to the pattern of the world, but to be transformed by the renewing of our mind (Romans 12:1-2). In this computer age we would say, "Take control over your body—don't think like those in the world think, and be transformed by the 'reprogramming' of your mind." We know from experience that if we program our computer with wrong information it will produce wrong results.

The same is true of our mind. Most people's minds have been programmed by their physical senses to operate in a "sense-ruled" physical world. It has been programmed to believe what it sees, hears, feels, tastes and smells; therefore, it has difficulty operating in the faith realm. It's all right to believe your senses when you are crossing a busy street, but when your senses contradict God's Word, you are to believe His Word. We have to reprogram our mind daily with the Word of God so that we think like Christ thinks. We need to think in line with God's Word in order to operate in cooperation with His spiritual laws.

Just as Michael Phelps was willing to submit his mind and body to a daily regimen of physical exercise to become an Olympic champion, so we are to submit our minds and our bodies to a daily regimen of meditation on the Word of God, in order that our inner man, our spirit man, may become strong and filled with faith.

(1) Built For Speed, by Alice Park, Time. New York: © Time Incorporated August 9, 2004, August 9, 2004. Vol. 164, Iss. 6; (pg. 72)

CHAPTER 4
THE SECULAR WORLD USES BIBLICAL PRINCIPLES TO SUCCEED

"But seek first the kingdom of God and His righteousness, and all these things shall be added to you" (Matthew 6:33).

LIVING WITHOUT GOALS

Like a lot of young people, I grew up without giving the future much thought. I had no defined long-term goals; I just did what seemed most advantageous to me at the time. Upon finishing high school, I went on to the university where I studied architectural engineering, and when I graduated from the university, I served a two year obligation in the U.S. Army. When I was discharged from the Army, I went to work for a large design-build construction firm. Eight years later I accepted a partnership in a small architectural firm and found myself in business for myself. I made these decisions not because they fulfilled my career goals—I didn't have any—but because these opportunities became available.

REALIZING A NEED FOR GOALS

I found that being in business for myself was quite different than working for a salary; now my livelihood depended not so much on my ability to complete the work, but on my resourcefulness in selling myself and my firm's services. For the first time in my life, I realized that I needed to establish some goals for my business and my personal life, but I wasn't sure how to go about it. I began to search out and read a number of popular secular success motivation books in an effort to produce prosperity in my business and find purpose and direction in my personal life. I sought these success principles because I thought that they would bring fulfillment to my life. These books generally offered a series of steps on how to develop self-discipline and establish specific financial goals for one's life.

Having been encouraged to do so by these success motivation books, I set a series of goals for my business and my personal finances. At the time I thought that if my company designed bigger projects, or perhaps if I had more people working for me, or if my firm produced bigger profits that it would satisfy the emptiness I sensed within me. But each year as we achieved our sales and profit goals, the satisfaction and fulfillment I had anticipated seemed to elude me. I reasoned that perhaps if I were to set more difficult goals, eventually I would find the promised satisfaction in life. In the eyes of others, I was successful; but inwardly I was empty.

SECULAR SUCCESS PRINCIPLES ARE BASED ON BIBLICAL PRINCIPALS

Then, as I pointed out in an earlier chapter, when I was forty-three years old, I became a born- again Christian and began to read the Bible, the "Creator's Handbook." Immediately, I began to recognize that the authors of the secular success books had obtained many of their "success principles" from the Bible. In fact some of these authors had actually quoted Jesus and used various biblical passages as the source of the principles which they taught. I believe it is important for you the reader to understand that if secular success motivation teachers (henceforth I refer to these teachers as SSMT) can use the spiritual principles contained in the Creator's Handbook to produce tremendous financial success in their followers, how much more should a Christian be able to use these same biblical principles to produce financial success in their lives when they have the Creator of the universe backing them?

WHY YOU NEED TO CHANGE THE WAY YOU THINK

The "curse of the law" which came upon mankind when Satan became the god of this world includes poverty, sickness and death. Mankind seems to have inherited a universal fear of this unholy trio. Every human being has suffered at one time or another from devastating effects of one or more of these three basic fears; we are fortunate if we do not suffer from all three. These fears attack our minds and cause our souls to become oppressed with a myriad of negative emotions that hinder our success in life.

Few of us emerge from childhood without the effects of some of these devastating emotions being imparted to our soul. Perhaps your parents were financially insecure, money was always a problem with them, and they told you over and over how bad things were. Perhaps your parents divorced or one of them died while you were quite young, or perhaps you grew up in a home where there was physical, emotional or sexual abuse, and therefore you perceive of yourself as having no value. The criticism of parents, teachers and friends, even well- meaning criticism, often leaves us with a low self-esteem and a poor personal image. Unless we initiate action to eliminate these negative emotions by changing the way we think, they will not only affect our success in the financial world, but our health and our social life as well. This is true because the dominating thoughts that we allow to inhabit our conscious minds will eventually manifest themselves in our lives.

MANKIND IS AN ETERNAL SPIRIT

The Creator's Handbook reveals a fascinating truth concerning the makeup of man that is unacceptable to the secular atheist world. The **truth** is that man is an "eternal spirit" who has a soul and lives in a mortal, physical body (1Thessalonians 5:23). It further reveals that before a man is born again he is spiritually dead (his "spirit" is separated from the Spirit of God), but he is still a "spirit being." It is because a man is a spirit being that he is capable of developing faith (natural human faith) in his ability to accomplish certain goals in life. Once we realize that man is a spirit, and that his spirit can develop faith, it opens up a whole new understanding of how to become successful in life.

The SSMT, on the other hand, have generally accepted the evolutionist view that man is a mortal being, and the Freudian view that man has a conscious and a subconscious mind. The secular world refers to man's soul (the thinking and reasoning part of man) as the conscious mind; it refers to man's spirit as the subconscious mind. They describe the conscious mind as the captain that sends commands to the subconscious mind, and the subconscious mind as the central operating system that stores and retrieves data much like the operating system of a computer. In their view, the subconscious mind (the spirit of man) does not think or reason; it merely obeys the commands it receives from the conscious mind and sets about to translate these commands into their physical equivalent.

YOU ARE TO MAKE YOURSELF PROSPEROUS

Most of us pray "God bless me and make me prosperous," but God told Joshua "you are to make **yourself** prosperous!" "This Book of the Law shall not depart out of your mouth, but you shall meditate in it day and night, that you may observe to do according to all that is written in it. For then you will make your way prosperous, and then you will have good success" (Joshua 1:8). God told Joshua to reprogram his mind by meditating on (thinking upon and confessing) the Word of God day and night, and do everything that is required by it...*for then you will make your way prosperous, and then you will have good success."*

"SSMT" ALSO TEACH SIMILAR PRINCIPLES

The SSMT have adopted success principles similar to those God gave to Joshua some 3500 years ago. They instruct their students to reprogram their minds by writing out a clear concise statement of the goals they wish to attain in life, addressing as a minimum the following: 1) the thing that they desire in life, 2) the date that they intend to possess the thing they desire, 3) a brief statement of the plan they intend to use to fulfill the thing they desire. Then they are instructed to confess these goals in the morning when they arise and in the evening, before they retire; and as they confess these goals they are encouraged to visualize themselves already in possession of the thing they desire. They are to meditate on (think upon and confess) the thing that they desire in life day and night. The SSMT even suggest securing a copy of their goal statement to the bathroom mirror so that they will be forced to read and confess it when they arise in the morning and when they retire in the evening. They do this because they have found that successful people have a clear mental vision of what they want in life. Unsuccessful people, on the other hand, are unsure of what they want to accomplish in life.

SUCCESS REQUIRES THE REPROGRAMMING OF YOUR MIND

Both secular and biblical success motivation principles involve the reprogramming of the mind. Secular success techniques reprogram the students' minds with positive success-oriented thoughts so that they habitually think in terms of success rather than failure.

Biblical success motivation teaching involves the reprogramming of our minds with the "Word of God" so that we think the way God thinks. Remember, He always thinks success and victory, and so should you.

MANY OF THE SSMT PRINCIPLES ARE TAUGHT IN THE BIBLE

As we have pointed out, many of the principles taught by the SSMT are actually taught in the Bible, and they often reference these biblical precepts in their books and teaching tapes. They have rightly concluded that there is a hidden part of man, which can cause mankind to become either a success or failure; however, they have wrongly concluded that this hidden part of man is a subconscious mind. The Creator's Handbook describes this hidden part of man as the spirit of man (the real man). Peter calls him "the hidden person of the heart" (1 Peter 3:4).

The SSMT have also rightly concluded that they can program this hidden man to either success or failure, by controlling the dominant thoughts he allows to occupy his conscious mind and the verbal affirmations that he speaks from mouth. One well-known SSMT states that the *"repetition of positive affirmations to your subconscious mind is the only known method of voluntary development of the emotion of faith."* In fact they use many of the same principles that we Christians use and they make many confessions that are similar to those we Christians make.

But faith's confession is not a formula for getting things from God. It is not a secular indulgence in new age, mind science activity. The SSMT may use some of the same scriptures we use, and make similar confessions to those we make, but they make their confessions based on their own desires and the ability of their subconscious mind to bring those desires into reality.

We Christians make our confessions based upon God's promises and His ability to bring His promises to pass. Theirs is an exercise of natural faith; ours is an exercise of the "God kind of faith" based on God's creative Word of promise. We humbly take our stand in a spirit of faith in God's person and His promise. God's Word is already established in heaven; but it's up to you to establish it upon the earth! (Psalms 119:89)

UNDERSTANDING THE CREATORS PROSPERITY PRINCIPLES

Let me make something clear: when applying God's principles for success, heart motivation is extremely important, and you need to stay in the middle of the road. On the one side of the road is a hyper-prosperity teaching in which we become motivated by "a desire for riches," forgetting that the real issue is stewarding God's resources for God's purposes rather than "getting rich." On the other side of the road is a pseudo spirituality which rejects financial prosperity, considering it as worldly pursuit detrimental to one's spiritual life. God is your Heavenly Father and it is his desire to give you good things, but He desires that you seek him for who He is, not for what you can get from Him. Jesus said it this way: "But seek **first** the kingdom of God, and His righteousness, and all these things will be added to you" (Matthew 6:33).

YOUR SUCCESS DEPENDS ON THE EXERCISE OF YOUR WILL

The Creator's Handbook teaches that there is an unseen spiritual world which is inhabited by a myriad of spiritual beings or angels which have the ability to influence our minds and affect the way we think. Some of these angels, which are under the authority of God, have the ability to influence people for good, while others, which are under the authority of Satan, have the ability to influence people for evil. These spirits influence us by impressing their thoughts upon our minds, in order to get us to accept them as our own and to yield to either good or evil. God has given mankind absolute control over their will, but unfortunately only a small percentage of men or women actually exercise that control. By exercising your will you have the ability to govern and control the thoughts which you allow to dominate your conscious mind. Therefore your success or failure in life depends on the exercise of your will.

CHAPTER 5
OVERCOMING FEAR

"...I heard your voice in the garden, and I was afraid..." (Genesis 3:10).

"For God has not given us a spirit of fear, but of power and of love and of a sound mind" (2 Timothy 1:7).

Fred Doerflein, a friend of mine, shared with me that in the middle of his business career he suddenly became fearful that his business would fail. There was no physical evidence that would lead him to believe that his business would fail; in fact, his business was doing quite well. But his mind became filled with fearful thoughts that his business would go bankrupt. This fear became so intense that there were days that he didn't want to get out of bed in the morning; going to work was torture. This went on for several months. One day Fred remembered the scripture "For God has not given me the spirit of fear but of power and love and of a sound mind (2 Timothy 1:7), and he began to confess this scripture to himself over and over again. After several days, Fred noticed that the "fear of failure" had diminished somewhat. After confessing the Word of God for several additional days, the spirit of fear left him and he was able to return to a normal thought-life.

It was not long after this experience that Fred began to feel physically tired. After several weeks of feeling exhausted and weak, his wife Joyce convinced him that he should go to the doctor for a physical examination. When Fred met with the doctor to review the test results, the doctor told him that he had leukemia. Immediately the fear of death attacked his mind, but only for a few seconds, because the faith of God rose up from within and drove off the spirit of fear that had attacked his mind. Fred told the doctor, "I am going to go home and pray about this." After prayer, Fred decided to believe God for his complete healing; he did not return to the doctor for eight years, and only then for a routine physical examination.

When Fred arrived home from the doctor appointment, his wife Joyce asked what the doctor had found. Fred simply said, *"The doctor said I have a blood disorder";* he refused to even say the word *leukemia.* That evening Fred remembered a story that a preacher had shared during a sermon, a story concerning a boy who asked his father for a new bicycle. When the father heard his son's request, he immediately agreed to give him a new bicycle. But the next day when the boy hadn't yet received the bicycle, he asked his father a second time. Each day thereafter he would again ask his father for the bicycle until his father became very upset by his constant nagging. Finally the father said, "Son, don't you trust me?"

Remembering this illustration, Fred asked his heavenly Father to heal him of the leukemia only once; thereafter he simply thanked God that He was healed. Fred says, "Sometimes we simply need to wait on God in faith, and not expect an immediate answer to our prayer." Within six months of asking God to heal him, the symptoms of leukemia had left Fred, and he is still healthy and vibrant today some twenty-five years later. Fred had learned that *"God has not given him the spirit of fear but of power and love and a sound mind.* (4)

When God created man, He gave him a free will, but sadly few people choose to exercise their will like Fred Doerflein did. The majority of men simply accepts every random thought as their own, and therein lies the secret of success and failure in life. In this chapter you will become aware of the absolute necessity of exercising your will to take control over your thoughts.

THE ORIGINATION OF FEAR

When Adam, the man whom God proclaimed to be His under-ruler on the earth (Genesis 1:28), collaborated with God's arch enemy Satan, he died spiritually. He became separated from God (Genesis 2:17), and the spirit of faith (the nature of God) was replaced by the spirit of fear (the nature of Satan), and therefore Satan became mankind's spiritual father (John 8:44). The spirit of fear and the host of negative emotions which are caused by it are so destructive to an individual's life and business success that we will spend this entire chapter learning to recognize and cope with them.

MANKIND IS UNDER A CURSE

When Adam sinned in the Garden, mankind came under a curse (Genesis 3:17). Paul refers to it in the book of Galatians as the "curse of the law" (Galatians 3:13). The law is contained in the first five books of the Bible and the "curse of the law" is summarized in Deuteronomy 28:15-68. This curse includes:

- ➢ Poverty
- ➢ Sickness
- ➢ Death

THE FEAR OF POVERTY

The "fear of poverty" is extremely destructive to one's business life. It can paralyze your ability to think, discourage you from developing faith in God's promises, and prevent you from obtaining victory in your business and personal life. It leads to torment in your mind and failure in your actions. Nothing brings mankind as much suffering as poverty does. The fear of poverty is so subtle and deeply rooted in our minds and spirits that we can go through life and never recognize its presence. I suffered from a subtle form of the fear of poverty for years; it caused me to be overly cautious and prevented me from making several profitable investments.

But thank God, Jesus has redeemed us from the curse of the law (poverty, sickness and spiritual death), so that we might receive the blessing of Abraham (prosperity health and eternal life) by faith. The Apostle Paul says emphatically that whatever is not of faith is sin (Romans 14:23 b). Faith is the antidote for the fear of poverty or, for that matter, any other fear.

JOB LIVED IN "FEAR OF POVERTY"

In the prologue of the book of Job a conversation between God and Satan is recorded for our admonition. Satan presents himself before God and challenges Job's piety, stating, "...Does Job fear God for nothing?" (Job 1:9). He goes on to suggest that if everything were taken away from Job, that Job would curse God. (Job 1:11) God said to Satan, "...Behold, all that he has is in your power; only do not lay a hand on his person" (Job 1:12). To the casual reader it would appear that God gave Satan permission to attack Job. But I believe God merely pointed out that Job was walking in fear (he was in sin) and was therefore out from under the protection of God. Job was in a position where the Devil could attack him. Job himself confirms this position when he confessed, "For the thing I greatly feared has come upon me, and what I dreaded has happened to me" (Job 3:25). Job was the richest man in the East, but he lived in fear, the "fear of poverty." Job feared that he would lose everything that he had accumulated, and that fear gave Satan access into his life. It allowed the devil to steal his wealth, kill his children, and attack his body (Job 1:13-19 & 2:7).

SYMPTOMS OF THE FEAR OF POVERTY

Perhaps you may be wondering if you suffer from the fear of poverty. Below are several symptoms of the fear of poverty that will assist you in making a self-diagnosis. If you…

- …suffer doubt that it is God's will for you to prosper
- …are overly envious of others who are successful
- …often worry about problems you are facing, lacking confidence that God will help you to succeed
- …have feelings of inferiority
- … are indecisive and often prognosticate in making decisions
- …are indifferent toward your work and suffer from lack of ambition or the desire to succeed
- …then you no doubt suffer to some extent from the fear of poverty, and you need to take steps to establish faith in God's Word concerning his promises and his desire to prosper you.

THE FEAR OF SICKNESS AND DEATH

The fear of sickness, old age, and death are all closely related. Fear of ill health is also reinforced by the fear of poverty. We think *if I should become ill, I could lose my livelihood and it could cost me my life savings.* In America, it is impossible to turn on the television or radio without hearing a drug manufacturer's advertisement proclaiming the benefits of their particular brand of cure and describing in vivid details the symptoms of some sickness or disease, reinforcing our innate fear of sickness and death. Among physicians, it is a generally accepted perception that a large percent of their patients are suffering from imaginary illnesses. It has been demonstrated that the **fear** of disease, even where there is not the slightest physical cause for that fear, may cause an individual to meditate on the disease until it produces physical symptoms of the very disease that the individual fears.

AN EXPERIENCE FROM MY OWN LIFE

A number of years ago I had an experience which brought home the power that our thoughts can have on our health and prosperity. One day the following thought flashed into my mind: *Now that you are getting older, you will probably have to start taking pills for sugar diabetes like your father used to take* (my father had passed away several years earlier). I really didn't dwell on the thought; I simply dismissed it. But several weeks later that same thought passed through my mind again. Again, I dismissed it. During the following year, that particular thought was impressed upon my mind again and again. Near the end of the year, I went to my doctor for a routine physical examination. Several days after the examination a nurse from the doctor's office called and said, *"You tested positive for sugar diabetes; we would like you to take a second test."* As I hung up the telephone, I turned to my wife Barbara and explained to her the nurse's report concerning my blood sugar levels. Then I asked Barbara to agree with me in prayer, and I proclaimed, *"In the name of Jesus, I rebuke the sugar diabetic condition!"* Then I boldly confessed *"My body is strong and perfect."* The following week I took a second blood test and my blood sugar level had returned to normal.

Several years after the above incident I was visiting with my mother and I related to her the above experience. Somewhat bewildered, she said, *"Where did you ever get the idea that your father took pills for sugar diabetes; he didn't have sugar diabetes!"* Where did I get that idea? While I had refused to receive the suggestion that I had sugar diabetes, I had come to firmly believe that my father once had it. The devil had sent one of his demon spirits of fear to sit on my shoulder and try to convince me that I was doomed to suffer from sugar diabetes because my father had it. I am convinced that if I hadn't taken control of the thoughts which I allowed to dominate my mind, today I would have sugar diabetes.

FEAR IS A SPIRIT

Fear is a spirit; it affects us from the outside. The root cause of virtually all the problems we have in life are caused by fear. When we allow fearful thoughts to dominate our conscious thinking, those thoughts will cause negative emotions such as envy, jealousy, bitterness, and anger to take up residence in our soul; and those emotions will eventually poison our spirit. These negative emotions are dangerous, because as we have explained elsewhere in this book, they prevent faith from developing in our spirit man. Allowing fear and negative emotions to develop in our spirit is a sin (Romans 14:23 b), and it will quench our relationship with God. It will not only affect our relationship with God and the people with whom we associate, but also our physical and mental health. Therefore, the elimination of fear (and its resulting negative emotions) is the number one task for the individual who aspires to be successful in life. Fear and negative emotions are the primary causes of under achievement and failure in life, particularly in the business world.

FEAR IS THE RECIPROCAL OF FAITH

The Manufacturer's Handbook describes both faith (2 Corinthians 4:13) and fear (2 Timothy 1:7) as spirits. Faith is the master over fear! It has been proclaimed: *"Fear knocked on the door, faith answered and there was no one there."*

Faith is information we get from God (his Word) to act on. Since fear is the reciprocal (opposite) of faith, it can therefore be considered information we get from the devil to act on. Here is how it works: A demonic spirit comes and impresses his negative thoughts of defeat and failure upon your mind. Thoughts such as *you will never make enough sales to keep your employees busy this month.* The next day he whispers, "S*ee you lost another sale…you are not going to make your goal…why call on more customers…you may as well go home and rest.*" If you are not aware of the source of these negative thoughts, you will accept them as your own. If you begin to think upon and confess these negative, fearful thoughts, you will begin to worry, and subsequently this will produce doubt in God's Word and His ability to help you. The spirit of fear will quench your faith and allow a host of negative, defeating emotions to become established in your soul. Those negative emotions will eventually poison your spirit and prevent you from taking the action which is required for you to succeed in life. You may not realize it, but as we pointed out earlier, when you act in fear, you are in sin and no longer in a position for God to help you. Without faith it is impossible to please God (Hebrews 11:6).

UNDERSTANDING HOW FEAR ATTACKS THE MIND

It is important for you to understand how the spirit of fear attacks your mind if you are to prevent its negative defeating effects from gaining a foothold in our life. You need to recognize the devil's methods so that you can take a stand against them. Paul says, "Put on the whole armor of God, that you may be able stand against the wiles of the devil" (Ephesians 6:11). In another place he says, "...for we are not ignorant of his (Satan's) devices" (2 Corinthians 2:11). We need to take a closer look at these verses as they describe Satan's strategies for attacking mankind; we need to recognize his strategies so that we can take a stand against them.

A number of years ago I read an excellent book entitled *Dressed to Kill* by Rick Renner (1) in which he discusses the root meaning of the word *wiles* and *devices* used in the above scriptures. He states that the word *wiles* used in Ephesians 6:11 comes from the Greek word *methodos* (meth-o-dos), from which we derive the word "method." However, **method** does not really convey its full meaning. Renner points out the word *wiles* is often translated as someone who is being crafty or full of trickery, but the most basic translation is "on a road." In other words, the devil does not have all the power or all the means he would like us to believe he has. In reality he has only one road or approach by which he can attack you. Renner goes on to explain that the English word *devices* used above in 2 Corinthians 2:11 is a translation of the Greek word *noemata* (no-e-ma-ta), a form of the word **nous**, which describes the mind or the intellect. The word *noemata* used by Paul in the above scripture carries the idea of a deceived mind. It actually depicts the insidious plot and wicked schemes of the devil to confuse and attack the human mind. Renner quoted one language specialist as stating that the word *noemata* suggests "mind games."

The devil and his demon spirits have only one road or avenue by which they can attack you; they play games with your mind. They impress their negative, evil thoughts on your mind in an attempt to get you to think upon and confess those thoughts. They attempt to manipulate your physical senses and your emotions to get you to believe something that is not really true. They try to make you believe the worst about your life, your family, your health, your finances, your business, etc. If you begin to think upon and confess the devil's lies, you will begin to perceive them as reality, and they will eventually become established in your life. Remember:

- The way you think...
- Determines what you believe in your heart (Proverbs 23:7a),
- Which determines the way you talk (Matthew 12:34 b),
- Which determines what you have in life (Mark 11:23).

Now let's take a closer look at how the spirit of fear works to gradually take over your thinking and eventually your entire body, soul and spirit.

DEPRESSION

When a problem arises in your life, a devilish spirit of fear causes you to think thoughts of failure and defeat that attack your mind; we commonly call this condition "depression." The demonic spirit causing you to become depressed is actually on the outside of you—this spirit is impressing his devilish thoughts on your mind. If you refuse his thoughts, and you meditate (think upon and confess) the Word of God concerning the answer to your problem, you will defeat him. If you resist the devil and his demons, and you refuse to allow his thoughts to dominate your mind, the spirit of fear will have to leave you (James 4:7, 1 Peter 5:9), just like it left my friend Fred Doerflein mentioned in the opening paragraphs of this chapter.

OBSESSION

If however, you begin to receive these devilish thoughts of fear and failure, and you meditate upon (think upon and confess) them until they dominate your thinking, you will give that demon spirit permission to enter your mind. When that spirit enters your mind, his thoughts will become your thoughts—they will become an obsession; they will dominate your every thought. Once a demonic spirit enters your mind, he can control it. Now that spirit is in you (in your mind) and you will require help in order to be set free from this spirit and his oppressive fearful thoughts.

It is my experience in praying for people around the world that often a very fearful and traumatic experience in one's life such as an accident or a physical attack on one's person may also allow a spirit of fear to slip into and obsess that person's mind or body. When a person experiences such a traumatic event, the spirit of fear will oppress them without that individual even recognizing the source of the oppression. While I was speaking in Japan in August of 2000, a woman in her fifties came to me for prayer and told me that the left side of her body was partially paralyzed. She explained that several years earlier she had been in an automobile accident in which her left side was painfully injured and had become paralyzed. She said she no longer had the sharp pain she once had, but the left side of her body was still partially paralyzed, and she explained that she was still extremely fearful of riding in automobiles. As she told me her story, I could see the spirit of fear looking at me through her eyes. I slapped her left side of her body with my hand and I proclaimed, "In the name of Jesus, I command the spirit of fear to come out of her." She began to scream at the top of her lungs; she grabbed her left side and continued to scream as I continued to demand that the demon of fear come out of her. In about two to three minutes the spirit of fear left her, and the woman was free. She was free of the fear and free of the paralysis.

After I had finished praying for her, she was very apologetic to the other people who were in the meeting because she caused such a disturbance. She said that she had never done anything like that before and she couldn't understand what had caused her to scream. But she was totally healed. Neither this lady, her doctors, nor her pastor or friends had recognized that it was a spirit of fear that held her in such physical and mental torment. They just thought it was an injury from the car accident. Certainly, the trauma of the accident had allowed the spirit to enter her body, but it was the spirit itself that caused the physical problem in her body.

POSSESSION

If a person allows his mind to be obsessed with negative demonic thinking long enough and does not get help, that demonic spirit may get down into his spirit, and completely take over his mind, spirit, and body. We use the word "possessed" to describe the state of such a person who is totally controlled by an evil spirit. In the more than thirty years that I have been praying for people, I have met very few individuals who are actually possessed, and they have all been non-believers. A person cannot be possessed and be a believer. Once a person is possessed by an evil spirit, they will definitely require help to be delivered and set free.

STAND AGAINST THE SPIRIT OF FEAR

The "good fight of faith" is not a momentary gust of faith to deliver you from a problem; it is a life style, a life-long commitment to meditate upon (to think upon and confess) "God's Word." It is a determined and committed state of the mind and heart. Paul admonishes the believer to be "strong in the Lord and the power of his might." We are to put on the whole armor of God and to stand fast in the face of every demonic attack. In Ephesians 6:10-18 Paul uses the various pieces of the Roman soldier's armor as a metaphor for applying the word of God. He says we are not be moved by adverse circumstances or the bad news that the devil tries to impress on our mind. We are to take the "sword of the Spirit," which is the Word of God, and pray and confess that Word right in the face of every problem. If we refuse to back off of our confession of God's Word, faith and patience will always produce victory (Hebrews 6:11-18).

FAITH IS PRESENT TENSE, FEAR IS FUTURE TENSE

Faith is always present tense—faith says it's mine; I have it now. Faith is established in your heart by meditating on (thinking upon and confessing) the promises of God. Satan tries to get you to think upon and confess your fears in order to quench your faith. He will try to impress thoughts of failure and defeat upon your mind so that you will doubt God's promises and fail to act on them. If you receive his devilish thoughts and begin to meditate upon (think upon and confess) them, those thoughts will replace the faith (faith that God will prosper you) that you have developed in your heart with the fear that you will fail. Fear and worry are always future tense.

Fear says, *"Even though the economy is good it may turn bad next year so don't try to expand your business."* Worry says *"I may have made an error on the bid for that new project; maybe I shouldn't go ahead with it. I don't know what to do."* Fear causes you to doubt God's promises. Doubting is to fear as believing is to faith. If you believe God's promises you will act on them, and that action shows God that you believe him. If you doubt God's promises you will fail to act on them, and your failure to act shows God that you do not believe Him. More importantly it shows the devil that he is winning the fight of faith.

DON'T EVER CONFESS YOUR DOUBTS AND FEARS

The devil is not omniscient; he cannot read your mind. The only way he knows if he is winning or losing the battle for your mind is by listening to your talk and observing your actions. The confession of God's Word from your lips, spoken in faith from your heart, will defeat the devil on every occasion and will give God dominion in your life; however, your confession of the devil's ability to hinder you and keep you from success will give the devil authority in your life.

If you are fearful, it is not something that is on the inside of you, it is something that is on the outside of you trying to get into you. The Creator's Handbook tells us more than seventy times "Fear not." God admonishes you and me to

"Fear not, for I am with you; be not dismayed, for I am your God. I will strengthen you, yes, I will help you, I will uphold you with my righteous right hand" (Isaiah 41:10). Never confess your fears; resist the spirit of fear and it will flee from you (James 4:7). Now, you may have doubts and you may even sense fear, but don't ever confess them. Confess God's Word concerning your situation instead. Confessing the Word of God one minute and speaking doubt and failure the next minute will cause confusion in your spirit; it will give the devil dominion over you and cause you to fail in life. Your actions must correspond with your confession.

Jesus said, *"I have told you these things, so that in Me you may have [perfect] peace and confidence. In the world you have tribulation and trials and distress and frustration; but be of good cheer [take courage, be confident, certain, undaunted]! For I have overcome the world. [I have deprived it of power to harm you and have conquered it for you]"* (John 16:33 Amplified Bible).

WORRY IS THE TRIUMPH OF FEAR OVER FAITH

As a businessperson you would never pay interest on money you have not borrowed. Why then would you worry? Worry is "interest paid on trouble that never happens."

Worry is simply the triumph of fear over faith. It is a subtle form of fear; it is meditating on all the things that might go wrong in the future. It is the misuse of the creative imagination that God has placed within each of us. It allows fear to take hold of your mind thought by thought and it will eventually paralyze your reasoning ability, destroy your self-confidence, and overcome your faith in God's ability to fulfill His Word. Worry is a sin because it is faith in the devil's ability to harm you, rather than in God's ability to protect you. Jesus specifically told us not to worry: "Therefore do not worry, saying, 'What shall we eat?' or 'what shall we drink?' or 'what shall we wear?' For after all these things the Gentiles seek. For your heavenly Father knows that you need all these things. But seek first the kingdom of God and His righteousness, and all these things shall be added to you. Therefore do not worry about tomorrow, for tomorrow will worry about its own things. Sufficient for the day is its own trouble." (Matthew 6:31-34) Those who are filled with fear and worry not only destroy their own ability to act, but if they express those fears to others, then **their** ability to act will be destroyed as well.

TAKE CONTROL OVER YOUR THOUGHTS

God has given mankind absolute control over but one thing... their will. Those who fail in life do so because they fail to exercise their will. They allow every negative thought to enter and inhabit their mind, while others of equal ability and training allow only positive, faith-filled thoughts to dwell in their minds. Because everything that mankind accomplishes begins with the way they think, we can readily understand how thoughts of failure and poverty can cause one to fail in life, and anxious thoughts of sickness and poor health can actually shorten one's life.

This last statement is substantiated by research accomplished by Ellen Idler, a sociologist at Rutgers University, and Stanislav Kasl an epidemiologist at Yale University School of Medicine, who co-authored the following study:

"A person's answer to the question, 'Is your health excellent, good, fair or poor?' is a remarkable predictor of who will live

or die over the next four years" according to their findings. *"A study of more than 2800 men and women 65 and older found that those who rate their health 'poor' are four to five times more likely to die in the next four years than those who rate their health 'excellent.'* <u>*This was the case even if examinations show the respondents to be in comparable health.*</u> *These findings are supported by a review of five other large studies, totaling 23,000 people, which reached similar conclusions,"* according to Idler and Kasl (3).

YOU MUST DEAL WITH YOUR NEGATIVE EMOTIONS

In an article in *Charisma Magazine* (a popular Christian magazine in America) entitled "God Doesn't Want You to Crash and Burn," the author states that *"negative emotions such anger, envy, and bitterness— as well as the mishandling of stress—can destroy ones health and life. Studies have shown, in fact, that anxious thoughts cause our bodies to release chemicals that actually suppress our immune systems."* That article goes on to state, *"The dangerous emotions that we must guard against are prolific and include jealousy, pride, envy, anger, and bitterness. It is important to understand what plays into each one of these emotions...One of the most dangerous of all emotions is anger. When anger is not dealt with immediately, it festers in our souls causing pain, isolation and eventually physically disease. That is why the Bible says not to "let the sun go down on your wrath" (Ephesians 4:26). Warning signs of anger include low self-esteem; being overly critical, controlling or confrontational; lacking in trust; blaming others for mistakes; and overreacting...If anger is not dealt with, bitterness sets in. You can choose to hold on to your hurt or pain and grow increasingly bitter, or you can deal with it, release it and feel better..."* (2) We deal with the issue of eliminating negative emotions such as jealousy,

pride, envy, anger, and bitterness in more detail Part III of this book.
(1) *Dressed to Kill*, Copyright © 1991 by Rick Renner (Pg. 243-244).
(2) "God Doesn't Want You to Crash and Burn." Janet C. Marccaro, *Charisma Magazine,* July 2003.
(3) "Patient Knows Best." *Reader's Digest Magazine,* August 1991
(4) Printed by permission, Fred Doerflein, Desert Hot Springs, CA.

CHAPTER 6
BEWARE OF NEW AGE MIND SCIENCE TEACHING

"But those who desire to be rich fall into temptation and a snare, and into many foolish and harmful lusts which drown men in destruction and perdition. For the love of money is a root of all kinds of evil, for which some have strayed from the faith in their greediness, and pierced themselves through with many sorrows" (1 Timothy 6: 9-10).

While traveling in third world nations, I have observed secular success books, which I knew to contain new age, mind science teaching, being sold alongside Christian success books in Christian bookstores. When I inquired as to why they were selling these secular books the book seller replied, *"These authors teach Christian principles."*

Several years before this, two men who worked for one of the large Fortune 500 companies in our area had shared with me a business training seminar to which their company had sent them. They were excited about the seminar because they thought the instructors were Christian since they had quoted a number of biblical scriptures and had even quoted the words of Jesus while presenting the seminar. But these instructors were not Christian; they were members of one of the new age, human potential organizations, which combine and synthesize many different religious and philosophical views into their business success teachings.

The final event that caused me to include this chapter in *Business by the Spirit* occurred when a Christian friend of mine excitedly related to me an event that had occurred in a recent sales training meeting sponsored by his multilevel marketing company. The sales trainer had been teaching the class that they could harness the power of the mind to increase and consummate their sales. In order to demonstrate this power, he had my friend sit in a chair in front of the class; he directed the other students to concentrate their thoughts on elevating him off the chair. My friend was quite excited as he related this story, because he had actually been lifted off the chair by what he considered to be the "combined power of the group's minds." Unfortunately my friend, even though he was a Christian, did not recognize that he had just been levitated out of the chair by a demonic occult power, a power that is often called upon by those involved in cultic religions.

NOT ALL "SECULAR SUCCESS TEACHING" IS SECULAR

It is important to recognize that not all secular success motivation teaching (SSMT) is secular; some of these success teachers have borrowed occult techniques and teachings from the metaphysical and mind science religions, and have repackaged them under the New Age Human Potential Movement.

"The New Age movement is a loosely structured network of individuals and organizations who share a vision of a new age of enlightenment and harmony (the "Age of Aquarius") and who subscribe to a common "world view." According to Ron Rhodes an editor with the Christian Research Institute in Charlotte, North Carolina, some New Age human potential seminars, such as *Lifespring, est, and The Forum* "teach attendees that "you are your own god" and "you can create your own reality." He reports that "Sometimes these seminars seek to induce an altered state of consciousness in attendees to lead them to question their *former* understanding of reality." (1)

In spite of these questionable practices, many Fortune 500 companies have been eager to use the New Age seminars because "they promise increased productivity, better employee relations, more creativity among workers, and—bottom line—*more sales.*"(1)

NOT EVERYONE WHO QUOTES THE BIBLE IS CHRISTIAN

The new age practitioners feel at home with the Judeo-Christian Bible and freely quote principles from the Bible and the words of Jesus, but they mix these teachings with the teachings of Buddhism, Hinduism, other religious doctrines, including the principals taught by some occult mystics. Often the immature Christian attending one of these seminars mistakes these human potential teachers for Christians because they teach some biblical principles. But the new age movement is syncretistic, combining many different practices and beliefs in religion and philosophy in an effort to gain compromise and unity. One of the first indicators that these teachers are not Christian is when you hear them refer to "the subconscious mind."

These secular success teachers often refer to a mysterious "universal intelligence" from which the subconscious mind may channel the energy and knowledge of the universe, in order to transmute one's desires into their physical equivalent. One SSMT states, *"You are surrounded by a universal mind that contains all the intelligent ideas and knowledge that ever existed or that ever will exist."* These SSMT teach their pupils that the secret to the ages, the key to health, happiness and prosperity can be theirs if they only learn to tap into this universal intelligence. Various SSMT call it by different names: Napoleon Hill, an early twentieth century SSMT, referred to it as "Infinite Intelligence"; Ralph Waldo Emerson called it "The Oversoul"; Madame Blavastsky a Russian occult practitioner who founded the Theosophy Society in 1875, called it "The Secret Doctrine"; Carl Jung, the Swiss psychoanalyst who was once an associate of Sigmund Freud's, called it the "Supra-conscious Mind." This doctrine has also been called by a number of similar names. Beware of such teachings; this "universal intelligence" by any name is simply a secular title for a principality of Satan's kingdom whose assignment it is to woo men away from the truth of the living God by helping them to become rich.

To the worldly Christian this "universal intelligence" sounds a lot like the Omniscient, Omnipotent, and Omnipresent God of the Bible; except that it makes no moral judgment and requires no moral commitment. I began reading these secular motivation books long before I became a Christian, and because of my lack of biblical knowledge, I like some of the readers of this book assumed that "universal intelligence" was the Christian God. Fortunately, I did not become heavily involved in these cultic philosophies, or I may never have recognized the truth and accepted Jesus Christ as my Lord and Savior.

SATAN WILL HELP WORLDLY MEN TO PROSPER

The SSMT move naturally into these mind science and cultic religious philosophies because they think that man is a mental and physical being. Most of them are completely ignorant of the fact that they are in reality dealing with evil, occult spirits. They teach that if one develops a burning desire, and a definite purpose in their subconscious mind, that this universal intelligence will give them the power and the information required to make them successful in life. They suggest that it may come as inner voice, a chance encounter with other people, or by creative ideas which will help them fulfill their goals in life; it may also come through an unpredictable event which manifests in their life.

One SSMT pioneer, who developed his philosophy of success in the first part of the twentieth century, began to hold imaginary meetings with great men of the past in which he solicited their wisdom and advice. He reportedly found that these meetings became so real that he became fearful of their consequences and discontinued them for several months. These meetings were what we in the Christian world refer to as a séance involving familiar spirits (spirits who were familiar with the lives of men from the past) who pose as the spirits of men from the past. (King Saul disobeyed the Jewish law and sought a séance to inquire of a dead spirit in the final days of his life...1 Samuel 28:7-19) This SSMT claimed that the ability to access this universal intelligence was a major factor in the tremendous success enjoyed by hundreds of extremely wealthy men and women that he had interviewed over the years.

The Bible states that the devil is the "god of this world." It is his desire to monopolize the wealth of the world financial system to prevent it from being used to evangelize the world for God. Therefore, it should come of no surprise that he will do everything possible to help worldly men and women to accumulate and hoard large amounts of wealth. The spirit of greed that motivates many of these worldly men and women to lust after wealth is the very spirit that often destroys them.

WEALTH WITHOUT GOD IS DECEPTIVE

The SSMT principles have helped thousands, perhaps millions of individuals to achieve great financial success in nearly every area of our society. In many cases however, the very riches they gained have led them to engage in ungodly activities that have eventually destroyed their lives. On the other hand, some wealthy men live reasonably moral lives and some even give large amounts of their wealth to charity, but if they die without accepting Jesus as their Savior, they sadly will spend eternity in hell, separated from the living God. It was this type of man that prompted Jesus to ask, "For what profit is it to a man if he gains the whole world, and loses his own soul? Or what will a man give in exchange for his soul?" (Matthew 16:26). In the parable of the unjust manager, Jesus equates the "love for money" with the service of Mammon. (Luke 16:9-13) (Mammon is generally considered to be the name of the demonic principality which dominates the world's financial system.) Paul says that "the love of money" is a root of all kinds of evil,..." (1 Timothy 6:10). Notice that Paul did not say, "money is the root of all evil"; he said, "the love of money." Money must be handled carefully and used wisely in order that the desire for it doesn't seduce us from true devotion to God. The Manufacturer's Handbook says, "The blessing of the Lord makes one rich, and He adds no sorrow with it" (Proverbs 10:22).

RICHES ARE NOT FOREVER

In this closing paragraph of Part I, "Getting Started in the Spirit," I would like to share a tragic story concerning the lives of seven successful and wealthy men; it is a story that has been told many times, but it's tragic ending makes it deserving of telling it once again. "In 1923 a group of the world's most successful financiers met at the Edgewater

Beach Hotel in Chicago. Collectively these men controlled more wealth than there was in the United States Treasury…"

They included the following:

- President of the New York Stock Exchange
- President of the largest independent steel company in the U.S.A.
- A member of the President's Cabinet
- President the Bank of International Settlements
- The greatest wheat speculator in the U.S.A.
- Head of the largest monopoly in the world
- The "Great Baron of Wall Street"

All these men knew the "secret of success." All were multi-millionaires. The policies they set in that meeting had an impact on the United States of America for many years in the future. But twenty-seven years later, their wealth had fled and had left them devastated.

- Richard Whitney—president of the New York Stock Exchange served time in prison and died shortly after he was released.
- Charles Schwab—president of United States Steel went bankrupt and lived on borrowed money the last five years of his life; he died penniless.
- Albert Fall—member of the President's Cabinet was pardoned from prison so that he could die at home.
- Leon Fraser—president of the Bank of International Settlements committed suicide.
- Arthur Cutten - the greatest wheat speculator was a fugitive from justice and died in a foreign land.
- Ivan Krueger—head of the greatest monopoly in the world committed suicide.

➢ Jesse Livermore—the "Baron of Wall Street" committed suicide.

All of these men had risen to the top of their various professions. All knew the thrill of high achievement. But these men had made money and success their god, and the desire for riches had caused them to compromise their integrity. When their riches failed them, these once-powerful men were devastated, and they had nowhere to turn. You see, it is important to remember Jesus' words:

"...it is hard for a rich man to enter the kingdom of heaven" (Matthew 19:23).

(1) New Age Movement, Copyright 1995, by Ron Rhodes (Pg. 7, 16, & 24).

INTRODUCTION TO PART II: UNDERSTANDING THE WORLD WE LIVE IN

Many people in America have made the government their god, and they look to it to supply all their needs. Our elected officials, wanting to gain favor with the electorate, have voted into law a number of programs which provide financial assistance to needy businesses and individuals. But every year, thousands of distressed leave businesses and needy individuals go without the available government assistance. Some go without it because they don't know that it is available; others go without it because they don't know how to obtain it; and still others go without it because they have no faith that if they were to apply for it, they would receive it.

In order to receive financial assistance from the government of a nation it is generally necessary to be a citizen of that government, to know the laws that provide for the assistance, and to understand the system that administers that assistance. The same is true in the spiritual realm. In order to obtain assistance from the kingdom of God, we must be citizens of that kingdom; we must know the laws and regulations that govern that kingdom; and we must understand the heavenly system that administers God's laws and regulations.

Many will be tempted to ignore this chapter because it may not appear to provide immediate benefits to their personal or business life. But your lack of understanding of the world in which we live will hinder your ability to fully implement the seemingly more exciting spiritual principles and laws taught in the later chapters of this book. In Part II "Understanding the World We Live In" you will learn:

- How your education and your Darwinian-Freudian mind can negatively influence what you believe and restrict the development of the God kind of faith.
- That the theory of Intelligent Design is rapidly overtaking the theory of Darwinian Evolution.
- That the primary reason God wants you to prosper is to help the poor and populate heaven by spreading the good news of Jesus Christ to the whole earth.
- How a wrong understanding of the creation, the fall, and the redemption of mankind can negatively influence the development of your faith.
- That the Abrahamic Covenant and the blessings of Abraham that it promises are available to every Christian believer by faith.

CHAPTER 7
THE ISSUES OF LIFE

"Keep your heart with all diligence, for out of it spring the issues of life" (Proverbs 4:23).
"Be careful what you think, for your thoughts run your life" (Proverbs 4:23 NCV).

Most of us grow up dealing with the daily problems that constantly press upon our lives—employment, the economy, marriage, raising a family, sickness, divorce—and we find little or no time to contemplate the larger issues of life. Where did the earth come from? Who is man? How did he get on the earth? Where did he come from? What happens when he dies? Few of us have spent much time contemplating the answers to life's most important issues. As you read the spiritual success principles taught in this book you may have concluded that I have always had a strong belief in the Christian-Judeo God, but nothing could be further from the truth. My university's "Darwinian-Freudian" education had severely retarded my belief in the supernatural nature of God; perhaps you also have experienced a similar condition. As we discussed in the opening chapters of this book, what you think and believe is extremely important because it affects what you have and where you are in life. In the following paragraphs, I relate my disillusionment with the supernatural nature of God, and my subsequent enlightenment to that nature, in hopes that it will help and encourage others who may have experienced a similar mindset.

MY EARLY YEARS

I grew up on my paternal grandmother's farm in a small community in the northwestern part of the United States. My father was an entrepreneur who owned and operated a small construction company. Dad started his company in 1932 at the height of America's great depression. Just as his business was beginning to flourish and he was able to spend more time with the family, along came World War II and once again he was required to be away from home, working long hours to further the war effort. From the time I was born until the time I was fourteen years old, I saw my father only on an occasional weekend or a special holiday. My mother was forced to raise our family of three active boys and one girl alone during the depression years of the thirties and the war years of the forties.

A TEST TO MY BOYHOOD FAITH

As a boy I enjoyed the outdoors and spent my summers in the farm fields planting and harvesting the crops. Mother would faithfully take me and my siblings to church every Sunday where I learned the basic tenants of Christianity. Growing up in the fields and forests of the Northwest made it easy to believe in God the Creator. How else could the earth exist? Who else could have made man? I never considered that there might be an alternative. That is until my younger brother died of acute appendicitis when he was four years old. It was then that my young mind was confronted with one of life's most perplexing questions: *if there is a God, why would He allow my brother to die?* My mother was devastated, but my brother's death never shook her faith in God. My father handled my brother's death by blaming the incompetence of our small town doctor.

My father, like many American men in the forty's, never accompanied the family to church. About the time I started to attend high school, I began to skip church and stay at home with my father, and gradually God became less and less important to me.

THE UNIVERSITY CHANGED MY THINKING

It was after I graduated from high school and went to the university to study architectural engineering that my university studies began to erode my faith in the concept of a creator God. My biology professors exposed me to a whole new theory concerning the origin of life. All the top scientific minds, they said, believed in Charles Darwin's Theory of Evolution, which surmised that man had evolved from a primordial soup by a process known as the survival of the fittest. They presented evidence collected by the world's most eminent scientists that proved the Darwinian Theory. At the same time my social science and psychology professors indoctrinated me with Sigmund Freud's theories concerning the conscious and unconscious mind. We no longer need to accept society's prudish morals concerning sex. Freud had discovered that our unconscious mind contained hidden primal sexual desires which controlled our actions independent of our conscious mind, therefore we should just let it "all hang out." Suddenly in a few short years everything my parents had taught me concerning the issues of life were brought into question. After all, I reasoned, my parents had never studied in the university, so how could they know about the latest scientific findings? Weren't these professors among the nations brightest? Certainly they must know the truth! I, like so many who attend the university, accepted the Darwinian and Freudian theories as a proven truth, and unknowingly became a theistic evolutionist. I simply changed my views on creation to believe that God used evolution to create the universe and everything in it. Perhaps you have had a similar experience.

CONFRONTED A SECOND TIME WITH THE ISSUES OF LIFE

In my second year at the university, I was once again confronted with what is undoubtedly the most important issue of life, the issue of *what happens when a man dies?* My brother, who was one year younger than I, suffered a severe head injury in an automobile accident. During the week following the accident our family spent a great deal of time in my brother's hospital room. My mother and her pastor spent considerable time in prayer. My father, who was otherwise not a religious man, dealt with the tragedy by letting my mother's pastor (and indirectly God) know that he would build him a new church if God healed my brother. My brother died a week after the accident. Once again my mother was devastated, but my brother's death did not shake her faith in God in any way. My father simply buried himself in his business activities. I was also devastated, and inwardly I wondered *if there is a God why didn't he answer my mother's prayer? Why didn't he heal my brother? What happens when a man dies? Is there life after death?* I simply didn't know.

IS THERE LIFE AFTER DEATH?

"For bodily exercise profits a little, but godliness is profitable for all things, having promise of the life that now is and of that which is to come" (1 Timothy 4:8).

Many men prosper in this life, but make no provision for the life which is to come, the life after physical death. You may be like I once was—you may not be sure that there is life after physical death. I definitely understand, as I once had the same doubts concerning the issue of life and death that you do. But the quest for the answer to the question "is there life after death?" is the most important answer that you will ever seek. Which view of mankind will you believe? Will you believe the Darwinian-Freudian view taught by my university professors that described mankind as a "mortal being" who has evolved from a primordial sea by a process called evolution; and that when a man dies, his consciousness simply ceases to exist...an individual whose unconscious mind contains primal desires which override his conscious will. Or will you believe the "Creator's Handbook" view that describes mankind as an "eternal spirit" who has a soul (mind, will and emotions) and lives in a mortal physical body, and is required by God to exercise his will against evil. The SSMT for the most part believe in the Darwinian-Freudian view of man, but I no longer believe in that view of man. I believe and teach in *Business by the Spirit* the biblical view of man, and in the provisions that the creator of the universe has made to bless mankind with every spiritual blessing in heavenly places in Christ (Ephesians 1:3). As you read the opening pages of this book you have a decision to make, a decision that will not only affect your prosperity in this life, but the life to come.

KOREA - AN EXPERIENCE WITH MASSIVE DEATH

When I graduated from the university shortly after the cessation of the Korean War, I was commissioned as a second lieutenant in the United States Army. Upon completion of my Officer's Basic Training, because I was a graduate architectural engineer, I was sent to Korea to help rebuild that nation's war-torn infrastructure. In order to maintain troop morale, the Army would rotate us to Japan every six to eight months for two weeks of rest and recreation. When it became my time to rotate to Japan, I had to wait until the next day for the Air Force to bring in another transport plane from Tachikawa Air Force Base near Tokyo. The Air Force plane that was to have transported me to Japan crashed and burned near the Hahn River as it was landing in Korea. There was very little left of the plane's burned out remains. This was not the first time that I had come face to face with death, but it was the first time that I had witnessed massive death, as every one of the young soldiers on that plane had been killed; no one had escaped. The plane they sent to transport us to Japan was called "the flying boxcar" by the Air Force, but we soldiers called it "the flying coffin." It had a reputation among the troops for crashing.

As I waited for that plane I couldn't get the image of that burned-out aircraft and those dead young men out of my mind. I wondered *what happened to those men when they died. Is there life after death? Is there a heaven and a hell?* I simply didn't know. Besides, it seemed there was no way a person could ever know for sure short of dying themselves. That trip to Japan and back to Korea was the worst airplane flight I have ever taken. For the first time in my life I realized that I had a fear of death. Once again I was confronted with the most important issue of life - is there life after death?

IT'S EASY TO IGNORE THE ISSUES OF LIFE

After I returned to the United States I put my thoughts concerning life after death out of my mind; they were simply too unpleasant and painful to ponder. Besides there were other things to occupy my mind—a new civilian job, marriage, raising children, working hard to become successful in business. Anyway, I figured, in civilian life, death never really occurred that often, certainly not among my young friends and the business people with whom I associated. God was only an abstract individual invented by primitive people to explain life, but in the twentieth century we knew the "truth," that there was no God. The headlines of the 1960's boldly proclaimed, "God is Dead." The concept that there was no God was readily accepted by my carnal (body-ruled) mind. If there was no God, then there were no absolute moral values, and if there were no absolute moral values, then I could live the way I wished, and I could simply follow my primal sexual urges.

When I returned to civilian life, I went to work in the construction industry, was married, adopted two children, bought a house on a lake, and launched out to live the American dream. When I was thirty-five years old, I was asked by two college friends to join them as a partner in their small architectural firm. I determined to make that firm a success, and over the next several years I was on the road constantly, driving or flying somewhere to obtain new business and to design new and exciting projects. Two years later my wife divorced me, and over the next several years both of my partners left the business. I was working harder and demanding more than any of them wanted to give. I had become very hard-driven; I had become like my father.

AN EXPERIENCE THAT CHANGED THE WAY I THOUGHT

As I mentioned elsewhere in this book, in February of 1975, I was attracted to a beautiful blond lady named Barbara, and in December of that same year we were married. When Barbara and I returned from our honeymoon I found a book on our living room table, which had been left by my new mother-in-law. It was entitled

Power in Praise and it was written by Merlin Carothers, a retired Lt. Colonel in the United States Army. Carothers had served with the famous 82nd Airborne; he was a master parachutist with over 90 jumps. He was my type of man. I thought *Power in Praise* was another success motivation book touting, *"If you praise your employees it will give you more power!"* But as I read the book, I realized that Colonel Carothers was not talking about success motivation principles in a conventional sense; he was talking about God's gift of eternal life.

He said, *"Many Church going people think of God's plan of eternal life as a ten-cent gift. They believe they have to struggle to live a good life to keep their "free gift." Trying hard to live a good life puts them under such a continual strain that they often wonder if trying hard to be a Christian is worth it. To them it just means going to church on Sunday, staying away from things that might be a lot of fun, and giving their hard-earned cash into the offering plate"* (1) Well, frankly that's what I thought Christianity was. I found the book extremely interesting, and I began to read it nearly every day. As I read and reread *Power in Praise,* it began to change the way I thought...and faith in God's word began to develop in my heart.

STARTING A NEW WAY OF LIFE

Then on the Sunday afternoon of March 8, 1976, I asked Jesus Christ to be my personal Lord and Savior. I remember the occasion vividly, because I sensed a peace within my soul, and I also knew that the fear of death of which I had become acutely aware during my service in Korea had departed from me. Most importantly, I knew that if I died I would be with in heaven with Jesus. You might ask how I knew those things. I don't know how to express it; I just knew it in my innermost being. I continued to read the book *Power in Praise* particularly the third chapter of that book entitled "Power Unlimited." In that chapter, Colonel Carothers described his experience in receiving what is referred among Christians as the "baptism of the Holy Spirit." In September of that same year, after reading that book another seven months, I also received the baptism in the Holy Spirit. As I prayed in my new-found prayer language, Jesus became very real to me.

I knew that he was alive, and I knew that the Bible was true. Suddenly the issues of life became clear. How could I have ever believed that man evolved from the slime of some primordial soup into an intelligent, conscious being with the ability to love and live in community and cooperation with others. Suddenly I knew there was a Creator God, and that he had given us a "Handbook" (the Bible) to guide and direct our lives. Regretfully, however, it has taken me far too many years to understand the details of that Handbook.

If you would like to know how a person can also be born again and baptized in the Holy Spirit turn to the final chapter of this book where I discuss it in further detail. But in the remaining paragraphs of this book I would like to share with you how my born again experience began to change the way I thought about the issues of life, and how the Holy Spirit has taught me to use the spiritual principles found in the Creator's Handbook to live a prosperous and fulfilled life.

DARWINIAN-FREUDIAN TEACHING: FACT OR THEORY?

So if you are as I once was, pondering the meaning of life, or if you have ever wondered as I once did if God is real, or if there is life after death, but are deterred by your Darwin-Freudian indoctrinated mind from believing in the creator God, let me share several truths with you.

Darwin's Theory of Evolution declares that life on earth arose from non-living matter by way of some unknown, unconscious, natural process, and then over billions of years proceeded to evolve into more complex life forms through the process of random mutation and natural selection. This theory of evolution is being taught in our schools as if it were an established scientific fact, but nothing could be further from the truth. More than one hundred and fifty years after Darwin first published his book *Origin of the Species*, science has still not been able to find the transitional forms (the so called missing links) in the fossil record that are required to substantiate his theory of evolution.

To the atheist evolutionist, man is a cosmic accident; therefore, it is not surprising that in an article in the *Scientific American* written by Stephen Jay Gould, one of America's leading atheist evolutionists, he quotes Sigmund Freud. Gould notes: "Sigmund Freud often remarked that great revolutions in the history of science have but one common, and ironic, feature: they knock human arrogance off one pedestal after another of our previous conviction about our own self-importance." Gould relates Freud's three examples: a) Copernicus's demonstration that the earth was not the center of the universe, b) Darwin's relegation of mankind to a mere branch of the animal world, and c) Freud's theory concerning the unconscious mind, which in his view exploded the myth of a fully rational mind. Both Gould and Freud regard the idea that a man's life has meaning because they are made in God's image as "human arrogance." In Gould's view, the Darwinian revolution remains woefully incomplete, because human thinking remains hopelessly teleological, which Gould perceives to be *"the last pedestal of human arrogance."* Teleological thinking is the belief that life has a purpose and that everything that we do has a plan and a design. To Gould and his atheistic evolutionist colleagues, mankind *"is but a tiny, late blooming twig on life's enormously arborescent bush –a small bud that would almost surely not appear a second time if we would replant the bush from seed and let it grow again"*(2). In other words, man is the result of thousands of linked events, any one of which could have occurred differently and eliminated the evolution of man as we know him.

Though Freud's basic theories have been largely discredited in the years since his death, he is still heavily quoted in many books on human behavior and in numerous news stories by the secular press. Freud theorized the human mind as an iceberg, the conscious mind being that small portion observable above the water, and the unconscious (subconscious) mind being the larger portion existing below the surface. His theories concerning the mind defied what the Judeo-Christian religion had taught for thousands of years, "that the devil was the perpetrator of evil," and that men were to exercise their will to resist evil. Freud taught that some aspects of the mind were not subject to our will, as the sub-conscious mind contained hidden primal desires which control mankind's actions independently of their conscious mind. Neurotic phobias and compulsions therefore were not the devil's work but that of unconscious primal forces over which man has no control.

Like they did with Charles Darwin's theory of evolution, the atheist intellectual community accepted Freud's theories with open arms. It was comforting to have their godless view of life confirmed, and to know that their sexual and aggressive actions were not the result of sin. According to Freud, they were caused by unconscious primal desires over which men have no conscious control. Therefore, men were free to live life as they desired, without a moral conscious and without the fear of divine retribution, especially as it related to their sexual activities. But Freud, the man who had weakened the faith of many, ended his own life discouraged, embittered, and gravely ill; he lived in constant pain. Near the end he asked his physician Max Schur to assist him in committing suicide, and on September 22, 1939, he lapsed into a coma and died the next morning. Freud's pessimistic view of human existence no doubt reflected the emptiness of his own Godless life.

Darwin and Freud's work are not established scientific facts as our university professors led us to believe; they are nothing more than unproven theories. In fact Darwinian Theory is rapidly being overtaken by a new theory called the "Theory of Intelligent Design." Intelligent Design is not really something new; it was declared to be a fact in the first chapter of the Creator's Handbook thousands of years ago. But for now because evolutionists generally control higher education, the scientific journals, and the media, Darwin's Theory of Evolution is still being taught in our schools and universities as an established fact.

PRESIDENT BUSH STIRS DISCUSION OF INTELLIGENT DESIGN

President George W. Bush in response to a question by a reporter in a group interview on Monday August 3, 2005, said that he believes that intelligent design should be taught along with evolution as competing theories: "Both sides ought to be properly taught...so people can understand what the debate is about," he said according to an official transcript of the meeting. Bush added: *"Part of education is to expose people to different schools of thought..."* (3) His remarks brought a firestorm of objection from the atheist evolutionist intellectuals. They objected to teaching of intelligent design because "it cannot be proven by the scientific method." But after more than a century and a half, these same evolutionists have been unable to prove Darwin's theory by the same scientific method.

OVER 500 SCIENTIST DISSENT FROM "DARWINIAN THEORY"

The American Public Broadcast System (PBS) in a 2001 television series entitled *Evolution* stated *"no scientist disagrees with Darwinian evolution."* In that same year the Discovery Institute first published its "Statement of Dissent from Darwin" as a direct challenge to the PBS pronouncement (4). As of March of 2006, more than 500 scientists from all disciplines had signed that statement. The list of 514 signatories includes member scientists from the prestigious US and Russian National Academy of Sciences. Signers include 154 biologists, as well as 76 chemists and 63 physicists. They hold doctorates in biological sciences, physics, chemistry, mathematics, medicine, computer science, and related disciplines. Many are professors or researchers at major universities and research institutions such as MIT, The Smithsonian, Cambridge University, UCLA, UC Berkeley, Princeton, the University of Pennsylvania, Ohio State University, the University of Georgia, and the University of Washington. The Discovery Institute's dissent maintained: *"The fact is, that a significant number of scientists are extremely skeptical that Darwinian evolution can explain the origins of life"* (4).

In the spring of 2008, Ben Stein released a documentary film entitled *Expelled: No Intelligence Allowed*. It exposes the incredible bias that exists in scientific and educational communities toward those who question Darwin's Theory of Evolution or believe that the complexities of life suggest an intelligent designer. In one particular scene the documentary takes the viewer on a visual tour showing the complexity of a single simple cell, which is like a miniature universe in complexity. Then a noted scientist points out that it might have been easy for Darwin to believe that life began with a single cell, but since we now know the incredible complexity of even the simplest single cell, it should be impossible for any honest scientist to believe that today.

LEADING ATHIEST CONVERTS TO THEORY OF INTELLIGENT DESIGN

Antony Flew, one of the world's leading atheist philosophers, recently changed his mind concerning Darwinian evolution as the source of life. He now believes that it is impossible to explain the origin of life without a creator and has become a believer in the theory of intelligent design. *The Times* of London has referred to Flew as "one of the most renowned atheists of the past half-century, whose papers and lectures have formed the bedrock of unbelief for many adherents." Flew won the prestigious John Locke Prize in mental philosophy. He has written twenty-six books, many of them classics like *God and Philosophy* and *How to Think Straight*. But while Flew no longer believes in Darwinian evolution, he says that he cannot become a Christian because he is unable to accept the idea that a loving God would send anyone to hell, therefore making Flew a Deist. A Deist is an individual who believes in the existence of God solely on the basis of reason. He believes that God created the universe, and after setting it in motion he abandoned it, and assumes no control over it (5).

TO THE ATHIEST, INTELLIGENT DESIGN IS "UNTHINKABLE"

Sir Arthur Keith, the famous British evolutionist who wrote more than twenty books defending evolution, stated, *"Evolution is unproved and unprovable. We believe it because it's only alternative is special creation, and that is unthinkable."*(6)

The atheist evolutionists have committed their lives to a godless worldview because they do not wish to submit their lives and their sinful desires to the God of scripture. The idea of a creator God is to them unthinkable.

WHICH UNDERSTANDING OF MAN WILL YOU BELIEVE?

If one wants to understand the make-up of man, they have two sources from which to obtain that information.

- ➢ The first source is the physiological and psychological studies of man made by our eminent scientists and psychiatrists.
- ➢ The second source is the Creator's Handbook, the Bible.

Scientists have used the scientific method very effectively to accurately observe, describe, and understand the physical laws that govern the earth, such as the law of gravity or the law of thermal dynamics. Other scientists have also made giant steps in accurately observing, describing and understanding the physical characteristics of the human body, but they have been decidedly less successful in accurately observing, understanding, and describing, the mental and spiritual aspects of man. Neither have they been able to prove the source of life, nor the probability of life after death.

Over the years I have come to favor the information provided by the Creator's Handbook concerning the origin of life, and how to successfully live our lives both in this world and in the world to come. The Creator's Handbook, like the Darwinian and Freudian theories, cannot be proven by the scientific method, and it is not written in the scientific language of our day, but it has been time tested over a period of thousands of years.

In order for you to successfully operate the Spiritual Laws described in this book, I believe that it is necessary for you to decide which understanding of creation and of mankind you will choose to believe.

Most secular success motivation teachers have adopted the Darwinian-Freudian view that man is a mortal physical body with a conscious and a subconscious mind. I have chosen to believe the Creator's Handbook's view, that man is an eternal spirit, who has a soul (mind, will and emotions) and lives in a mortal body.

In order to develop strong faith in God's desire and ability to prosper his people, you may need to change the way you think about the world you live in.

(1) Power in Praise, © 1972 by Logos International, Merlin Carothers (Pg. 20).
(2) Stephen Jay Gould, "The Evolution of Life on Earth" *Scientific American* © 1994 Scientific American Inc., October 1994, (Pg. 91).
(3) Peter Baker and Peter Slevin, Washington Post Staff Writers, Wednesday, August 3, 2005; (Pg. AO1).

(4) Discovery Institute Website, http://www.discovery.org
(5) Article entitled "Thinking Straighter" by James A. Beverley, © 2005 *Christianity Today*, April 2005, Vol. 49, No.4, (Pg. 80).
(6) Sir Arthur Keith, *Evolution and Ethics*. New York: G. P. Putnams Sons, 1947 (Pg. 230).

CHAPTER 8
THE PURPOSE OF PROSPERITY

"And let them say continually, 'Let the Lord be magnified, Who has pleasure in the prosperity of His servant'" (Psalms 35:27b).

At the time I became a Christian, my wife Barbara and I attended a mainline denominational church that emphasized going to church on Sunday, giving money into the offering plate to support the minister and maintain the church building, and trying to live a good moral life. Like most American churches there was little or no emphasis placed on winning those outside the church to Christ.

But soon after becoming born again, I attended a meeting of the Greater Seattle Chapter of the Full Gospel Business Men's Fellowship, a Christian businessmen's organization, whose stated mission was to call men back to God, introduce them to the power of the Holy Spirit, and train and equip them to fulfill the great commission. The president of the chapter which I attended had a global vision for the work of God; at every meeting he would enthusiastically ask *"How many of you have a suitcase?"* Nearly everyone would raise their hands to indicate that they had a suitcase. Then he would ask *"How many of you have a passport?"* Only a few in the meeting would respond in the affirmative. Next he would enthusiastically challenge the people to get a passport, and then he would have them stand as an act of faith while he prayed that God would provide the finances required to participate in one of the many mission trips that the Greater Seattle Chapter sponsored. These mission trips, which were called "airlifts," were designed to win the businessmen of the nations to Christ, introduce them to the power of the Holy Spirit, and teach them to also lead other men to Christ. I had been a Christian for a little over a year and had gone to the Fellowship meetings for only a few months when I decided to participate in an airlift to Europe. Since that time, I have traveled to dozens of nations starting Fellowship chapters, speaking in churches, praying for the sick, casting out devils, and providing financial resources to help reach the lost in those nations. Because I was encouraged to go to the nations within months of my being born again and baptized in the Holy Spirit, it never occurred to me that I needed a formal bible school education or that I had to be an ordained minister in order to do the works of Jesus (Matthew 9:35). *Doing the works of Jesus* has been as much a part of my life as that of operating my business.

Recently I attended a seminar taught by John Garfield entitled "Releasing Kings for Ministry in the Marketplace." I picked up a copy of a book co-authored by John Garfield and Harold Eberle by the same name (1). In their book they make the following observation:

Think about the great names that you know from the Bible. Perhaps Abraham, Isaac, Jacob, Joseph, Moses, Joshua, or David comes to mind. Now, list all the priests you can remember. Draw a blank? You may think of one or two prophets, but leaders identified strictly as priests do not stand out. Why is this? The reason is that God always has used kings as the movers and shakers in the kingdom.

Priests (pastors, teachers, and other church leaders) play an important role in the Temple (Church), but it's a role that has a maintenance implication. They keep families healthy by feeding them the Word. They counsel, encourage, heal, marry, and bury. They shepherd, feed, and equip God's people. Pastors naturally gravitate to a peaceful, healthy atmosphere and have a godly motivation to keep congregations happy and maturing.

In contrast, kings go to war. They establish their authority. They move people into new territories – stretching people out of their comfort zones to expand the Kingdom of God on this Earth.

Historically, kings have been leaders who worked closely with people and prophets. They were talented people with the resources to get things done. They also were well-versed in God's word and occasionally could operate in prophetic ministries themselves.

In the Old Testament, we see that Daniel spent his life in a governmental (kingly) role but used a prophetic gift to interpret dreams. Abraham was a businessman who raised livestock and became the most powerful man in his day. Moses was a national leader. Joshua was a military leader. They all had a calling as kings to possess the inheritance God gave His people.

In the New Testament, we see the Lord pressing major initiatives with kings again. Neither Jesus nor any of his twelve disciples came from priestly lines. The major players were kings in the ministry sense. They had influence and power in the marketplace; some even had significant wealth.

Notice that the kings did more than provide for the Temple of God. This is important because some of the church leaders today want to release the kings, but they think the king is to use all his profit to provide for the Priest and the Temple. Of course, the kings will be blessed financially, and they will be generous in providing for God's house, but they are called to do more than that. Kings have a calling of God to extend the rulership of Jesus Christ into all of the world. They expand the Kingdom to fill the earth with His glory (1).

I agree with the authors of *Releasing Kings in the Marketplace*. God has called those of us who work in the marketplace to expand the kingdom of God in the earth, both by going to the nations ourselves and by providing for his missionaries to go. Paul says that the Lord "Himself gave some to be apostles, some prophets, some evangelists, and some pastors and teachers for equipping the saints for the work of the ministry, for the edifying of the body of Christ" (Ephesians 4:11-12).

THE PURPOSE OF PROSPERITY

If we expect God to make us prosperous, then we should endeavor to use our prosperity to accomplish His will and do His work. The apostle Peter points out that it is not His will that any human being should perish (2 Peter 3:9), and Jesus Himself said, "For God so loved the world that He gave His only begotten Son, that whoever believes in Him should not perish but have everlasting life (John 3:16). It is God's primary purpose in the earth to save the lost and populate heaven, and therefore His primary purpose for prospering His people is to evangelize the world.

Before you read any further, perhaps you should examine your motives. Why do you want God to prosper you? Is it to help finance the work of God or is it to enjoy the luxuries of life—a big home in an upscale neighborhood, expensive foreign cars, a vacation home in Florida, personally tailored clothes, and entertaining in the cities most expensive restaurants? I am not suggesting that these things in themselves are wrong, God wants you to live an abundant life, but what I am asking you is this: is your primary motive to become wealthy so you can live a luxurious lifestyle or is it to help evangelize the world?

When God makes you wealthy, He would have you use your wealth wisely. Paul admonishes his young follower Timothy to "Command those who are rich in this present age not to be haughty, nor to trust in uncertain riches but in the living God, who gives us richly all things to enjoy" (1Timothy 6:17). The word command used in this verse is the Greek word paranggello which means to "charge or to command" (2). Paul's admonition to the rich Christian is a requirement; it is not a negotiable option. The word rich used in this scripture is the Greek word plousios, and it describes someone who possesses incredible abundance, extreme wealth, and enormous influence (2). God wants His people to have abundance, enough to not only meet their own needs but to abundantly meet the needs of others as well.

If you are financially blessed, praise God for it, but be careful to separate who you are from what you own. If you are willing and obedient, the Holy Spirit will direct you as to how to best use the resources that He has provided to you. The eyes of the Lord go throughout the earth to find an individual through whom He can funnel His financial resources to advance His kingdom.

And if you know others who are financially blessed, don't covet their wealth. Instead rejoice with them and pray that they will have the wisdom to use their wealth to advance the kingdom of God in the earth.
(1 *Releasing Kings for Ministry in the Marketplace-*. John Garfield and Harold Ebrele. Worldcast Publishing (June 2004) (Pg. 16 & 17).

(2) *Sparkling Gems from the Greek*; ISBN 0-9-97254-2-5 Copyright © 2003 by Rick Renner P.O. Box 702040, Tulsa OK 75170-2040 (Pg. 893).

CHAPTER 9
UNDERSTANDING THE WORLD WE LIVE IN

"Now all these things happened to them as examples, and they were written for our admonition, upon whom the ends of the ages have come" (1 Corinthians 10:11).

I recently read in a prominent Christian newsletter that 65 percent of the American population consider themselves to be born again Christians, but only 3 percent of those who consider themselves born again have a biblical world view; a world view defined by the Christian Judeo Bible. The Creator's Handbook (the Bible) reveals that we live in two worlds, a natural, physical world which we contact with the five physical senses and an invisible, spiritual world which we contact with a sixth sense, a sense called faith (Hebrews 11:1). It also reveals that the unseen spiritual world is inhabited by spiritual beings called angels—the angels of God who dwell in heaven and do God's will, (Psalms 103:19-22) and the angels of Satan who were cast out of heaven war against God's will (Ezekiel 28:11-19). These spiritual beings have the ability to influence human beings, and we are admonished to resist the influence of evil spirits (1 Peter 5:8&9). The spiritual world, while invisible to our physical senses, existed before the physical world, which is temporary, and is more real than the physical world because it is eternal (Romans 1:20; 2 Corinthians 4:18).

Because people are not familiar with the Bible, they often blame God for sickness, the death of loved ones, poverty, and natural disasters such as earthquakes, hurricanes, and floods. But poverty, sickness, death and natural disasters are the result of the fall of mankind, and their author is Satan. When mankind fell in the Garden of Eden, Satan became the god of this world (2 Corinthians 4:4). His evil rule resulted in a curse upon the earth, a curse which eventually caused God to bring a worldwide flood, a cataclysmic event that destabilized the very foundations of the earth and brought natural disasters such as earthquakes, hurricanes, and floods on the earth. The source of many of mankind's problems can be clearly seen in the book of Job. Satan caused the Sabeans to kill Job's servants and steal his oxen and donkeys; he caused fire to fall from heaven and consume Job's servants and his sheep; he caused a great wind to destroy Job's older son's house, and kill all his sons and daughters; and he caused the Chaldeans to kill his servants and steal his camels (Job 1:13-19). Jesus clearly describes Satan as "the thief who comes to steal, kill and destroy" (John 10:10). When hurricanes, tornados, earthquakes, and plagues strike the earth, people often use the term "the judgment of God" to describe these events, but most biblical judgment is simply the inevitable, built-in consequences of man's sin and separation from God, which forces God to remove His hand of protection and allow Satan to unleash his fury upon mankind.

MANY CHRISTIANS ARE THEISTIC EVOLUTIONISTS

Many in the western world who consider themselves Christian are confused concerning the origin of life and the world in which we live. For nearly a century now the "Theory of Evolution" has been taught in our schools and universities not as a theory, but as a proven fact; but that theory stands in direct opposition to the description of creation revealed in the Bible. Because of our educational bias toward evolution, many (like I once was), have become "theistic evolutionists"; that is, they believe that God used evolution to create the universe and everything in it. By believing in at least some aspects of evolution they are able to gain scientific respectability, and also satisfy an inward belief that there must be a God. But reinterpreting scripture to make it compatible with evolution contradicts most Old Testament writers, all New Testament writers and Jesus Christ Himself, and will produce a weak faith which cannot bring the power of heaven to earth to work on your behalf.

THEORY OF INTELLIGENT DESIGN

As pointed out in the last chapter, science, for the most part, has embraced the atheistic and materialistic approach to creation; they have adopted Darwin's Theory of Evolution which offers only a mechanical explanation of the universe and the world that we live in. They believe that man is a cosmic accident the result of thousands of linked events, any one of which could have occurred differently and eliminated the evolution of man as we know him.

But during the latter part of the twentieth century, a significant number of scientists have become extremely doubtful that the Theory of Evolution can explain the origins of life, and this theory is being rapidly overtaken by that of Intelligent Design. Many of the leading scientists have concluded that "the world we live in" is so complex and intricately interwoven that it cannot possibly be explained without a creator, an Intelligent Designer.

But science will never be able to locate this Intelligent Designer because He is a spirit; therefore, He cannot be contacted through man's central nervous system or his physical senses. When mankind committed treason in the Garden, he died spiritually; he became separated from his Creator, and he is no longer able to communicate with

God who is a spirit. If mankind is to understand creation, then the Creator must reveal Himself to mankind.

WHY IT IS IMPORTANT TO UNDERSTAND THE WORLD WE LIVE IN

In order to exercise the spiritual laws which are described in other chapters of this book, it will be helpful, if not necessary, to understand what the Bible has to say about the following five biblical events: 1) why the universe was created; 2) how that creation became separated from its Creator; 3) why the Creator found it necessary to destroy His creation through a worldwide flood; 4) why the Creator made a covenant with a Hebrew named Abraham; and 5) why the Creator sent His Son Jesus Christ to the earth.

THE REASON FOR THE EARTH IS MAN

The Manufacturer's Handbook is the Creator's revelation of Himself and his creation to mankind. It was not written in the scientific language of our day; it was written in a simple but descriptive language that would transcend time. In Genesis, the first chapter of that Handbook, the Creator describes the origin of the universe, the origin of the solar system, the origin of the atmosphere, the waters above the earth, the waters under the earth, the origin of life, the origin of humanity, the origin of evil, the origin of language, government, culture and religion. It further declares that the earth is the reason for the universe (Genesis 1:14-19), and that mankind is the reason for the earth, for after God created man His creative activities ceased (Genesis 1:26-2:2).

UNDERSTANDING THE CREATION OF MAN

On the sixth day God created man; He made him in His own image and His own likeness; He made him an eternal spirit so that man could communicate and fellowship with Him (Genesis 1:26). He formed a physical body for man from the elements of the earth (Gen. 2:7), so that man could function in the physical world. Then He breathed His Spirit into man and man became a living soul with a mind, a will, and emotions that allowed him to operate independently in the physical world (Genesis 2: 7 & 1 Corinthians 15:45). When God breathed His Spirit into man, He gave him a measure of His faith, just as He does today, when a man or woman becomes born again (Romans 12:3). When God made mankind, he designed him in His image to be His earthly king, to take dominion and reign over His earthly creation (Genesis 1:27-28). Eden was a realm in which Adam, as God's earthly under ruler, imitated God, where Adam walked by faith and "called those things which do not exist as though they did" (Romans 4:17- 22), and his faith gave substance to his hope (Hebrews 11:1 NEB).

GOD, THE FATHER, DESIRED SONS AND DAUGHTERS

God was revealed as the King of glory or the King of heaven in the Old Testament, (Daniel 4:37 & Psalms 24:7), but when Jesus Christ, the Son of God, came to the earth He revealed the father nature and the love nature of God (Matthew 6:6-13 &1 John 4: 8 &16). It was His love nature that motivated the King of heaven to desire sons and daughters with whom he could share His love. He created mankind in His image, the image of a King, with the ability to reign over the earth as His earthly under-ruler. The King of heaven desired to extend His heavenly spiritual kingdom to an earthly physical kingdom by delegating His authority over the earth to His sons and daughters.

GOD GAVE MEN A FREE WILL

From the beginning He wanted sons, not servants; therefore he gave mankind a free will because He wanted His earthly children to love Him, fellowship with Him, and obey Him out of love and affection, not out of obligation or compulsion. Even though God's spirit dwelt in Adam to guide and help him, he was free to choose whom he would love and obey. God's original plan was to create a family to whom He could relate as a father—a family of sons and daughters whom He could guide by His Spirit to extend His spiritual kingdom in heaven to His physical kingdom on the earth.

EVERYTHING THAT HE HAD MADE WAS EXCELLENT

"...And God saw that everything that He had made was very good" (Genesis 1:31). It was excellent! It was excellent because there was no poverty, sickness, or death in the earth; these curses had no place in God's original plan for creation. But Adam found no one among the creation that was a suitable companion for him, so God took flesh and bone from Adam's side and made a woman whom He called Eve, and she became Adam's wife. Then God blessed Adam and Eve and gave them every herb and tree that bears fruit to eat, with one prohibition: they were forbidden to eat of the tree of "Knowledge of Good and Evil." God warned Adam…"in the day that you eat of it, you shall surely die" (Genesis 2:17).

THE EARTH WAS PERFECT UNTIL MAN COMMITTED TREASON

The earth was a perfect place until a fallen angel named Satan tempted Adam and Eve to doubt God's word and eat of the forbidden tree of Knowledge of Good and Evil. Satan said to Eve, "You will not surely die for God knows that in the day you eat of it your eyes will be opened, and you will be like God, knowing good and evil." Eve ate of the fruit of the tree of the Knowledge of Good and Evil and gave some of it to her husband Adam and he also ate of it. Mankind had disobeyed the only prohibition which their Creator had given to them (Genesis 3:1-7). Adam, God's earthly king, obeyed Satan; he committed treason, and in so doing he turned the legal authority of God's earthly kingdom over to Satan. When Adam obeyed Satan, he became Satan's slave (Romans 6:16), and Satan became the god of this world (2 Corinthians 4:4). When Adam sinned, the spirit of faith, the nature of God, departed from Adam. He became spiritually dead; his spirit became separated from the Spirit of God (Genesis 2:17). Satan, a fallen angel, became mankind's spiritual father (John 8:44), and consequently the spirit of fear, the nature of Satan, entered into mankind. Adam's first words after he sinned were: "I heard Your voice in the garden, and I was afraid."

MAN LOST HIS KINGDOM

When man sinned, he lost his kingdom and became a slave to Satan, a cruel dictator. Man was no longer a citizen of the kingdom of God, and he had been expelled from the spiritual realm, from the faith realm; now he had to rely solely on his human abilities. He then had to work with his mind and his body in order to survive. Mankind was under a curse (Genesis 3:17-19). The "kingdom of

God" in the earth had been replaced by the "kingdom of darkness"! Satan became the god of this world, and he continues to rule that kingdom by blinding the eyes of men so they cannot see God (2 Corinthians. 4:4). The whole earth is under the sway of the evil one (1 John 5:19); it is filled with poverty, sickness and death. Because of sin, mankind became separated from God, and he was under a curse. Mankind, who was created to rule the earth, had turned over his kingship to a cruel dictator, and the Spirit of God could no longer dwell in men. He could not help himself; he was in need of a liberator, a redeemer.

GOD IMMEDIATELY INITIATES A PLAN TO SET MANKIND FREE

Immediately after Adam and Eve committed treason, God confronted Satan, mankind's deceiver, with the following words: "And I will put enmity between you and the woman, and between your seed and her Seed; He shall bruise your head, and you shall bruise His heel" (Genesis 3:15). The God of heaven looked into the future and proclaimed that a specific man, born of a specific woman, would deliver Satan a fatal blow! Satan would wound the man, but the man would conquer Satan! This prophetic statement by the **King of heaven** announced His plan for the redemption of mankind and the future restoration of the kingdom of heaven to the earth.

The Old Testament is the unfolding story of God's plan to redeem mankind from the curse, and to restore the kingdom of heaven in the earth. While Satan did not have a full understanding of God's plan to redeem mankind, he knows that if he is to prevail he must control the mind of fallen man, and he must eliminate the knowledge of God in the earth.

GOD BRINGS A WORLDWIDE FLOOD

Nearly 1700 years after mankind committed treason in the Garden, the human race had become so utterly wicked that the knowledge of God was nearly eliminated from the earth (Genesis 6:5-7). Only one man, Noah, still served God (Genesis 6:8&9). In order for a righteous line of men to be maintained in the earth through which God at the right time in history could bring forth the promised redeemer, He was forced to destroy that entire wicked generation. God revealed to Noah that he planned to destroy mankind through a great flood, and gave him instructions for the building of an enormous ship, an ark, by which he, his family, and a male and female of every living thing that breathed air, would be saved from the destruction of the flood (Genesis 6:18 &19; Genesis 7:13-15).

The biblical description of the flood in the book of Genesis describes it rather briefly, it does not describe the cataclysmic changes that will forever effect and destabilize the very foundations of the earth and bring future disasters such as earthquakes, hurricanes, tornados and floods upon the earth. "...in the second month, the seventeenth day of the month, on that day all the fountains of the great deep were broken up, and the windows of heaven were opened. And the rain was on the earth forty days and forty nights" (Genesis 7:11-12). The waters increased and lifted up the ark, and it rose high above the earth... The waters prevailed fifteen cubits upward, and the mountains were covered (Genesis 7:17&20). "And the waters prevailed on the earth one hundred and fifty days" (Genesis 7:24). *Notice that the flood water was actually on the earth for over a year.

Dr. Walt Brown, a creation scientist and author of the book *In the Beginning: Compelling Evidence for Creation and the Flood*, describes the violent changes that occurred in the earth, its atmosphere, and indeed in the physical universe itself at the time of the flood:

"The flood begins suddenly with all the fountains of the great deep busting open on one day. "Geshem rain" begins. (Genesis 7:11) - Rupture phase: A crack propagates around the earth in 2-3 hours, releasing subterranean water, fountains of muddy water jet high above the earth. Mammoths are frozen in super cold, muddy hail falling from above the atmosphere. The highest velocity water escapes earth and forms comets. Launched rocks become asteroids and meteoroids. - 40 days and 40 nights of Geshem rain" ends (Genesis 7:4, 12) - Flood Phase: Rising waters blanket and suppress the high jetting fountains of the great deep. Animals and plants are buried in sediment from muddy water. - Flood waters rose until the 150th day when they covered all preflood mountains. (Genesis 7:19-24) High-pressure water continues to gush up into the flood waters. Liquefaction sorts sediments and dead plants and animals. Salt domes, coal, and oil begin forming. Continental-Drift Phase: Mid-Atlantic Ridge buckles up; Atlantic floor rises and western Pacific subsides, so the hydroplates accelerate downhill, sliding on a layer of lubricating water. When the massive hydroplates decelerate, they are crushed, thickened, buckled, and heated in a gigantic compression event. Over thrusting occurs in some places. 150th Day: A wind passes over the earth. Waters begin to subside. Ark lands on the mountains of Ararat. (Genesis 8:1-4) Continents take on present shape. As major mountains form, air is displaced, causing a great wind. The earth slowly rolls 35° – 45°, and the poles shift. 150th – 371st Day: Passengers remain on the Ark; Recovery Phrase: Hostile environment: earthquakes, inner earth heated, oceanic

trenches and methane hydrates form, flood basalts and volcanoes erupt, water drains, continents shift, vegetation reestablished, and Ice Age begins. Lowered sea level facilitates land migration and allows the formation of table mounts and submarine canyons. Plateaus form. Large continental canyons form by dam breaching 371st Day: Ark off-loaded (Genesis 8:15-19)" (1).

The destabilization of the very foundations of the earth that occurred as a result of the flood still affects the earth to this day.

GOD RE-ESTABLISHES HIS COVENANT WITH MANKIND

Four hundred years after the Flood, the most important event in human history until the birth of Christ took place. God established a covenant with a Hebrew named Abraham. He cut a Blood Covenant of Friendship with Abraham and his seed (Genesis 15:7-18). That covenant meant that everything that Abraham owned was God's, and everything that God owned was Abraham's if either needed the other's assistance. That covenant, which we call the Abrahamic Covenant, is important to us Christians because it is the legal foundation upon which we may receive the blessings of Abraham (prosperity, healing, and eternal life) by faith (Galatians 3:14). Because this covenant is so important, we have included a detailed description of it in the next chapter of this book.

THE DECENDANTS OF ABRAHAM PRESERVED THE KNOWLEDGE OF GOD

For another two thousand years after God made the covenant with Abraham, He used the descendants of Abraham, the Hebrew nation of Israel, to preserve the knowledge of God in the earth. He protected the Israelites from harm, He provided for them during times of famine, He delivered them from slavery in Egypt, and He gave them the Law of the Covenant and a system of sacrifices to cover their sin if they broke the law. He did all this in order that he might preserve them as a righteous remnant, through whom in the fullness of time He might bring the promised Redeemer into the earth (Psalms 105:7-45; Ephesians 1:10). God used the physical descendants of Abraham to maintain the knowledge of God on the earth until the Seed of Abraham, the Christ (Galatians 3:16), would appear to redeem mankind from the curse of the law (Galatians 3:13), and so that the Gentiles in Christ Jesus (Christians) might also receive the blessings of Abraham through faith (Galatians 3:14).

JESUS, THE PROMISED REDEEMER, RE-ESTABLISHISHES THE KINGDOM

At just the right time in history, the King of heaven sent His Son Jesus Christ to re-establish His kingdom in the earth. *"...When the fullness of time had come, God sent forth His Son, born of a woman, born under the law, to redeem those who were under the law, that we might receive adoption as sons"*. And because we are sons, God has sent the Spirit of His Son into our hearts. (Galatians 4:4-6). Jesus Christ was born of a woman, thus he was a man; but the woman was not impregnated by the seed of a man, but by the Holy Spirit (Luke 1:30-38). Therefore Jesus Christ was a man, but he was not born of a natural generation. He was a not a descendant of Adam, and therefore was not under the dominion of Satan. Christ walked on earth with the authority of a man (Mark 2:10), yet as a man who was without sin—a man who could legally pay the penalty for mankind's transgression, a man who conquered Satan (Colossians 2:15), and a man who delegated His victory to every man who would believe in Him (Matthew 28:18-20; Mark 16:15-18). Christ redeemed mankind from the curse of the law (paid the price for mankind's sin), so that the blessing of Abraham might come upon him through faith (Galatians 3:13-14). By believing that Christ, who knew no sin, became sin for us, we become the righteousness of God in Him (2 Corinthians 5:21).

IS GOD CAUSING YOUR PROBLEMS?

When reading the Creator's Handbook, an individual can readily become confused if he does not judge what he reads about God in the Old Testament by what Jesus said about God in the New Testament. For instance, the Old Testament describes the curses that would come upon the Israelites if they did not obey the voice of the Lord (Deuteronomy 28:15-68) as follows: "The Lord will send on you cursing, confusion, and rebuke…(verse 20). The Lord will make the plague cling to you…(verse 21). And The Lord will strike you with consumption, with fever, with inflammation …(verse 22). These curses are referred to in Galatians 3:13-14 as the "curse of the law"; they lead us to believe that God Himself puts sickness, plagues, drought, calamity and the other curses mentioned in the Old Testament upon His people. If God is the one who puts sickness on people, as is implied in these Old Testament verses, then why does the New Testament say that "God anointed Jesus of Nazareth with the Holy Spirit and with power, who went about doing good and healing all who were oppressed by the devil" (Acts 10:38)? If God is the one who puts sickness on people, then Jesus the Son of God spent His entire earthly ministry healing the sick and destroying the works of God. Obviously something is wrong here. I believe the answer lies in an explanation given by Dr. Robert Young, author of Young's

Concordance, in his out-of-print book entitled *Hints to Bible Interpretation*. In that book, Dr. Young states that in the original Hebrew manuscripts, the verb was in the permissive sense rather than the causative sense. In other words these verses should have been translated the *Lord will permit these curses to come upon you*. Dr. Young's explanation has settled the issue for me. I believe that you must also settle this issue if you want to develop strong faith, because if you believe that it is God who is causing your problems, it will be harder for you to develop faith, the type of faith required to get you out of the problem.

If we sin and violate God's spiritual laws, we get out from under the protection of God, and He will permit the devil to attack us. It is the same with fear. Fear is the opposite of faith. While we may not understand it, if we allow fear to dominate our thinking, we are in sin. The Bible says fear is sin (Romans 14:23), and fear will stifle your faith and allow the enemy of your soul to wreak havoc in your life.
Such was the case with Job, for he was walking in great fear, which allowed Satan to bring calamity upon his life. "For the thing I greatly feared has come upon me, and what I dreaded has happened to me." (Job 3:25).

SATAN'S STRATEGY IS TO BLIND GOD'S PEOPLE

Satan's strategy has been to blind God's people with a false and misleading philosophy concerning the stewardship of property and material things—a philosophy which condemns material prosperity as a worldly pursuit that hinders one's spiritual development. Satan wants the Christian to reject the wealth of the material world and the stewardship of it because he wants it for himself and his kingdom. The result of this philosophy in the Christian world has been a lack of finances—finances to help those in need as well as to proclaim the Good News of our redemption throughout the world. It has prevented the heathen, godless nations that Satan holds in captivity from hearing the Good News that Christ has redeemed them from the curse.

SATAN IS THE GOD OF THE WORLD FINANCIAL SYSTEM

Make no mistake about it: Satan has a monopoly on the world's financial system (Matthew 4:8&9). Mankind motivated by satanic greed will do almost anything to gain worldly wealth. Man is so avaricious that every conceivable law has been passed to safeguard men from each other. The newspapers and the television screens are full of men who have been caught circumventing these laws in order to increase their financial statements with millions of dollars in unearned wealth.

THE SILVER AND THE GOLD BELONG TO GOD

But throughout the scriptures, God declares Himself to be the rightful owner of the earth and all its riches. "for the earth is the Lord's, and all its fullness" (1 Cor.10:26; Psalms 24:1; Psalms 50:12). "The silver is Mine, and the gold is Mine,' says the Lord of hosts." (Haggai 2:8). The earth's riches are God's because He made them; they belong to Him even though they are not presently in His possession. In the remaining pages of this book, I will share with you some of the strategies and weapons that God has given to you and me to take back our portion of those riches and use them to expand the kingdom of God on the earth.

(1) Excerpt from Table 21. Comparison of Biblical Chronology with Major Events of the Hydroplate Theory – from the book In the Beginning: Compelling Evidence for

Creation and the Flood (7th Edition) by Dr. Walt Brown. Copyright © 1995-2007, Center for Scientific Creation. All rights reserved.)

CHAPTER 10
ABRAHAM'S BLESSINGS ARE YOURS

"And he said, 'Lord God, how shall I know that I will inherit it?' So He said to him, 'Bring Me a three-year-old heifer, a three-year-old female goat, a three-year-old ram, a turtledove, and a young pigeon.' Then he brought all these to Him and cut them in two, down the middle, and placed each piece opposite the other; but he did not cut the birds in two" (Genesis 15:8-10).

"And it came to pass, when the sun went down and it was dark, that behold, there appeared a smoking oven and a burning torch that passed between those pieces. On the same day the Lord made a covenant with Abram..." (Genesis 15:17-18).

There is a recurring message that runs from Genesis to Revelation; it is that God has made a covenant with Abraham and with his seed, a covenant which He remembers forever. It is a covenant of blessing. It is a sacred covenant of friendship which was established with blood; therefore, it is the "blood covenant of friendship" between God and Abraham.

This is good news! It is news that every Christian should be excited about, but little is known in twenty-first century Christianity regarding either the existence or the sacredness of this blood covenant of friendship that God made with Abraham.

A number of years ago I came across a book by Dr. H. Clay Trumbull entitled *The Blood Covenant* (1). That book not only illuminated for me the sacredness of a "blood covenant" but the importance of the covenant that God cut with Abraham and with his seed. In his book, Dr. Trumbull presents overwhelming evidence that there has been a blood covenant practiced by all primitive people from time immemorial; and because the practice of the blood covenant is so widespread, it has the marks of an original revelation from God (1).

UNDERSTANDING THE BLOOD COVENANT

Sir Henry Stanley and Doctor David Livingston were two men who stirred the imagination of English speaking peoples throughout the world in the middle part of the nineteenth century. Doctor Livingston was a Scottish missionary who left Scotland in 1841 to explore the continent of Africa. His mission was to open the interior of Africa to colonization, extend the Gospel of Jesus Christ in that same region, and abolish the African slave trade. After nearly fifteen years in Africa, he returned to England on a furlough. Then in 1866, he departed on his last and most famous exploration of the Dark Continent. Little was heard from Livingston during the next five years, and many became concerned for his safety. In 1871, Henry Morton Stanley, a reporter for the New York Herald, embarked on a mission to Africa to find Dr. Livingston. Upon finding him near lake Tanganyika, Stanley uttered his now famous words, "Doctor Livingston, I presume?" Stanley, in his books describing his African journeys, relates that he cut a blood covenant of friendship with various African tribes more than fifty times.

On Stanley's first trip to Africa, he came in contact with a powerful equatorial tribe. They were very war-like, but Stanley was not in a position to fight them. Finally, his interpreter asked him why he didn't make a blood covenant with the chieftain of the tribe. Stanley asked what making a blood covenant would involve, and was told that it meant drinking each other's blood. Stanley revolted from such a rite, but conditions kept growing worse, until finally the young African man asked again why he didn't cut a blood covenant of friendship with the old chieftain. Stanley asked what the results of such a covenant would be, and the interpreter explained. "Everything the chieftain has will be yours if you need it."

This appealed to Stanley and he investigated further, after several days of negotiation, he and the chieftain arrived at a covenant. Stanley was in poor health, and he had brought along a goat to provide milk for his nourishment, but during the negotiations the old chieftain seemed to want nothing but Stanley's goat. Finally Stanley gave up the goat, and in return the old chieftain handed him his seven-foot copper-wound spear. (Stanley thought he had been cheated, but he found later that wherever he went in Africa with the old chieftain's spear, every tribe bowed and submitted to him).

When the negotiations were complete, two men were selected as substitutes for Stanley and the chief. Then a priest stepped forward with a cup of wine, made an incision in both men's wrist, and let the blood drip into the cup of wine. Then the wine was stirred and the two men's blood was mixed. As the two substitutes drank from the cup, the act bound Stanley and the chieftain, as well as Stanley's men and the chieftain's warriors, into a blood brotherhood that was indissoluble.

At the conclusion of the ceremony the old chieftain stepped forward and shouted, "Come, buy and sell with Stanley, for he is our blood brother." A few hours before, Stanley's men had to stand guard over their bales of cotton cloth and bags of trinkets, but now he could leave his goods lying in the roadway and nothing would be disturbed. For anyone to steal from his or her blood brother was a death penalty. The old chieftain couldn't do enough for his newfound brother. Stanley couldn't understand the sacredness of it, and years later wondered about it.

There was another very important feature of this ceremony. As soon as the two young men had drunk each other's blood, a priest stepped forward and pronounced the most awful curses that Stanley had ever heard—curses that were to come upon Stanley and his men if they broke the covenant. Then Stanley's interpreter stepped forward and pronounced the curses that would come upon the old king, his wife, his children and his tribe if they broke the covenant with Stanley (2).

While the method of cutting the blood covenant varies from region to region, in many places the method is similar to that described above by Stanley. In some societies, rather than drinking the blood, those making a covenant may put their wrists together or touch their tongues to the blood flowing from each other's incision as a means of consummating the covenant. In South America, primitive tribes cut a blood covenant in a manner similar to that in Genesis (Genesis 15:9&10), by slaying the sacrificial animal, cutting it in half and laying the two halves of the animal opposite each other. Then both of the individuals who are cutting the covenant walk between the two halves of the slain animal to consummate the blood covenant (1).

However, it is not the method used that is important; it is the fact that whenever the blood covenant was pronounced, it was considered a sacred agreement to be honored by the individuals partaking in it, and most often the penalty for breaking the covenant was death. But even more important, the moment the blood covenant ceremony is consummated everything that a blood covenant brother owns is at the disposal of his covenant brother, if he needs it. Neither brother however, would ever think to ask anything of the other, unless he was driven by circumstances to require it.

GENESIS - THE MOST IMPORTANT BOOK IN THE BIBLE!

Dr. Henry Morris, a scientist and biblical scholar, makes a strong case that the book of Genesis is the most important book in the Bible. He observes that if the book of Genesis were removed from the Bible, the rest of the Bible would make no sense. Genesis describes to us the origin of the universe, the origin of life on the earth, the origin of evil, the origin of the Jewish people…and gives meaning to life itself. The book of Genesis devotes more than half of its fifty chapters to the call of God upon one individual, a rancher and businessman named Abram. In fact, in the book of Genesis, God made some sixty promises to this man.

GOD CALLED ABRAHAM AND HIS OFFSPRING TO BE HIS PEOPLE

Two thousand years after the fall of mankind and four hundred years after the Flood, the human race were worshipping idols again. But God had a plan; He called a man named Abram (Abraham's name before God changed it) to leave his home in idolatrous Mesopotamia and go to a land where He would make him the father of many nations.

Then twenty-five years after God called Abraham out of Mesopotamia to establish the Hebrew nation, the greatest event in human history until the birth of Christ took place:

God cut a blood covenant with Abraham (Genesis 15:7-18). The Hebrew word for covenant *"beriyth"* means "to cut." It suggests an incision where blood flows, thus the name "blood covenant." The "blood covenant of friendship" that God cut with Abraham is referred to in scripture as the Abrahamic Covenant, and because of it, Abraham is the only man in the Old Testament called the friend of God (2 Chronicles 20:7; Isaiah 41:8).

It is important for Christians to understand the Abrahamic Covenant, because it is the legal foundation upon which every blessing which God has promised to the Jew and the Christian is based.

GOD CUTS A "BLOOD COVENANT OF FRIENDSHIP" WITH ABRAHAM

The fifteenth chapter of Genesis is one of the most important chapters in the most important book of the Old Testament because it depicts the establishment of the Abrahamic Covenant. God came to Abram in a vision and said, "Abram, I am your shield, your exceedingly great reward"(Genesis 15:1). But Abram said, "Lord God, what will You give me, seeing I go childless, and the heir of my house is Eliezer of Damascus?" (Genesis 15:2). Let me paraphrase Abram's response: "So if you give me the whole world, what good is it to me, for I have no descendant through whom I may establish my posterity." So God said, "...but one who will come from your own body shall be your heir." Then God took Abram outside his tent and said, "Count the stars if you are able to number them... So shall your descendants be" (Genesis 15:4&5). And Abram "believed in the Lord, and He accounted it to him for righteousness" (Genesis 15:6). He received God's promise by faith.

Two verses later God said, "As for me, bring a three year old heifer...and a young pigeon." Abram brought them and cut them in two down the middle, and he placed each piece opposite each other, but he did not cut the birds in two (Genesis 15:9&10). In the evening, God appeared as a smoking oven and a burning torch and passed between the pieces, consuming the offering, to consummate the "blood covenant of friendship" with Abram (Genesis 15:9-12&18).

You see, God is a spirit. He didn't have any blood, so He had Abram shed the blood of innocent animals as a substitute for His blood. And after consuming the offering by fire, God proclaimed that He had made a covenant with Abram (Genesis 15:18).

ABRAHAM CUTS THE BLOOD COVENANT OF FRIENDSHIP WITH GOD

When Abram was ninety-nine years old, God appeared to him and changed his name from *Abram*, meaning "exalted father," to *Abraham*, meaning "father of many nations" (Genesis 17:1-6). Then God commanded Abraham and his male descendants to consummate the "blood covenant of friendship" with their own blood, by cutting the flesh of their foreskin (circumcision). God said that their circumcision would be the sign of an everlasting covenant between Him and Abraham and his descendants, and that He would be their God (Genesis 17:7-14). God further proclaimed to Abraham that he was to no longer call his wife by the name *Sarai*, but by the name Sarah, and that He would bless Sarah and through her give Abraham the son which He had promised to him some twenty-five years earlier. Then God told Abraham to name his son Isaac, and proclaimed that He would establish His covenant with Isaac as an everlasting covenant (Genesis 17:19&21).

Abraham cut the blood covenant of friendship with God with his own blood, and now everything that God possessed was Abraham's and everything that Abraham had was God's...even his life. (1)

ABRAHAM RECEIVED THE PROMISED SON

Abraham was one hundred years old when his son Isaac was born. Finally, after twenty-five years, Abraham had received his most cherished possession, a son from his own body, by his wife Sarah. Isaac was the "son of promise" who would assure Abraham's posterity—a son through which Abraham's name would be preserved to future generations (Gen. 21:1-7).

GOD TESTS ABRAHAM'S FAITH

Have you ever wondered why God tested Abraham? When God cut the covenant (old covenant) with Abraham, all the angels of heaven and all the demons of hell knew that God was capable of keeping His part of the covenant; but could and would Abraham keep his part of the covenant?
If Abraham would not have kept the covenant, then no legal agreement between God and Abraham would have existed; and without a covenant with a man, God would have no legal basis to provide mankind a substitute sacrifice, a redeemer to pay the price for man's transgression.

Justice demanded that God test Abraham's ability to keep the covenant; otherwise Satan (the god of this world) would have a legal claim against God's right to provide mankind a Redeemer. Abraham had to prove to the angels of heaven and the demons of hell that he would keep the covenant. Abraham had to prove that everything he possessed was God's should God require it.

THE TESTING OF ABRAHAM

Abraham had believed God for a son for some twenty-five years before Isaac was born. Then when Isaac was in his late teens, God tested Abraham by asking him to sacrifice his only son Isaac on a mountain as a burnt offering (Genesis 22:1&2).

When they arrived at the mountain which God had shown them, Isaac said to Abraham, "Look, the fire and the wood, but where is the lamb for a burnt offering?" (Genesis 22:7).

Abraham prophetically says, "My son, God will provide for Himself the lamb for a burnt offering." (Genesis 22:8). God provided a lamb for Himself in the person of Jesus Christ the Son of God. John the Baptist proclaimed Jesus to be "...The Lamb of God who takes away the sin of the world" (John 1:29). In the book of Revelation, Jesus is proclaimed to be "...the Lamb slain from the foundation of the world" (Revelation 13:8).

ABRAHAM FOUGHT THE GOOD FIGHT OF FAITH

The writer of Hebrews tells us that when God asked Abraham to sacrifice his son Isaac on the mountain, Abraham's faith reasoned that God was able to raise Isaac from the dead in order to keep the covenant (Hebrews 11:19). But Satan, no doubt, tried to steal God's Word out of Abraham's heart. Anyone who has attempted to believe God under difficult circumstances knows the mind games that the devil plays in order to get a believer to doubt God. I am sure that Abraham went through the same kind of mental testing that you and I do. I can just imagine some of the thoughts that went through Abraham's mind during that three-day trip to Mount Moriah: *What are you going to tell Sarah when you come home without Isaac?...The authorities will have you in jail as soon as you get home!...Don't you remember what God said to Cain when he killed Abel?*

ABRAHAM PASSED THE TEST

As Abraham took the knife to slay his son Isaac, the angel of the Lord called to him from heaven: "Do not lay your hand on the lad, or do anything to him; for now I know that you fear God, since you have not withheld your son, your only son, from Me" (Genesis 22:12). After Abraham passed the test, the angel of the Lord called to Abraham a second time out of heaven, and said, "'By Myself I have sworn, says the Lord, because you have done this thing, and have not withheld your son, your only son-" (Genesis 22:15-16). Then God made more promises to Abraham and his seed (Genesis 22:17-18):

- I will bless you…
- I will multiply your descendants…
- Your descendants shall possess the gates of their enemy…
- In your seed (singular), all nations of the earth shall be blessed because you have obeyed my voice.

"…because you have done this thing, and have not withheld your son, your only son-" (Genesis 22:16)—God Himself, the entire corporate power of heaven, became the surety of the Abrahamic Covenant. God had found, in Abraham, a man that would keep the covenant, a man with whom He could legally enter into relationship with mankind, and a man through whom he could legally bring the promised Redeemer into the earth.

GOD GAVE THE ISRAELITES THE LAW

After God delivered the Israelites from Egypt, He made them a sovereign nation; and then through Moses, He instituted the Law and gave them a system of sacrifices which tied the "blessings of Abraham" to the keeping of the Law. He did this in order to preserve the Jewish people by providing a method by which they could atone for their sin until the promised Redeemer would come.

WE HAVE BEEN REDEEMED FROM THE CURSE

God proclaimed that the Abrahamic Covenant was an everlasting covenant (Genesis 17:7&19). Everlasting means that the Abrahamic Covenant is still in effect today. Not only did God make a promise to Abraham and his seed, but He also swore an oath, so that by two unchangeable things—His promise and His oath—we might have great confidence in His covenant promises (Genesis 22:16; Hebrews 6:17-18).

Here is the exciting news: in the New Testament book of Galatians, Paul proclaims that **Christ** is the seed to which the Abrahamic promises were made. "Now to Abraham and his seed were the promises made. He does not say, "And to your seeds" as of many, but as of one "And to your Seed" who is Christ" (Galatians 3:16). In this verse, Paul refers to the promise that God made to Abraham in Genesis 22:18. Then a few verses later, Paul makes it clear that if you belong to Christ, you are Abraham's seed and heirs according to the promise (Galatians 3:29). What promise? The promise that God made to Abraham!

A few verses earlier Paul had proclaimed that "Christ has redeemed us from the curse of the law," and that "the 'blessings of Abraham' might come upon the Gentiles in

Christ Jesus, that we might receive the promise of the Spirit by faith" (Galatians 3:13&14). The Gentiles in Christ Jesus are Christians, and the promise of the Spirit was that we Christians might receive the blessings of Abraham. How do we receive the blessings of Abraham? The same way we receive everything from God...by faith.

WHAT ARE THE BLESSINGS OF ABRAHAM?

In his book entitled "WHAT ARE ABRAHAM'S BLESSINGS ANYWAY? Dr. Jay Snell state's "From Genesis to Revelation, the God of Scripture specifically singled out from the rest of humanity only one group of people, Abraham and his seed, to whom he specifically committed himself in the form of Sixty Promises. Because of this commitment, God embraced Abraham and his seed in a way in which he embraced no other group of people in recorded history." (3) Snell points out elsewhere that many of the sixty promises use the terms *bless, blessed,* or *blessing,* and that the root Hebrew word translated "bless, blessed, or blessing" is **barak** which "means to endue with power for success, prosperity, fecundity, longevity, etc." (5). (Fecundity means to be fruitful in childbearing)

The "blessings of Abraham" are summarized in the first fourteen verses of the twenty-eighth chapter of Deuteronomy. The first two verses tell us: "Now it shall come to pass, if you diligently obey the voice of the Lord your God, to observe carefully all His commandments which I command you today, that the Lord your God will set you high above all nations of the earth. And all these blessings shall come upon you and overtake you, because you obey the voice of the Lord your God." Verses 3 to 14 summarize the "blessings of Abraham" that would come upon the Israelites if they would keep God's commandments. From these verses we can see that the "blessings of Abraham" promise the seed of Abraham:

- Success in Life
- Material wealth [at the very least having all our needs met]
- Physical health and longevity
- Spiritual life (right standing with God)
- Many Children

The "curses of the Law" are summarized in the last fifty-three verses of that same chapter. "But it shall come to pass, if you do not obey the voice of the Lord your God, to observe carefully all His commandments and his statutes which I command you today, that all these curses will come upon you and overtake you" (Deuteronomy 28:15). Verses 16 to 68 describe the curses that would come upon the Israelites and overtake them if they failed to observe God's commandments. From these verses we can see that the curse of the Law includes problems in every area of life:

- Poverty
- Oppression
- Defeat
- Spiritual death (separation from God)
- Disease and death

JEWS ARE TAUGHT TO SUCCEED

Jesus acknowledged that worldly men are often more shrewd in their generation (in dealing with the production of wealth) than spiritual men (Luke 16:8). But that was not necessarily so in the Old Testament. During the periods of history that the Israelites honored the God of the Covenant, the Jewish Patriarchs were very wealthy men.

They attributed their wealth to the blessing that God had promised to Abraham and to his seed.

Even today, the Jewish people who live in the United States of America enjoy a greater degree of prosperity than the general population as a whole. The "Forbes Four Hundred" is a list published annually of the four hundred wealthiest people in America. Every year, fifteen to twenty-five percent of the names on that list are Jewish, yet the Jewish people represent only two and one half percent of the population of America (4).

The Jewish people are successful because they have been taught that they are the seed of Abraham, they are therefore heirs of the blessings that God promised to Abraham, and that God takes pleasure in the prosperity of his people. And perhaps most importantly, unlike many of us Gentiles, they have been taught that business is an honorable profession (4).

THEN WHY DON'T MORE CHRISTIANS ENJOY THE BLESSINGS?

If the Old Covenant saints enjoyed health, wealth, and salvation, and the New Covenant saints do not, then the New Covenant must not be as good as the Old Covenant. Wrong! The writer of Hebrews says the New Covenant is a better covenant based on better promises (Hebrews 8:6). Then the next question becomes *why don't the majority of Christians live the abundant life of health and wealth as well as salvation?*

Since the blessings of Abraham are received by faith, we must conclude that Christians have not received the blessings of health and wealth because they do not have faith to receive these blessings. Most Christian denominations believe and teach that Christ has redeemed mankind from spiritual death, and therefore we may receive salvation of the soul, by faith; but not all believe and teach that we may receive prosperity and healing by faith. Since faith is information we receive from God to act upon, the reason most Christians do not have faith for prosperity and healing is that health and prosperity are never preached or taught in most churches. How then can the Christian have the faith to receive the blessings of Abraham, if they have never heard what the blessings of Abraham are and that they belong to them?

(1) *The Blood Covenant.* Author: H. Clay Trumbuill. Copyright ©1975 Impact Books, Inc. 137 W. Jefferson, Kirkland, MO. 63122. All Rights Reserved (pg. 4,5,6,7,&10).
(2) *The Blood Covenant.* Author: E.W. Kenyon Fourteenth Edition, Copyright ©1969 by Kenyon's Gospel Publishing House. (Page 11,12,13).
(3) *What Are Abraham's Blessings Anyway?* Volume 1, Author: Jay Snell; Copyright ©1989 by Jay Snell Evangelistic Association, PO Box 59, Livingston, Texas 77351 (Pg. 21)
(4) *THOU SHALL PROSPER – Ten Commandments For Making Money,* Copyright © 2002 by Rabbi Daniel Lapin. All Rights reserved (Pg. 10, 17).
(5) Theological World Book of the Old Testament Vol. 1, (page 132).

INTRODUCTION TO PART III: UNDERSTANDING THE LAWS OF THE KINGDOM

There are three types of laws that influence the affairs of men in the earth: man-made laws, physical laws, and spiritual laws. In order to live happy, fulfilled and successful lives, it is important that we understand those laws. In Part III of *Business by the Spirit*, we will familiarize you with five laws of the kingdom of God which influence your success in your life.

It is hard for a person who lives in a democracy to understand the way a kingdom operates. A kingdom is the domain over which the king has dominion; it is a domain over which he has absolute authority. The king makes the law, and the king is the judge and the jury concerning the law--he is sovereign. According to the law of the Medes and Persians, the king's word once spoken could not be altered. Not even the king himself could change it, for the king's word was the law of the Mede-Persian Empire (Daniel 6:8).

It is the same in the kingdom of heaven. When God speaks, His Word becomes the law of heaven; it cannot be rescinded. God's Word is His will; it is the law of heaven. Jesus said, "Heaven and earth will pass away, but My words will by no means pass away" (Matthew 24:35). The psalmist proclaimed "Forever, O Lord, Your Word is established in heaven." (Psalms 119:89); but it is our responsibility to establish His Word in the earth.

God has given human beings a will, and as long as they live on the earth they are allowed to exercise their will. Mankind can choose to believe and obey God's Word or to doubt and disobey His Word. If a man disobeys God's Word, and later confesses his disobedience, God is faithful to forgive his disobedience (1 John 1:9).

But angels do not have a choice; they exist to do God's will, and to obey His law. God's Word is the law of heaven, and the angels of God must obey His Word. When Satan and his angels disobeyed God's law, they were cast out of the kingdom of heaven (Luke 10:18).

When you and I take our stand in faith, on God's Word, and refuse to yield to doubt and unbelief, the angels of God will come along side of us to bring His Word to pass in the earth. In the following pages we will discuss the Law of Success, the Law of Seed Time and Harvest, the Law of Giving and Receiving, the Law of Love, the Law of Faith, as well as the importance of **hope** in the operation of these laws.

CHAPTER 11
OUR LIVES ARE GOVERNED BY LAWS

"Heaven and earth will pass away, but My words will by no means pass away" (Matthew 24:35).

There are three types of laws that influence the affairs of men in the earth: man-made laws, physical laws, and spiritual laws.

YOU MAY VIOLATE A MANMADE LAW AND NOT GET CAUGHT

If you violate a man-made law such as a speed limit or a stop sign, you may not get caught, at least not every time you speed or fail to stop at a stop sign.

BUT YOU CANNOT ESCAPE A PHYSICAL LAW

If you violate a physical law, however, such as the "law of gravity," you will get caught every single time, because the law of gravity is in effect everywhere in the earth, twenty-four hours a day, seven days a week, three hundred and sixty-five days a year. If you throw an object off the roof of a ten-story building in Tokyo, Japan, it will fall to the sidewalk below with the same force it would if you threw it off a ten-story building in Moscow, Russia. It doesn't matter if you know about the law of gravity or whether anybody ever told you about the law of gravity when you were growing up. The law is neutral; it affects every human being, Christian and non-Christian, because they both have physical bodies and live in the physical realm.

NEITHER CAN YOU ESCAPE A SPIRITUAL LAW

The spiritual order of the universe which is established on spiritual laws is just as true as the natural order which is established on natural laws. You have learned to trust God's law of gravity without even questioning it, but you must learn to trust God's spiritual laws in the same way.

Spiritual laws, such as the law of faith, are also in effect one hundred percent of the time even though their operation cannot be observed in the physical realm. If you violate the law of faith you will get caught every single time, because the law of faith is in effect everywhere on the earth, twenty-four hours a day, seven days a week, three hundred and sixty-five days a year. It doesn't matter if you know about the law of faith or whether anybody ever told you about the law of faith when you were growing up. The law is neutral; it works for every human, Christian or non-Christian, because both are spirit beings and subject to spiritual law. Christians, of course, should have more understanding of spiritual laws because they have been introduced to the Manufacturer's Handbook, but sadly most Christians spend little time studying the handbook.

IGNORANCE OF THE LAW IS NOT A DEFENSE!

If you fail to stop at a red light and your car is hit broadside by another car, you wouldn't go to the director of streets in your city and tell him you didn't know that you had to stop at a red light would you? And you wouldn't demand that the city repair your car because you didn't know about the law concerning stoplights would you? You wouldn't make that type of demand because the government has made it your responsibility to know the traffic laws before you are authorized to drive on a public street.

IT IS YOUR RESPONSIBILITY TO KNOW GOD'S LAW

But many times Christians fail to spend time studying the Creator's Handbook, and are therefore ignorant of God's spiritual laws. Then when they violate one of His laws and problems develop in their lives they say, "Oh God why are you letting this happen to me..." The truth is that God has sent His Son Jesus to redeem you from the "curse of the law" (poverty, sickness, and spiritual death) so that you might receive the "blessings of Abraham" (prosperity, health and eternal life) by faith (Galatians 3:13&14). And He has given you His Word to enlighten you and to produce in you the faith required to receive those blessings (Romans 10:8). He has given you his Spirit to teach you all things (John 14:26). It's not up to God to do something about your problem; it's up to you to do something about your problem. God has made the blessings of Abraham (wealth, health and eternal life) available to every Christian, but these blessings are received by understanding and exercising His spiritual laws.

"Beloved, I pray that you may prosper in all things and be in health, just as your soul prospers" (3 John 2).

The Creator's Handbook tells us that God wants His people to prosper in all things, and He wants them to be physically healthy. But notice that He qualifies prosperity and health with the words "even as your soul prospers." From the above scripture it is apparent that the qualification for receiving God's blessing is the prosperity of the soul (the mind, the will and the emotions). Therefore if you are more interested in becoming rich than in serving God, you are reading the wrong book, because the purpose of this book is to teach you to apply God's Word so that you may prosper by cooperating with the Spirit of God. In order to obtain prosperity by the Spirit of God. you must esteem spiritual things more highly than earthly things. God gives us the power to get wealth in order that he may establish and confirm the Covenant that He made with His friend Abraham (Deuteronomy 8:17-18). God wants your needs to be met, and He wants you to have the desires of your heart; but after your needs are met and the desires of your heart fulfilled, He desires that you use your abundance to help those in need, and to take the Good News of Jesus Christ to all the nations of the earth.

CHAPTER 12
THE LAW OF SUCCESS

"This Book of the Law shall not depart from your mouth, but you shall meditate in it day and night, that you may observe to do according to all that is written in it. For then you will make your way prosperous, and then you will have good success" (Joshua 1:8).

God revealed the "law of success" to Joshua shortly after he took over the leadership of the nation of Israel from the Old Testament patriarch Moses. He admonished Joshua four times in the first chapter of the book of Joshua to "be strong and of good courage." After he had proclaimed the "law of success" to Joshua he added, "Have I not commanded you? Be strong and of good courage; do not be afraid, nor be dismayed, for the Lord your God is with you wherever you go."

The "law of success" found in Joshua 1:8 states:

- ➢ Confess My Word from your mouth continuously...
- ➢ Meditate upon My Word day and night...
- ➢ Do all that is written in My Word...
- ➢ Then you will make ***yourself*** prosperous, and then you will be successful.

David reiterates the "law of success" in slightly different words: "Blessed is the man who walks not in the counsel of the ungodly, nor stands in the path of sinners, Nor sits in the seat of the scornful; But his delight is in the law of the Lord, And in His law he meditates day and night. He shall be like a tree planted by the rivers of water that brings forth its fruit in its season, whose leaf also shall not wither; and whatever he does shall prosper (Psalms 1:1-3).

These scriptures affirm the importance of guarding the thoughts we allow to inhabit our mind and controlling the words we allow to be spoken from our mouth as they will determine our success or failure in life.

MEDITATION

When the Creator's Handbook uses the English word *meditation* it is translating the Hebrew word *hagah* (hah-gah) (Strong's #1897). *Hagah* means something quite unlike the English meaning for meditation which is a mental exercise only. In Hebrew to meditate means to reflect, to ponder, to mutter, to contemplate a thought as one quietly repeats the words to themselves (while utterly abandoning outside distractions). It means in today's vernacular to "think upon and confess." Meditation (thinking upon and confessing) is the quickest way to renew your mind and to receive revelation knowledge concerning the Word of God. It is the way that God has given you and me to build strong faith in your heart.

F.F. Bosworth, an early twentieth-century evangelist, said, "Most Christians feed their body three warm meals a day and their spirits one cold snack on Sunday, and then they wonder why they are so weak in faith."

MEDITATION IS THE DIGESTIVE SYSTEM OF THE SOUL AND THE SPIRIT

When we eat natural food our body's digestive system assimilates that food into a form that produces strong bodies. Similarly when we meditate on the Word of God day and night, faith becomes established in our heart and produces a strong spirit. Meditation is the digestive system of the soul and the spirit. As words are contemplated in the mind and spoken from our mouth, they are digested by the soul and established in the spirit. Just as it takes time for natural food to digest and strengthen our physical body, so it takes time for the Word of God to digest and strengthen our spirit. It takes time for meditation on (thinking upon and confessing) the Word of God--"the word of faith"--to develop faith in our inner man.

I remember the first time I heard my voice on a tape recorder. I was a teenager and tape recorders were not the small handheld electronic types we have today; they were quite large and very bulky, and the tape itself was a fine stainless steel wire. I could hardly believe that the deep male voice I heard on the tape recorder was actually my voice. You see I had never heard my voice with the outer ear. I had always heard my voice with my inner ear, but everyone else in the room had heard me with his or her outer ear. They knew what I really sounded like and they assured me that the voice on the tape recorder was mine. God has created mankind with two sets of ears. Each of us has an outer ear and an inner ear. The inner ear is made up of a bone structure inside your head. I believe that when you speak, the inner ear feeds your voice directly to your inner man, your spirit man. This makes the words you speak to yourself much more important than the words that others speak to you. Faith comes more quickly when you hear yourself confessing **God's Word** than when you hear others speaking it to you.

When you think upon God's Word, the mental picture developed in your mind is impressed upon your spirit; and when you confess God's Word with your mouth, your spiritual ear hears it, and your spirit man begins to produce faith in that word. If you meditate upon (think upon and confess) God's Word concerning prosperity, your spirit man will develop faith for prosperity. If on the other hand you meditate on God's Word concerning healing, your spirit man will develop faith for healing. If you want to produce success in your life, you must first determine the area of your life in which you want to become prosperous and successful. Next, you need to find God's Word promising you those things. Finally, you need to meditate on those words night and day until they become established in your heart.

Since May of 2003, I have disciplined myself to spend an hour or more each day meditating on (thinking upon and confessing) God's Word. Every day I arise early and meditate on God's promises to prosper me, to heal me, to protect me, to guide me. I meditate on the authority over Satan that Jesus has delegated to the believer. I am in effect meditating on my rights and privileges as a citizen of the kingdom of God. When I first started this daily routine in 2003, I faced a major financial challenge in my business. (I discuss this challenge in detail later in this book.) As I meditated on God's Word, my spirit began to grow stronger, and as faith in God's promises to prosper me became firmly established in my spirit, that faith produced a fifty percent increase in sales, and it generated the highest annual profit that the company had ever experienced.

You see, as I was feeding my spirit "faith food," I was building it up so that I could overcome the devil, the world and the flesh. As I travel around the world and pray for others to receive the baptism in the Holy Spirit, healing or deliverance, I am amazed at the boldness that this daily meditation in the Word of God has produced in my spirit. The Word of God will produce the same boldness in your spirit if you will only take the time to meditate upon it.

CHAPTER 13
THE LAW OF SEEDTIME AND HARVEST

"While the earth remains, Seedtime and harvest ...Shall not cease" (Genesis 8:22). "Do not be deceived; God is not mocked; for whatever a man sows, that will he also reap" (Galatians 6:7).

I lived the first eighteen years of my life on a farm located in the fertile Chehalis River Valley in the Pacific Northwestern part of the United States of America. About half of our farm land was located in a low area over which the nearby river flooded each year depositing a new layer of rich silty soil each spring. These fields with their rich silty soil produced an abundant harvest each year. The other half of the farm was located on a plateau which was some thirty to forty feet above the surface of the river. The surface of this upper land had a thin layer of rocky topsoil located over a fifty to sixty feet deep layer of gravel. This upper area of the farm would only grow grass for grazing the farm animals and even that required constant irrigation of the fields. The rocky topsoil located over the gravel subsoil acted as a giant drain which allowed the moisture from the rain and irrigation to quickly drain to the water table below. Every spring we tilled the soil and planted the seed, and in the fall we harvested the crop. It took time for the crop to germinate, grow and produce ripe grain, but we never had a crop until we planted the seed.

Every farmer knows that seed produces after its own kind. If he sows corn seed, the soil will produce a crop of corn; if he sows wheat seed, the soil will produce a crop of wheat. He never considers how the soil and the seed interact to produce a crop; he just knows it will.

In a similar way if you sow strife in your relationships, it will produce more strife; if you sow love in your relationships, it will produce a love crop in your relationships. The seed you plant determines the crop you reap. If you plant the Word of God--"the word of faith"--it will produce faith in your heart.

THE MOST IMPORTANT PRICIPLE JESUS EVER TAUGHT

One day while Jesus was teaching by the sea, so many people were crowding around Him that He had to get into a fishing boat and push off from the shore so that the crowd could see and hear Him. From that boat He related what He proclaimed to be His most important parable (Mark 4:3-20; Matthew 13:3-23; Luke 8:4-15). After He had told the parable to the people in the crowd, he explained privately to the twelve disciples: "To you it has been given to know the mystery of the kingdom of God; but to those who are outside, all things come in parables." The word *mystery* used in this verse is the Greek word *musterion* (moos-tay-ree-on) (Strong's #3466). In biblical Greek it means **truth revealed**. It denotes something that is hidden to the unbeliever but is revealed to the believer-- something an individual could never know by their own understanding, as it demands a revelation from God.

Next He said to the twelve, "Do you not understand this parable? How then will you understand all of the other parables?"

Jesus went on to explain that words are the seed, and that man's heart is the soil that produces a harvest in a man's life. Jesus said the parable was specifically talking about sowing the Word of God in the heart of men (Mark 4:14).

The Word of God is referred to by the Apostle Paul as "the word of faith" (Romans 10:8). Therefore we can readily see that the thirty, sixty, one hundred-fold crop that Jesus is referring to in the parable of the sower is faith. The "word of faith" (the seed) that is sown in the heart of man produces "faith" in the heart of man. Everything that we receive from God we receive by faith; therefore being able to understand how faith is produced is of primary importance to doing business by the spirit. Here is another truth which Jesus spoke that is extremely important for you to grasp: the "kingdom of God" is within you, it is in your heart (Luke 17:21). Jesus taught that the kingdom of God (which is in your heart) produces faith in a similar way that the soil in your garden produces a crop.

YOUR HEART IS YOUR GARDEN

Your heart is a garden, which God has provided for you to produce faith for the things that He has promised you in His Word. In the parable of the sower, Jesus spends considerable time discussing the manner in which the various types of soil found in men's hearts affects the size of the faith that they develop.

He described some men's hearts as being hard (bitterness, rejection, deep inner wounds, and anger). When the Word of God is sown in a man's hard heart, he can't understand the Word, and the devil comes immediately and steals the Word out of his heart (Matthew 13:19).

Other men have shallow rocky soil in their heart (envy, jealousy, and pride). When people's hearts are filled with envy, jealousy and pride, they immediately receive the Word with gladness, but because the soil is shallow, the Word develops no root, and so when problems and tribulations arise for the Word's sake, immediately they stumble. You can be sure of this one thing: when you begin to believe God's Word, Satan will immediately bring tests and trials into your life in an attempt to stunt the growth of your faith. He doesn't want you to develop strong faith in God's Word.

Still others have hearts filled with thorns (the cares of the world, the deceitfulness of riches, and the desires for other things), which enter in and choke the Word and it becomes unfruitful. Some Christians are concerned about their children; others are worried about their health, and other cares of the world. Still others are concerned about accumulating things; they desire a bigger house, a more expensive car, a vacation in the Bahamas, and they simply have no time to meditate on the Word of God. Their desire for other things chokes the Word and prevents it from ever producing strong faith.

But some men's hearts contain good soil--they walk in love, they obey God's Word, they meditate upon the Word of God day and night, and they live their lives in accordance with the word. They develop strong faith, faith that produces the thing for which they are believing God, "some thirtyfold, some sixty, some a hundred" (Mark 4:20).

Six verses later Jesus relates another parable describing the kingdom of God. He states, "…The kingdom of God (which is in your heart) is as if a man should scatter seed on the ground, and should sleep by night and rise by day, and the seed should sprout and grow, he himself does not know how. For the earth yields crops by itself; first the blade, then the head, after that the full grain in the head. But when the grain ripens, immediately he puts in the sickle, because the harvest has come" (Mark 4:26-29).

Smith Wigglesworth was a great man of faith in the early part of the twentieth century. They called him the "Apostle of Faith" because of the miracles which occurred as he ministered to the sick. People would often ask Wigglesworth how they could develop the kind of faith which he had. Wigglesworth would reply "First the blade, then the head, then the full grain in the head." Wigglesworth understood the parable of the sower; he understood that it is the Word of God planted in the heart of man that produces strong faith. It is said that Wigglesworth would go no more than fifteen to twenty minutes without opening his New Testament and reading the Word of God.

Jesus' words in this most important parable should give us reason to guard the thoughts which we allow to be established in our hearts because the condition of your heart will determine the size of your faith.

When our thinking is right, our heart will contain fertile soil in which we may plant the "word of faith," the kind of soil in which the Word of God will grow and produce a thirty, sixty, or a one hundred-fold crop of faith, which in turn will provide you with whatever God has promised in his Word.

He has given us His Word to transform our thinking and to root out the negative emotions (the hard, ground, the rocky soil, and the thorns and thistles) that weaken our faith and cause us to under-perform and fail in life. But even good soil will produce the wrong crop if we plant the wrong seed.

BE DILIGENT TO PLANT GOOD SEED

As we pointed out earlier you can plant good seed, the Word of God, or bad seed, the negative depressing words of the devil. The seed that you plant is up to you. If you continually think upon and confess, "God has redeemed me from the curse of poverty, therefore everything I do shall prosper," your spirit will develop faith for prosperity. If you continually confess, "The Spirit of God dwells in me, and guides me into all truth; therefore I have perfect knowledge of every business circumstance and situation that I come up against," then your spirit will develop faith to excel in your business affairs.

Your spirit man never sleeps; when you think and talk like God thinks and talks, your spirit man will search for ways to prosper you because you are agreeing with the Spirit of God who dwells in you. Therefore, His Spirit will teach your spirit to make wise decisions; and He will give you inside information which will help you to prosper in life. God will guide the man or a woman who agrees with his word, to prosperous business contacts and new business opportunities, and the angels of God will influence men to give you the new sales you need to prosper.

But if you continually think upon and confess "Everything I try fails; I never seem to do anything right," you will develop doubt and fear in your heart which will cause you to fail in life.

This is the law of seedtime and harvest as it relates to words sown in the heart of man. Be careful of the seed that you plant in your heart. Set a guard over your mind and your mouth. Make sure that you think upon and confess only those things that agree with the Word of God!

IT TAKES TIME TO PRODUCE A HARVEST

It takes time for a crop to germinate, grow and produce ripe grain. The Creator's Handbook states that "Faith comes by hearing, and hearing by the Word of God" (Romans 10:17). Faith comes by hearing God's Word over and over and over. When we meditate upon (think upon and confess) God's Word (the seed), it takes root in the soil of our spirit. As we continue to meditate upon God's Word, it irrigates that seed with "the water by the word" (Ephesians 5:26), and our faith grows stronger and stronger until the harvest is ready. "First the blade, then the head, after that the full grain in the head" (Mark 4:28). When our faith is complete, the harvest will come; and the thing we have believed God for will manifest in our life.

As you develop faith in God's Word in your heart, and as you speak that faith out of our mouth, it will cause heaven to move the mountain that is standing in the way of your success in life (Mark 11:23). But remember, it takes time to produce a harvest.

"And let us not grow weary while doing good, for in due season we shall reap if we do not lose heart" (Galatians 6:9).

CHAPTER 14
THE LAW OF GIVING AND RECEIVING

"But this I say: He who sows sparingly will also reap sparingly, and he who sows bountifully will also reap bountifully. So let each one give as he purposes in his heart, not grudgingly or of necessity; for God loves a cheerful giver. And God is able to make all grace abound toward you, that you, always having all sufficiency in all things, may have an abundance for every good work." (2 Corinthians 9:6-8)

"'Bring all the tithes into the storehouse, That there may be food in My house, And try Me now in this,' says the Lord of Hosts. 'If I will not open for you the windows of heaven and pour out for you such a blessing that there will not be room enough to receive it. And I will rebuke the devourer for your sakes, So that he will not destroy the fruit of your ground, Nor shall the vine fail to bear fruit for you in the field,' says the Lord of Hosts." (Malachi 3:10-11).

In the following paragraphs we will address the "Law of Giving and Receiving" by exercising faith in the promises of God. God, however, is sovereign, and He could "if the Spirit wills" grant you a financial blessing through a manifestation of the gifts of the Spirit, a manifestation similar to the miracle the widow of the prophet received, when God greatly multiplied her jar of oil (2 Kings 4:1-7). Most Christians, however, will go through life and never experience a manifestation of a gift of the Spirit in the area of finances; they can, however, receive the financial blessings promised by the word of God "by faith" at any time.

Through the centuries much of organized religion has considered material prosperity a worldly pursuit which would hinder a Christian's spiritual development. But in the latter part of the twentieth century, God began to refresh His people through the "Charismatic Renewal" which was followed closely by the "word-faith movement" which taught the importance of the "word of God" in the development of faith, and the importance of faith in receiving the promises of God. Kenneth E. Hagin, founder of Rhema Bible Training Center, is considered to be the father of the modern word of faith movement.

Hagin taught that God is not glorified by poverty, and He doesn't want His people or His preachers to be poor, and he has authored several books on the subject of biblical prosperity. But near the end of his life, Hagin began to observe that many preachers were distorting the biblical prosperity message by teaching what I refer to elsewhere in this book as a "hyper-prosperity gospel," to support a lifestyle of greed and selfish indulgence. Four years before he died Hagin called many of the prosperity teachers to a conference in Tulsa, Oklahoma, in which he attempted to correct many of these abuses. A year later in 2000 he published The Midas Touch - A Balanced Approach To Biblical Prosperity (1), a book in which he attempted to present a balanced, biblical view concerning money and the prosperity message, and condemned many abuses and extreme teachings used by the "hyper-prosperity gospel" preachers.

MANY CHURCHES TEACH PROSPERITY

The prosperity message taught in many churches emphasizes tithing and the giving of offerings to the work of God. Some also teach that the purpose of God's prosperity is to expand the kingdom of heaven in the earth; and many of these churches teach their people how to develop faith in God's promises to prosper them. All of these teachings are important and they are certainly in line with God's Word, but I believe most churches by emphasizing the tithe have omitted some very important New Testament principles concerning giving and receiving.

God's Old Testament people, the Israelites, received the "blessings of Abraham" by keeping the law, and the tithe referred to by the prophet in Malachi 3:10&11 is the law. The New Testament says very little about tithing and there is considerable disagreement in the church as to whether it is actually a New Testament doctrine. But if it is God's primary purpose in the earth to save the lost and populate heaven, and it is our desire to please Him, why would we object to giving ten percent of our income to win the lost to Jesus? Perhaps the more important question should be "is the place I give my ten percent actually winning the lost to Christ?" Jesus, referring to giving and receiving, promised that "... with the same measure that you use, it will be measured back to you" (Luke 6:38).

PAUL HOWEVER HAS A GREAT DEAL TO SAY ABOUT GIVING

The Apostle Paul, however, had a great deal to say about New Testament principles of giving and receiving in 2 Corinthians chapters 8 and 9. He emphasized that we are not to give because of a commandment or out of compulsion (8:8; 9:7), or even according to what others give, but in a manner that does the will of God from our heart (8:5). He encouraged believers to give: abundantly (9:6); as a 'grace' (8:7); out of love (8:8); out of a sincere desire (8:8;8:10;8:11); willingly (8:12, 9:7); joyfully (8:2); generously, even beyond our ability (8:3;8:12); in response to Christ's gift to us (8:9; 9:15); and as evidence of the reality of our confession of Christ (9:13). From the above scriptures, it is clear that the Lord is more concerned with the condition of our heart, than the amount of our gift. Paul assures us that if we give bountifully and cheerfully as we purpose in our heart, and not grudgingly or of necessity, that God is able to make all grace (the entire corporate power of heaven) abound toward us, so that we will always have enough to meet every need (9:8-9). He is able to make us rich in every way, so that we can be generous on every occasion (9:10-11). I personally love the preceding scripture, and it is a promise that I have spoken before heaven and hell many times throughout my business career.

MANY CHURCHES TEACH TITHING AS THE LAW

The tithe is taught in many churches as a mandatory law, a minimum requirement, which precedes free-will giving. But if we give to keep a mandatory law, we are violating the New Testament principles concerning giving taught by Paul, as well as the following scriptures which clearly teach that sons and daughters of God are to be led by the Spirit of God. "For as many as are led by the Spirit of God, these are sons of God" (Romans 8:14). "But if you are led by the Spirit, you are not under the law (Galatians 5:18). Don't misunderstand me; I have not pointed these scriptures out so that you can avoid the giving of the first ten percent of your income to God. If you will yield to the Spirit of God, He may well ask you to give much more than ten percent. God delights in giving good gifts to his children just as we delight in giving good gifts to our children; but when He blesses us financially, He wants us to freely share those blessings with his ministers and others.

SOME NEVER EXPERIENCE THE PROMISED INCREASE

Earlier in this book I remarked that in the thirty years in which I have been a born-again Christian, I have observed a number of Christian men and women who have tithed and given offerings faithfully for years, some perhaps for most of their life but have never experienced anything extraordinary in the way of financial increase. Most of the individuals I have heard testify of God's blessing and increase were not working for a salary; they were generally involved in outside sales, operated some sort of business, or were in a ministry that taught tithing and giving to other Christians. I have wondered about this disparity for years; perhaps you have also, as it is particularly startling in light of the promises of both the Old and New Testaments.

Unfortunately, many Christians, particularly young immature Christians, who have heard teaching on Malachi 3:10-11, have been left with the impression that God is going to open the literal windows of heaven and rain down a financial blessing upon them that they cannot contain. But Malachi 3:10-11 does not teach that God will open the windows of heaven and pour out enough grain, fruit, and herds to fill the farmer's barns. No, it teaches that He will pour out a blessing on the seed the farmer plants and herds the farmer tends, and He will cause them to increase.

God spoke the words recorded in third chapter of Malachi to the people of Judah, an agrarian society, most of whom were farmers and ranchers. When they heard the words of the prophet Malachi, they understood precisely what he was saying; but to the twenty-first century urban dwellers, the meaning of his words bounce off of their minds like rifle bullets off an armored vehicle.

FARM BOYS LEARN TO FARM BY OBSERVING AND DOING

As a child, the Jewish farm boy would carry food and water to the fields where he watched the harvest crew's work. As he grew older his father taught him how to tend the herds, how to prepare the soil, plant the crop, and how to cultivate and harvest the crop. By the time he inherited the land from his parents, he was a seasoned farmer. He understood that after he had paid the tithe, the rest of the increase was available for him and his family to use--everything, that is, except a portion of the newly harvested seed (usually the best seed) which would be required to plant the next year's crop.

His father had also reinforced in him the "Law of Moses": he understood that it required him to give "a tithe" of the harvest to the Lord. He believed that his obedience to the law would cause God to bless the produce of his ground and the increase of his herds (Deuteronomy 28:4), cause Him to give rain to his land in its season (Deuteronomy 28:12), and to protect his crop from the curse of the law: the locust (Deuteronomy 28:38), the worm (Deuteronomy 28:39), and your enemies (Deuteronomy 28:31).

Therefore, the Israelite must have shuttered when he heard the prophet Malachi proclaim, "You are cursed with a curse, for you have robbed Me, even this whole nation." He knew that the curse had removed God's protective shield from his land, and had allowed the devourer (the devil) to bring drought, hail, windstorms, rain storms, floods, insects and blight to devastate his crop, and cause his harvest to fail.

THE JEW HAD TO ACT IN FAITH ON GOD'S LAW

When the Jewish farmer heard the word of the Lord concerning giving a tenth of his increase to the Lord, he had to fight the same mental battle that you and I fight. "I hardly have enough to live on now; if I give ten percent of my harvest (my income) to the Lord, how will we make it to the next harvest (the next paycheck). He knew that the Word of God promised prosperity, but the circumstances he observed with his physical senses disagreed with the law. Like you and me, the Jew had to believe and act on God's Word to receive the promise. He had to believe that if he gave the tithe to God, God would bless the seed which he planted and the herds which he tended, and bring him an abundant increase the following year. Like everything that man receives from God, the Jewish farmer had to exercise faith in God's promise to receive it.

Unlike some Christians, the Jewish farmer understood that God was not going to literally pour down grain and herds out of heaven; he had to prepare the soil, plant the seed, harvest the crop, and tend the herds. God's part was to send rain in the proper season and to protect the crop from the devastating effects of weather, predators, insects and disease.

MOST OF US LIVE IN THE CITY

In the twenty-first century few of us actually live and work on a farm. We live and work in an urban environment and are employed in industrial, technological, professional or service types of jobs. Most of us get a paycheck every couple of weeks instead of a crop every season.

Most average American Christians work hard, earn a good salary, live in a nice house, and own a late model car; but they are in debt up to their eyeballs. They have adopted a worldly lifestyle that devours their seed. After they have given their tithes and offerings and paid their bills there is no seed left "to plant," or as we would say in our urban world "to invest."

Unlike the Jewish farmer who taught his son to save the best seed to plant as next year's crop, most American fathers have failed to teach their sons and daughters how to save a portion of their paycheck to invest in order that they may harvest a crop in the urban financial environment. Their fathers didn't teach them, because their fathers hadn't taught them. We have turned the job of teaching our children over to the public school system, and they have done little to prepare this generation for the realities of the world financial system. Giving to God is not a magic, get-rich scheme to replace study, skill and hard work, any more than it was for the Jewish farmer.

When the average person graduates from high school or college, he has no knowledge of the financial realities of life. Today's graduates don't understand how to read or prepare a financial statement; they don't understand the difference between principle and interest. They simply don't understand the basic realities of personal finance. They think as long as they are making their monthly payments to the finance company then they are succeeding in life.

PROSPERITY MESSAGE IN MOST CHURCHES DOESN'T GO FAR ENOUGH

The prosperity message taught in many churches is good, but it doesn't go far enough. Have you ever heard a sermon on the pitfalls of fulfilling the lust of the eyes, the lust of the flesh, or the pride of life using excessive consumer debt? Have you ever heard a sermon on saving a portion of the harvest (the paycheck) for seed? Have you ever heard a sermon on the necessity of sowing seed (investing), in order that God might have something to bless, something He can cause to increase? Perhaps most importantly have you ever heard a sermon which taught that it is just as important for a Christian man or woman to become financially literate, as it was for the Jewish farmer to learn how to plant and harvest his crop or tend to his herd?

In Part V of this book entitled "Developing Wisdom for Wealth," we discuss some of the fundamental financial principles necessary to the creation of wealth. We also instruct you on how to prepare and read a basic financial statement, we caution you on the pitfalls of consumer debt, and we discuss some basic investment principles and guidelines for planting your seed (investing) in the urban environment.

The creation of wealth requires some start-up capital (the seed) and the knowledge of how to use that capital to bring increase. But the factor which turns these ingredients into wealth is faith! Anyone who wishes to participate in the free enterprise system has to be willing to work first, and then believe for a reward.

The same is true in the kingdom of God! The New Testament principles of giving and receiving are built upon faith, and anyone who wishes to participate in that system has to be willing to give first and then believe for a return. However, our primary motivation for giving should be because we love God and want to please Him by being obedient to His Word and helping Him to fulfill the great commission.

THE LAW OF USE

There is another kingdom law that relates closely to the "law of giving and receiving," and it is sometimes called "the law of use." Jesus illustrated the law of use in a parable about a rich businessman traveling to another country. He said that the kingdom of heaven was like this rich man who distributed his financial resources to his three managers and told them to "do business until I return" (Matthew 25:14-30). Two of the managers invested the resources they had been given, while the third did not. When the rich businessman returned, he asked for an accounting. He praised the two managers who had invested his money wisely and rewarded them richly for their diligence. But the rich businessman was very angry toward the manager who operated out of fear and insecurity, and did nothing with his money. He called him a wicked and lazy servant, took his property away from him, and gave it to the manager who had invested his resources wisely. As Jesus completed this parable, He announced a law of the kingdom: "For to everyone who has, more will be given, and he will have abundance; but from him who does not have, even what he has will be taken away."

This parable and others like it make an important point; Jesus expects His sons and daughters to deal wisely with money and the material things of this world while He is gone. Many other scriptures in both the Old and New Testaments confirm this principle.

(1) Reprinted by permission. The Midas Touch, A Balanced Approach To Biblical Prosperity, By Kenneth E. Hagin, ©

2000, Rhema Bible Church/Kenneth Hagin Ministries, Tulsa, OK. All rights reserved.

CHAPTER 15
THE LAW OF LOVE

"...You shall love the Lord your God with all your heart, with all your soul, and with all your mind.' "This is the first and great commandment," And the second is like it: 'You shall love your neighbor as yourself.' "On these two commandments hang all the Law and the Prophets" (Matthew 22:37-40).

LOVE TRUMPS ALL OTHER LAWS

One day a lawyer desiring to test Jesus asked him the following question: "Which is the greatest commandment in the law?" Jesus didn't hesitate, He immediately replied, "'You shall love the Lord your God with all your heart, with all your soul, and with all your mind.' This is the first and great commandment," and the second is like it: 'You shall love your neighbor as yourself.' "On these two commandments hang all the Law and the Prophets" (Matthew 22:37-40).

Perhaps you have never noticed that the Law of Love is the master law of the universe. Failing to walk in love and harmony with God and your neighbor will hinder your ability to be successful in life. It will hinder your ability to successfully walk in any of the other spiritual laws. "Upon the law of love hang all the Law and the Prophets."

Don Ostrom, a friend of mine and owner of a company that owns and operates nursing homes, shares the following incident from his business life in his book entitled *Millionaire in the Pew*: (1)

Many years ago, I learned the graphic lesson that harboring unforgiveness stops the flow of God's blessings. I lost thousands of dollars, not knowing that my bitterness was the cause.

I had a close friend whom I had helped to become successful in winning others to Christ. We had worked together for years, going overseas to help reach people with the gospel. In the course of events, he was accused of wrongdoing, things I knew he would not do. I defended him. As time progressed, certain men treated him with dishonor, and I built up a bad attitude toward them. I criticized them and talked about them to others. My attitude became so bad that I didn't want to see them at meetings. I avoided them. It was really none of my business, but I took offense for my brother. I wanted to defend him, to protect him, but inadvertently I became secretly bitter toward his accusers. I harbored unforgiveness in my heart toward them. Criticism invaded every area of my life. Soon, I was criticizing my wife, my pastor, my employees, and my friends.

One day, unexpectedly, I heard the Lord say to me, "Ask forgiveness of those men for your attitude." "No way!" I responded, "They should be coming to me asking forgiveness." I was stubborn and refused to obey the Lord. The very next day, a friend from another country sat beside me and said that he had noticed that I had changed from my usual happy self. He said that something "not so good" was coming out of my life. He caught me totally by surprise when he said to me, "Don, I think you should go to those brothers and ask forgiveness for your attitude." It was like a knife going through me. Here was a friend telling me the same thing the Lord had spoken. It was too much! I knew the Lord was being patient and gracious to get me to repent.

I knew I had to obey if I wanted God's blessings on my life.

I called the leader of the group and asked to meet with him. We did meet, and I asked him to forgive me. I told him I would fly to the board meeting and ask all of these men for forgiveness. He accepted my apology and said he would relay it to the others. I felt good as I left the room. Now I could face these men without fear or disgust. As I walked to my room, I heard the Lord say, "Now your beds will fill at the nursing home in Bremerton." I was shocked! What did those twenty empty beds have to do with my asking forgiveness? I couldn't believe there was any connection. We had been struggling financially for several months. I had been rebuking the devil, and calling those beds full, but nothing was happening.

Two days later, I called Sam, our administrator in Bremerton, and asked him how things were going. He said, "Don, we've started taking residents again." I asked, "When did that start?" He said, "Two days ago." Within two months our facility was full. We had lost about $60,000.00 that year. It was a very expensive problem. I learned the lesson, however, that unforgiveness and bitterness can block the blessing and protection of the Lord in our lives. We must maintain godly character and be quick to forgive. We must not harbor resentment. We must let it go. The sooner we do the better..." (1)

BITTERNESS CAN AFFECT YOUR HEALTH AS WELL AS YOUR BUSINESS

My wife Barbara and I first learned the importance of guarding our hearts against bitterness and resentment when we were speaking in Ireland in 1984. An incident that occurred in Dundalk, a small town located just south of the border between Southern and Northern Ireland, dramatized the importance of forgiving others if we want to keep our bodies free of sickness and disease. Father Hampsch, a Catholic Priest from America, was traveling with our team. He had just finished speaking on the importance of forgiving others if we want God to forgive and heal us, when an Irish lady in her late forties approached my wife and me for prayer.

It appeared that every joint of her body was swollen from rheumatoid arthritis; it was obvious that she was in severe pain. I asked her if she understood what Fr. Hampsch had just taught concerning the importance of forgiving others if we want God to forgive and heal us; she related that she understood. I asked her if she was holding bitterness toward anyone, she replied, "Yes, many people." We led her in a simple prayer in which she asked her Heavenly Father to forgive her for the bitterness and resentment she had harbored toward these people, and she named the people quietly before the Lord. I reminded her that Fr. Hampsch had taught that it was important that she contact each of these people and ask them to also forgive her. She agreed she would do so. When she finished her prayer, we prayed for her healing, but there was no apparent change. Her joints were still filled with pain.

Frankly, I left the meeting that afternoon thinking the lady hadn't received a thing from the Lord. That night my wife and I traveled to Northern Ireland where we would speak in a number of meetings in and around the city of Belfast during the following week.

On the following Friday, Barbara and I returned to Dundalk to speak in a Christian businessmen's meeting, which was to be held in the same restaurant in which we had prayed for the woman with arthritis the previous week. When we walked into the restaurant there was the woman, and she was smiling from ear to ear. In fact she had brought ten or twelve other people with her. She ran to Barbara and me, threw her arms around us, and exclaimed, "I visited the doctor yesterday, and all the arthritis is gone." Since that experience in Ireland, I have observed Christian people all over the world who have allowed bitterness and resentment to become established in their heart, and it has hindered their prayers and allowed the enemy of their souls to inflict their bodies with disease and pain.

OBEDIENCE CAUSES THE BLESSINGS TO COME UPON US

Having witnessed the negative effects that bitterness and resentment can have on a person's health and business success, I would like for you to clearly understand the following important principle taught in the Creator's Handbook:

Moses proclaimed this important principle to the Israelites in the book of Deuteronomy: "Now it shall come to pass, if you diligently obey the voice of the Lord your God, to observe carefully all His commandments which I command you today,..."And all these blessings shall come upon you and overtake you, because you obey the voice of the Lord your God:" (Deuteronomy 28:1 & 2). Then in the next thirteen verses he describes blessings of prosperity, health, and abundant life that would come upon the Israelites if they carefully observed all the commandments of the law. These blessings describe what is referred to in the New Testament as the "Blessings of Abraham"

(Galatians 3:14). Everyone wants prosperity, health, and abundant life; but in order to receive them, it is necessary that we obey the law of the Lord.

DISOBEDIENCE ALLOWS THE CURSES TO COME UPON US

After Moses proclaimed the blessings of Abraham, he declared the curse of the law: "But it shall come to pass, if you do not obey the voice of the Lord your God, to observe carefully all His commandments and statutes which I command you today, that all these curses will come upon you and overtake you" (Deuteronomy 28:15). The curses named in the next fifty-three verses included poverty, sickness and death. They include eleven specific diseases, and "Also every sickness and every plague, which is not written in this Book of the Law..." (Deuteronomy 28:61). These verses describe what is referred to in the New Testament as the "curse of the law" (Galatians 3:13).

A NEW COMMANDMENT I GIVE UNTO YOU

The Old Testament believer, the Israelite had over six hundred laws to obey, but you and I as New Testament believers have only one law to obey, the "Law of Love." Jesus said, "A new commandment I give to you, that you love one another; as I have loved you, that you also love one another." (John 13:34). The Apostle Paul declares says, "For all the law is fulfilled in one word, even in this: You shall love your neighbor as yourself" (Galatians 5:14; Romans 13:8-10).

UNFOGIVENESS CAN HAMPER YOUR BUSINESS LIFE

While I understood that negative emotions such as resentment or bitterness would affect a person's health, it never occurred to that it could affect one's success in the business world, not at least until very late in my business career. The construction industry tends to be a rather rough and tumble industry. Looking back, I can recall a number of occasions when I have allowed anger or resentment to develop toward an individual who was acting in a very adversarial manner toward me or my company. Knowing what I now know, I am sure that my negative attitude toward these individuals not only affected my judgment in dealing with them, but hardened them against us. Perhaps even worse, it prevented my faith from producing victory in the situation.

One incident in particular stands out in my mind. A man had done something to me that was not right and in fact not even lawful, and I became offended. I decided to teach this individual a lesson and I started a major contention with him. One evening I was reading my Bible when I came across the following admonition: "For you, brethren, have been called to liberty; only do not use that liberty as an opportunity for the flesh, but through love serve one another. For all of the law is fulfilled in one word, even in this: You shall love your neighbor as yourself. But if you bite and devour one another, beware lest you be consumed by one another!" (Galatians 5:13-15). I immediately saw that I had gotten out from under the law and had opened myself up to sickness and disease. I dropped to my knees and asked the Lord to forgive me. The next morning at 7:30, I called this man (he lived about a thousand miles from me) and asked him to forgive me. He was so shocked he didn't know what to say. I don't believe he ever said that he forgave me, but I got the bitterness out of my heart, and it was very liberating.

When problems arise in our personal or business lives, they may not always be caused by the devil; they might be caused by bitterness and resentment on our part. We can become the problem through unforgiveness and fleshly actions or reactions. When we teach about faith we often use Mark 11:23 & 24 to describe and demonstrate the "God kind of faith." But we nearly always overlook the next verse: "And whenever you stand praying, if you have anything against anyone, forgive him, that your Father in heaven may also forgive you your trespasses. But if you do not forgive, neither will your Father in heaven forgive your trespasses"(Mark 11:25 & 26). You simply cannot get an answer to your prayer if you are harboring unforgiveness in your heart toward another. It is often the little things that keep our faith from working and our prayers from being answered. Often it's bitterness against another that keeps our voices from being heard in heaven.

WALKING IN LOVE TOWARD OTHERS IS DIFFICULT

Walking in love toward others, particularly those who are not being kind to you, is an area of the faith walk which I have personally found to be the most difficult. However, it is an important part of the faith message, and we must learn to walk in the love of God if we want to experience the blessings of God in our lives and our businesses. It certainly is not easy to walk in love toward someone, especially when they are not being kind toward you, but I know from personal experience that it is the right thing to do if we want God's blessings in our lives.

LOVE NEVER FAILS

Several years ago my office manager, a woman who had worked with me for a number of years, had a rather sharp disagreement with one of my vice presidents. During the verbal exchange he apparently cursed at her and said some rather unkind things. She became very upset and angry and filed a sexual harassment complaint against our company with the Federal Government. She was in poor health at the time, and was experiencing marital problems, which no doubt contributed to her anguish.

In America, a sexual harassment lawsuit can be very expensive for a company to defend against, and it could have cost our company a great deal of money. Several weeks after she filed the complaint she resigned from her position and prepared to leave the company. I decided that even though she was suing our company that we would organize a company luncheon in her honor and present her with a nice going away gift (something we normally did when a long-term employee would leave the firm). She was apparently so embarrassed by the fact that we were blessing her, even though she was in essence cursing us, that she feigned sickness and asked to be excused from attending the luncheon. Following the luncheon we sent the gifts to her home and a week later she withdrew the sexual harassment charge. The Manufacturer's Handbook says, "Love never fails" (I Corinthians 13:8).

FAITH WORKS THROUGH LOVE!

"And now abide faith, hope, love, these three; but the greatest of these is love" (I Corinthians 13:13). As we have said many times in previous chapters, "faith is important," but the Creator's Handbook clearly says that love is greater than faith. Furthermore, the handbook states that faith works through love (Galatians 5:6). If faith works through love then it is essential to your success that you develop and walk in the "God kind of love."

The English word **love** used in the above scriptures is the translation of the Greek word **agape** (ag-ah'-pay). But the English word **love** doesn't accurately reflect the full meaning of **agape**. Agape describes the "God kind of love," wherein God makes a deliberate choice to exercise love toward us. The agape love, to which we are to aspire, requires no special relationship, and even responds in love toward those who wrong us. It is quite unlike human love, which loves only those with whom we have a relationship and those who love us. The thirteenth chapter of Corinthians encourages us to overlook the faults of others and refuse to react to the unkind things that others may do or say to us. Thinking and talking about the wrongs and hurts that other people have inflicted upon us causes anger, bitterness, strife and resentment to become established in our hearts, and those negative emotions in turn cause us to react negatively toward others. Even worse, it allows the demon forces of hell to attack our minds and our bodies, and hinder the development and exercise of our faith.

LOVE IS NOT LOVE UNTIL IT IS SPOKEN

Faith must be in your heart, and in your mouth, to be effective (Romans 10:8). It is the same with love; it must be in your heart and in your mouth to produce results. You can have a heart full of love for your wife or sweetheart, but you must confess your love to her and act upon your love for it to produce results. Your love is not love until it is confessed and acted upon. Walking in love toward others is not easy. It requires you to change; it requires a new way of life.

"And then take on an entirely new way of life--a God-fashioned life, a life renewed from the inside and working itself into your conduct as God accurately reproduces his character in you"(Ephesians 4:22-24 MSG).

ONE FINAL ADMONITION

One day the apostle Peter asked Jesus "How often shall I allow a person to sin against me, and I forgive him? Up till seven times?" Jesus answered, "Not seven times, but up to seventy times seven." Then Jesus related the following story which has a surprisingly harsh ending about a man who would not forgive. In the story, Jesus compared the kingdom of heaven to a king who decided to collect all the debts that were owed to him (Matthew 18:23-35). One of the king's debtors owed him a great deal of money, the equivalent of $10,000,000 in today's currency. But the man could not repay the king, and the king ordered that everything the man owned, including the man, his wife, and his children be sold, and the money gained from the sale be applied toward the man's debt.

The man fell at the king's feet, begged him earnestly to have patience with him, and promised that he would repay all he owed to the king. The king was moved with compassion for the man and forgave him all his debt. Now, later the man whom the king had forgiven this extremely large debt, began to settle accounts with his own debtors. One of them, a poor man, owed him the equivalent of $20.00 in today's currency, but could not repay it. The debtor begged the man, "Give me time, and I will pay you all of it." But the man whom the king had forgiven the $10,000,000 debt was unwilling to forgive his debtor the $20.00 debt, and had him thrown into prison until he should pay his debt. The king, upon hearing about the incident, was very upset and had the man whom he had forgiven brought before him. The king said to the man, "I forgave you all that debt, because you asked me. Shouldn't you have had had compassion and done the same to your fellow servant?" The king was very angry and delivered him over to the tormentors until he should pay all that was due to the king.

Jesus said, "So My heavenly Father also will do to you if each of you, from his heart, does not forgive his brother his trespasses" (Matthew 18:35). In this illustration, Jesus makes it very clear: if we do not forgive our fellow man, our Heavenly Father will not forgive us! He will remove his protective shield and allow the tormentors (the demon spirits of hell) to exact their deadly toll on our mind and body.

(1) Reprinted by permission. *Millionaire in the Pew*, by Don Ostrom, copyright 2004, All rights reserved. (Pg. 132-133).

CHAPTER 16
THE LAW OF FAITH

"...If you have faith as a mustard seed, you will say to this mountain, 'Move from here to there,' and it will move; and nothing will be impossible for you" (Matthew 17:20).

Gunnar Olson, a Swedish industrialist in the plastics field, is the Founder and Chairman of ICCC, International Christian Chamber of Commerce. I met Gunnar in 1979, at the time he was an International Director of the Full Gospel Business Men's Fellowship. Our local Seattle chapter had invited fifteen leaders of the Fellowship from Europe to spend a week in our city for training and fellowship. Gunnar stayed in our home along with a man from Germany.

At the time Gunnar stayed in our home, I had been a Christian for only three years, but I remember vividly a story that Gunnar shared with my wife and me concerning an aluminum pot and pan business he owned. The company had produced a warehouse full of thousands of pots and pans, and sales had been very slow. The company was running out of working capital; the situation was desperate. In his Friday night prayer group one of the members shared a Bible scripture which inspired Gunnar to speak to his mountain (the warehouse full of pots and pans). His prayer group joined in agreement with Gunnar, and in the name of Jesus he commanded the pots and pans to move out of his warehouse. Within days new sales came into Gunnar's Company and the warehouse was emptied. Years later, when I was faced with a serious lack of sales in my business Gunnar's simple testimony shared in the living room of our home inspired me to speak to my mountain. While I didn't see immediate results, as I continued to stand on the word of God, we were awarded the largest project our company had ever received, and the next year we sold six times the work we had sold in the previous year.

Subsequent to Gunnar Olson visiting Seattle in 1979 he sold the aluminum pots and pan factory and purchased a plastics factory named Alfapac. Gunnar relates the following story:

Alfapac produces huge plastic bags in which farmers store their silage. Alfapac had introduced these plastic bags to farmers as a cost-effective method for storing the silage and they very soon dominated the market. "One year, however Alfapac experienced an enormous problem with the silage bag production. Production had begun in December and the first shipments of the bags were scheduled for the end of April. When it came time to ship, we had our storage yard full of thousands of silage bags worth several million dollars. I had no idea that anything was wrong until my brother, who was the general manager, came to me. He looked troubled.

"Gunnar, I think we've come to the end of the road at Alfapac," he told me. "Whatever do you mean?" I asked.

I listened as he explained that all the bags, which had been produced during the last five months, were faulty. Something had happened to the plastic molecules during the processing and instead of producing a bag with two sheets of plastic; they had laminated together forming a single sheet of plastic. After heat-sealing the bottom of the bag, we had an automatic folding machine which had made it impossible to discover the problem until it was too late. Over one thousand pallets of silage bags were standing in the yard ready to go, but not one could be used! That week, engineering and manufacturing experts had been called in from all over Europe but no one could suggest a solution. Our production was totally useless, and the reject bags could only be used by recycling.

My poor brother was almost sick with worry from it all, as he had been carrying this burden of this problem for over a week. We had been producing bags for over five months and no one had noticed the problem until it was time to ship! He knew that Alfapac was ruined. The company could not sustain such a great financial loss, and we would never be able to regain the market. I told my brother to go home and relax. I knew that our answer was to be found in prayer, and I knew that my brother couldn't pray effectively feeling as he did.

I assembled the family and shared the news. Then we decided how we would deal with the problem in prayer. We would simply present the situation to the Lord and then listen to His Holy Spirit because after all we had given the company to Him.

"Lord," I prayed, "You know what's happened. What shall we do?" Then we waited on the Holy Spirit. After a short time of praying, each person shared what he or she sensed the Lord was saying. We began with Git, our youngest. She said, "This situation is not from God; it was the work of the enemy and we should stand against it in the name of Jesus." Mats agreed, and my wife Asther said, "If Jesus could turn water into wine, then plastic bags are no problem!" I felt that if we had faith the size of a tiny mustard seed we could command this "mountain of a problem" to be

thrown into the sea. And so we all agreed. We weren't going to receive the problem, even though it was a fact in the physical world. By faith we were going to receive the solution. Just as we finished our prayer, the phone rang. Someone was calling from London; it was a man I had met earlier in China.

"Listen," he said, "I don't know what's going on, but I have a word for you. You must speak to the invisible."

This word of encouragement was just what we needed, and our faith was strengthened. Then the man continued, "If you can't deal with the small things, how are you going to deal with China?" At that time, I had some plans for China, and his words really spoke to me. How we praised the Lord and thanked Him for answering our prayers! That phone call had reassured us of God's love and His faithfulness, and I felt the pressure of the burden lift away. I immediately phoned my brother and told him to relax with his family and go and play a round of golf.

"What's up with you?" he asked. "How can you tell me to relax at a time like this? Don't you understand you're finished?"

"Just go and play golf," I replied. "There's not going to be a problem." My brother had told me the bad news on Friday, and the first opportunity we had to visit the factory and see the pallets was Sunday evening. Driving out to the factory, we agreed that we would not allow even the tiniest piece of sealed plastic to remain after we had prayed. As we stood holding hands in the yard, I was glad I hadn't seen all the pallets before. They were everywhere! To the natural eye, it was overwhelming. For a while, we stood and praised the Lord for His faithfulness and mercy. Then I yelled at the top *of my voice, "Listen heaven and earth! Who is the Lord over Alfapac? His Name is Jesus! In the name of Jesus, I command all those plastic molecules to come back into line!"*

Praying in tongues, we laid hands on each pallet and after three hours we had finished the job. We went home. On Monday morning, my brother ordered the whole factory staff to open all the boxes and check their contents. And to the glory of God, not one plastic bag was sealed! What a mighty God we serve! This is the glory element which becomes visible as we submit every aspect of our lives to Him. There is a joy which carries us through every difficulty as we work with Him, and He is excellent in everything He does. (1)

Gunnar says there is a difference between a secular business and one that's given over to the Lord: "There is a glory dimension to a Kingdom business which distinguishes it from the secular business! It is a dimension which should be normal for a Christian businessman, but I had to learn about this as the Lord brought us through various situations at our company Alfapac." (1)

Gunnar's obedience in speaking to his mountain caused God to manifest a miracle in his company and no doubt saved Alfapac from financial ruin.

FAITH PLEASES GOD

"But without faith it is impossible to please Him, for he who comes to God must believe that He is, and that He is a rewarder of those who diligently seek Him" (Hebrews 11:6).

Many desire the promises of God's Word, without living a life that is submitted to God's Word. In the book Business by the Spirit, we emphasize the importance of faith, as well as the development and exercise of your faith. Faith is certainly important, because the writer of Hebrews says that "without faith it is impossible to please God." Yet it is also true that in order to please God you must also live your life in accordance with the moral tenants of His word. In the above scripture from the book of Hebrews, the writer is obviously speaking about the "God kind of faith"-- the kind of faith that comes by believing and living in accordance with God's Word.

If we cannot please God without faith, and we want God's blessing in our lives and our business, then we need to understand what the "God kind of faith" is, and how to develop and release it in our lives.

FAITH IS INFORMATION WE RECEIVE FROM GOD

Let me share with you what I believe is the best human definition of faith that I have ever heard. "Faith is a noun; it is information. It is something you have... you get a set of instructions or information from God which becomes your faith. Believe is a verb; it is something you do...your acting is your believing." (2) Believing is an action you take as a result of the faith you have in your heart. "You do not believe in the Biblical sense without acting on your faith." (2)

When you meditate upon (think upon and confess) a promise that God has given you in the Creator's Handbook, or word spoken into your heart by the Spirit of God, it plants a seed of hope in your heart and that seed begins to grow. When the Word of God is fully established in your heart it becomes your faith. Your faith, the information you get from God to act on, tells you in advance what the will of God is concerning a matter. God's Word is His will.

The eleventh chapter of the book of Hebrews is often referred to as the "faith chapter." The writer of Hebrews gives us several examples of Old Testament men and women of faith such as Noah, Abraham, Sarah, Moses, and others. All of these men and women received information from God, information that told them in advance what they were to do. That information became their faith, and they demonstrated that they believed God by acting on their faith. As an example, Noah received advance information from God concerning a worldwide flood which He was going to bring upon the earth. God also instructed Noah as to how to construct an ark whereby Noah, his family and two of every creature might escape the flood. It was that information that became Noah's faith. Noah acted on his faith by building the Ark, and by doing so he became an heir of the righteousness that is according to faith. (2) (Hebrews 11:7) Acting on your faith (the information you get from God) is the only way that God will account you righteousness, and when you are righteous you are in right standing with God.

In the twenty-first century we usually get our information from God in two basic ways: (1) we get it from the Scriptures and God may speak a "Rhema word" directly to our spirit.

EVERY CHRISTIAN HAS THE "GOD KIND OF FAITH"

When you were born again the Spirit of God moved into your spirit. Speaking to the believers in Rome, Paul said,

"...God has dealt to each one a measure of faith"(Romans 12:3). Paul was talking about a measure of the "faith of God" that was given to you when you were born again. God starts every believer off with the same amount of faith; it is yours to be used and developed in your daily life. The measure or the amount of faith that God gave to you when you were born again can be increased - it can grow (2Thessalonians 1:3). However, you are the one who increases it - not God. You can increase your faith by:

- Meditating upon (thinking upon and confessing) the Word of God, and
- Exercising your faith, by putting it to work in your daily life and business affairs.

THE LAW OF FAITH DEFINED

One day Jesus and his men were walking from the town of Bethany on their way to the city of Jerusalem when He became hungry. In the distance Jesus saw a fig tree, and He approached the tree to see if perhaps He might find some figs on it. Finding no fruit He said to the barren fig tree, "let no one eat fruit from you ever again!" (Mark 11:14). The next morning as He and His men were passing by the same fig tree, Peter noticed that it had dried up from its roots. Peter remembered and said to him, "Rabbi, look! The fig tree which you cursed has withered away" (Mark 11:21). Jesus used the incident to teach his men concerning faith, and said to them, "Have faith in God." One modern translation says, "Have the faith of God." Jesus had demonstrated the "God kind of faith" when He cursed the fig tree. Then Jesus went on to explain the "God kind of faith": "For assuredly I say to you, whoever says to this mountain, 'Be removed and cast into the sea', and does not doubt in his heart, (his spirit), but believes that those things he says will be done, he will have whatever he says. Therefore I say to you, 'Whatever things you ask when you pray, believe that you receive them and you will have them'" (Mark 11:23 - 24). These two verses define the Law of Faith, and in the above incident with the fig tree Jesus, gave us a practical demonstration concerning the exercise of the Law of Faith. First, our faith must be in our hearts and in our mouths to get results; second, our faith must be in God, based on God's promises (remember - "faith is information we get from God to act on"); thirdly, Jesus' words those things means that the "Law of Faith" will produce whatever things that God has promised us in his word; fourthly, you can either say your faith or pray your faith.

On another occasion Jesus spoke the same principle to his men using slightly different words: "... for assuredly, I say to you, if you have faith as a mustard seed, you will say to this mountain, 'Move from here to there,' and it will move; and nothing will be impossible for you" (Matthew 17:20). Think about that! If you develop the "God kind of faith" in your spirit concerning prosperity in your business affairs, "...nothing will be impossible to you."

YOU MUST KNOW WHEN TO RECEIVE

Most of us get the believing and confessing part of the law of faith right, but we miss it in the receiving part. Jesus taught that we are to receive the answer to our prayer when we pray (Mark 11:24). After we pray we are to think and act like we have received the thing for which we prayed. This is the area of the faith walk in which I experienced the most difficulty in the early years of my Christian business career. I would believe that God had given me a certain thing, and would even confess that I had it, but I didn't think and act as if the thing for which I had prayed was mine. When problems developed and doubt began to bombard my mind, I would think my faith wasn't working and become discouraged. The receiving of the thing for which I believed was always in the future.

The thing we pray for becomes a fact in the spiritual world when we believe that we receive it, but it may not manifest in the physical world until a later time. I have found that believing God for finances is generally a process. It takes time, because our faith grows gradually. First the seed, and then the blade, then the head, after that the full grain in the head, and when the grain ripens the harvest comes (Mark 4:26-29).

Most Christians have a measure of faith, but they are not using the faith they have, because they don't know how to release their faith.

YOU CANNOT SAY JUST ANYTHING TO YOUR MOUNTAIN

The Law of Faith states "...Whosoever shall say unto this mountain, Be thou removed, and be thou cast into the sea; and shall not doubt in his heart, but believe that those things which he saith shall come to pass, he shall have whatever he saith." (Mark 11:23 KJV). In his book "HOW TO OBTAIN ABRAHAMS BLESSING'S" Dr. Jay Snell explains: "In this verse the words "say and "saith" occur twice each. "Say and Saith are different forms of the same word in the Greek text. The Greeks had different words for "saying" or "speaking". In this scripture, the word translated say and "saith" is the Greek word LEGO which emphasizes the content of what is said. Jesus could have used the Greek word LALEO which would have emphasized the way the speech was strung together. But, he used LEGO to stress the content of what they are to say to the mountain. And what was the content of what we are to "say" to "this mountain"? The content of their saying to the mountain was limited by the information they must receive in advance from God concerning the mountain,..." (2)

What we are to say to our mountain must be limited to the information that we receive in advance from God concerning our mountain. You see, it is limited to our faith. We cannot just say anything to our mountain. If we want our mountain to move, we must say the same thing that God has said about our mountain. In other words, we must first find a promise which God has made in His word or a word that God has spoken into our hearts concerning our mountain. Suppose you have a financial problem...let's say your business needs money to make the payment on its bank loan. In order for you to speak to your financial mountain you must first find a scripture that promises that God will meet your financial needs (scriptures like Luke 6:38; 2 Corinthians 9:6-8; Philippians 4:15-19). Then you must meditate (think upon and confess) on that promise day and night until faith for finances is established in your spirit. Faith comes by hearing, and hearing by the Word of God (Romans 10:17). You might also receive a word of knowledge or a word of wisdom spoken directly into your spirit from the Spirit of God guiding you as to what you should speak to your mountain.

Faith comes by hearing, but faith is released by speaking.

FAITH MUST BE IN THE HEART AND IN THE MOUTH

Paul expresses the "law of faith" in another way in Romans 10:6-8 "But the righteousness of faith speaks in this way... But what does it say? The word is near you, in your mouth and in your heart" (that is, the word of faith which we preach):" Notice that Paul calls the Word of God "the word of faith" (Romans 10:8). The "God kind of faith" is developed in our spirit by meditating upon (thinking upon and confessing) the word of faith. But the "God kind of faith" is released from our spirit by speaking it from our mouth.

You may have great faith for a thing in your heart, but for it to produce results you must speak the faith you have for that thing from your mouth, and not just once, but continually until you receive the thing for which you are believing. The Word of God must be believed in your heart and confessed with your mouth to bring the manifestation of your faith to pass in your life.

In the next verse Paul, talking about the born again experience continues: "That if you confess with your mouth the Lord Jesus and believe in your heart that God has raised Him from the dead, you will be saved. For with the heart one believes unto righteousness, and with the mouth confession is made unto salvation" (Romans 10:9 & 10).

Notice that a person must confess that he has salvation, before he actually receives it. This is the touchstone of the "Law of Faith," and it applies to everything that we receive from God. We must confess that we have it before we receive it. We must believe that we have received it, and confess that we have it before it actually manifests in the physical world (Mark 11:23 & Mark 11:24).

The English word salvation used in the above verse is the translation of the Greek word Solteria (Strong's #4991), and it means deliverance, preservation, soundness, prosperity, happiness, rescue, and general well-being. The word is used both in the material, temporal sense and in the spiritual, eternal sense.

Therefore Romans 10:9&10 could just as well have been written, "That if you shall confess with your mouth the Lord Jesus, and believe in your heart that He has redeemed you from the curse of poverty, you shall become prosperous. For with the heart one believes unto redemption, and with the mouth confession is made unto prosperity."

A MAJOR HINDERANCE TO YOUR FAITH

Jesus is the Son of God; He is the express image of God's person, and He upholds all things by the word of His power. (Hebrews 1:3) The creation trusts God's word because God is faithful to His words. In order for you and me to walk in the God kind of faith we must also be faithful to our words. The Pharisees developed elaborate rules regarding the making of promises or vows, declaring that only those employing the name of God were binding. Yet Jesus declared, "let your 'yes' be 'yes' and your 'no' be 'no.' He pointed out that you shouldn't need to swear by the name of God; your word ought to be good enough.

If you are careless with your words, you will also doubt God's word! To be careless with your words is to care less about them; it means you place little or no value on the integrity of your word. If you do not have faith in your own words, how can you develop faith in God's Word? If you are not faithful to your words, it is because you do not really know Him, because He is faithful. I have found the younger businesspeople to be particularly careless with their words; they agree to complete a task at a certain time and do not keep the deadline, they say they will meet at a certain time and routinely show up twenty to thirty minutes late. They say that they will attend a particular meeting but do not show up. When one tries to contact them by telephone they are greeted by their voice mail, and they do not return your call, when one sends them an email it goes unanswered; they seem to think that they can ignore your attempts to communicate with them and still maintain a normal relationship. They place little value on the integrity of their words.

In order for you to become successful in business you must be faithful to your words even when it will cost you to do so. In the Psalm 15 David says, "Lord who may abide in Your Tabernacle? Who may dwell in Your holy hill?" (Psalm15:1). David describes five traits of those who dwell in God's presence. I deem the fourth trait cited by David to be extremely important to your success in business: "He who swears* to his own hurt and does not change;..." (Psalm 15:4). The fifteenth psalm concludes by declaring: "He who does these things shall never be moved." *A footnote in my Bible concerning verse 15:4 explains: "Swears - refers to a man's giving his word on a business deal that turns into a deficit, but in which he still keeps his word."

During my many years of experience in the business world there have been several situations where my verbal business agreements have turned into a deficit, but I have always honored my word even when it was quite costly to do so. I know that because I keep my word, God has honored me and prospered me because my faith was not compromised.

YOUR FAITH IS CONTINGENT UPON YOUR LOVE AND YOUR HOPE!

"And now abide faith, hope, love, these three; but the greatest of these is love" (I Corinthians 13:13). Faith is important, but as we have discussed in the previous chapter the Creator's Handbook describes the God kind of love is greater than faith. Notice that in the preceding verse of scripture that Paul includes faith, hope, and love all in the same context.

The New English translation says, "And what is faith? Faith gives substance to our hope, and makes us certain of realities we do not see (Hebrews 11:1 NEB). According to this scripture, hope is important for without it faith would have nothing to give substance to. Therefore it is important that we understand hope and how to obtain hope even in seemingly impossible situations. We discuss hope in more detail in the next chapter.

(1)BUSINESS UNLIMITED, Copyright 2002 J. Gunnar Olson Published by ICCC, International Christian Chamber of Commerce Hjalmarbergets Foretagscenter SE-702 31 Orebro, Sweden www.iccc.net (Pg. 110, 111,112).

(2) HOW TO OBTAIN ABRAHAM'S BLESSINGS, Volume 4, Author: Jay Snell; Copyright 1989 by Jay Snell Evangelistic Association, P O Box 59, Livingston, Texas 77351 (Pg. 17, 18, 43, & 44).

CHAPTER 17
HOPE IS A PARTNER TO YOUR FAITH

"Let us hold fast the confession of our hope without wavering, for He who promised is faithful" (Hebrews 10:23).

FAITH AND HOPE WORK TOGETHER

"And now abide faith, hope, love; these three, but the greatest of these is love!" (1 Corinthians 13:13). In an earlier chapter we talked a great deal about how love works with faith to produce victory in your life. Now, let's look at how faith, and hope work together to cause our desires to become a reality in our lives.

"Now faith is the substance of things hoped for, the evidence of things not seen" (Hebrews 11:1).

In the above scripture what "things" is the writer of Hebrews talking about? The things you hope for! What things are we to hope for? We are to hope for those things which Jesus Christ has made available to us when he redeemed us from the curse of the law (Galatians 3:13&14). We are to hope for those things that God has promised us in his word.

FAITH GIVES SUBSTANCE TO THINGS HOPED FOR

I like the way the New English Bible translates this same verse, "AND WHAT IS FAITH? Faith gives substance to our hopes, and makes us certain of realities we do not see" (Hebrews 11:1).

"Faith gives substance to our hopes"--I like that. We live in a physical world. Therefore, until our hope is given substance, it is of no value to us. Substance is the matter from which our physical world is constructed.

WITHOUT HOPE, FAITH HAS NOTHING TO GIVE SUBSTANCE TO

Biblical hope is often misunderstood; it is not an optimistic outlook or wishful thinking without any foundation like the world's hope. The word translated *hope* in Hebrews 11:1 is **elpis** (el-peece): hope - confident expectation based on solid certainty (Strong's #1680). Biblical *hope* is based on God's promises. Hope is not inferior to faith; it's a partner with faith. Faith is the present possession of grace. Hope is confidence in grace's future accomplishment.

Faith is always now; hope is always future. Hope is the goal-setter for our faith!

OUR HOPE IS A PARTNER TO OUR FAITH--IT SETS THE GOAL

If we have no hope, then our faith will have nothing to give substance to! Paul describes Abraham's battle (in the face of contrary evidence) to believe God's promise that he would have a son. "Who, contrary to hope, in hope believed, so that he became the father of many nations, according to what was spoken, 'So shall your descendants be.' And not being weak in faith, he did not consider his own body already dead (since he was about a hundred years old) and the deadness of Sarah's womb. He did not waiver at the promise of God through unbelief, but was strengthened in faith, giving glory to God, and being fully convinced that what He had promised He was able to perform" (Romans 4:18-21).

Abraham was ninety-nine years old, and his wife Sarah was eighty-nine years old when God told Abraham that he would have a son by his wife Sarah. It was then also that God changed his name from *Abram* (meaning exalted father) to *Abraham* (meaning a father of many nations).

The scripture says that there was no hope, but Abraham **in hope**, believed. What did he believe? Where did Abraham get his hope? He believed the word that God had spoken to him, and he received supernatural hope. When we hear Abraham's name in English we hear "Abraham," but when Abraham heard his name in Hebrew he heard "father of many nations." God arranged it so that every time that Abraham spoke or heard his name he heard "father of many nations."

When there was no natural hope, Abraham got supernatural hope from the word that God had spoken to him. The confession of his hope (the promise of God that he would be "the father of many nations") produced faith in his heart. Subsequently, that faith in his heart, spoken from his mouth gave substance to his **hope**.

HOW I FOUND HOPE IN THE WORD OF GOD

As I describe in the next chapter, by December of 2003, my consulting firm had been losing money for over thirteen months. The company had lost more than one hundred percent of its net worth. I had to borrow money on two occasions to keep the consulting firm in business. (The only way the company could borrow money was for my wife and I to pledge our personal wealth as collateral.)

Our backlog of work was extremely low; we could only keep about half to two thirds of our staff productively employed. Our overhead costs were eating us up. Each month we were falling farther and farther behind. There was no natural hope that we could turn the business around.

My managers were discouraged; some of them were saying that I should give up and close the business down. They were ready to give up. Unknown to me Joseph, the man I had been grooming to take over and purchase the company, was searching for a position with other companies. Even my wife (after particularly discouraging news) suggested that I close the business.

But I continued to meditate (think upon and confess) the Word of God day and night, and like Abraham, I got supernatural hope from God's Word. When all natural hope was gone, I found hope in God's Word. I continued to confess that hope (the hope I found in God's Word) without wavering (Hebrews 10:23). Gradually that hope became my faith, and my faith gave substance to my hope, and by October of 2004, the business had turned around and it posted the best financial year that it had ever experienced. It was so good, in fact, that I was able to sell the business for the price which I established.

HOPE WORKS LIKE A THERMOSTAT

I have worked in the construction industry most of my life and my company has specialized in the design of buildings. Let me give you an illustration from the building industry that I believe will help you to understand hope. (While no illustration from the physical world can perfectly describe the operation of a spiritual principle, I think the following example will help you understand the necessity of confessing your hope.) A heat, ventilation and air conditioning system produces and controls the interior climate in all modern buildings. We commonly refer to this system as the HVAC System. The HVAC equipment is the heart of the building's climate control system; it is designed to produce whatever temperature the thermostat requests of it.

A thermostat is generally located in each area or room of the building in which we wish to control the temperature. The thermostat is a device that sends a command to the HVAC equipment identifying the temperature that it is to establish in the room. The thermostat is the goal-setter for the HVAC system. The HVAC system merely obeys the command given by the goal-setter (the thermostat). If the thermostat is set at 60°F (18°C) and you want to increase the temperature in the room to 70°F (22°C), you reset the thermostat to the higher temperature and it signals the HVAC system to send more hot air to the room. Now let's say that the room temperature is 80°F (27° C), and you reset the thermostat to 70°F (22°C). The thermostat will send a signal to the HVAC system causing the HVAC system to send cool air into the room until the room reaches the lower temperature.

YOUR SPIRIT PRODUCES THE HARVEST

Your spirit is like the HVAC equipment; it is designed by God to develop the faith that will give substance to your "hope goal." You go to the Word of God and find a promise that He will to prosper you, and on the basis of that promise you establish a "hope goal" to increase your sales and your profits by twenty percent next year. Then by an act of your will, you begin to meditate on (think upon and confess) God's promise to prosper you; and your hope goal to increase your sales and profits by twenty percent next year. As you think upon and confess your hope goal, it will produce faith in your heart. You are to hold fast to the confession of your hope (Hebrews 10:23), because it will take time to produce faith in your heart. As your faith is complete, it will give substance to your hope, even when your business is shaken by an attack of the devil.

Paul said it this way: "Therefore take up the whole armor of God that you may be able to withstand in the evil day, and having done all, to stand. Stand therefore..." (Ephesians 6:13 &14). The evil day is the day that the devil and his demons come to attack your business. Furthermore, Paul said "Therefore be imitators of God as dear children, And walk in Love..." (Ephesians 5:1 & 2), and in another place he says that "God who ... calls those things which do not exist as though they did;" (Romans 4:17); therefore you and I are to call things that do not exist as though they **do** exist.

You are to speak your hope like Abraham did. Even when it looks like there is no natural hope, you go to the Word of God to find supernatural hope. You confess that your sales are twenty percent higher than last year. And you continue to speak prosperity and increase right in the face of apparent lack. You plant the seed (your "hope goal" based on the Word of God) in your spirit (the garden that God has given you to produce faith) by speaking your hope.

God has designed you so that your voice, heard by the inner ear, sends the signal for what you desire in life directly to your spirit. You confess your hope continually until you see the confession of your hope come to pass.

"Let us hold fast the confession of our hope without wavering, for He who promised is faithful" (Hebrews 10:23).

DON'T CONFUSE YOUR SPIRIT

Now let's go back to the illustration of the building HVAC System. Perhaps someone set the thermostat at 70°F (22°C) and a few minutes later he changed it to 80°F (27°C). But then a little while later he changed it again, this time to 60°F (18°C). The HVAC system will not work properly if you constantly change the thermostat. It will overheat and shut itself down.

Christians often send confusing signals to their spirit. They hear someone teach the principles taught in this book and they immediately begin to confess their hope. "My business is prosperous and successful, because my God meets all my needs according to His riches in glory"(Philippians 4:19). After several weeks, they look at the adverse business conditions and the slow cash flow and fear enters their mind. They pray, "Father, I don't have enough money to make the payroll, it looks like your word isn't working. I don't know what I am going to do." Then several days later they pull themselves together and begin to confess, albeit somewhat fearfully, "My God meets all my needs." They keep changing the thermostat! Once you have to set the "hope thermostat" to where you want it, leave it there regardless of the circumstances. The confession of your hope must be constant and consistent. Then your faith will work day and night to produce the goal that your hope sets for it. Faith gives substance to our hope.

INTRODUCTION TO PART IV: DOING BUSINESS BY THE SPIRIT

"But recall the former days in which, after you were illuminated, you endured a great struggle with sufferings" (Hebrews 10:32).

In the first seventeen chapters of *Business by the Spirit*, I trust that your mind has been illuminated by the Word of God so that you now understand the necessity of meditating on (thinking upon and confessing) the Word of God and doing all that is required by it in order to become successful in life because:

- The way you think.
- Determines what you believe in your heart (Proverbs 23:7).
- Which determines the way you talk (Mathew 12:34b).
- Which determines what you have in life (Mark 11:23).

If you haven't already started to do so, it is now time to begin applying these principles to make yourself prosperous and have good success.

When I first visited the nation of Russia in September of 2000, I had been in business for over thirty years, and had practiced many of the success principles included in *Business by the Spirit*, but I had never taught them to others. The Russian Christians who'd been without both Christianity and capitalism for over seventy years literally begged me to teach them business principles. I agreed to do so and struggled through several eight to twelve-hour business seminars using examples from my many years of business experience. Then over the next several years I refined and expanded this material into a two or three-day seminar. As I taught these seminars, God began to illuminate my mind, bringing back many principles He had taught me over the years and reminding me of a number of situations from which He had delivered me, and He began to give me new revelation concerning doing "business by the Spirit."

Then boom! It seemed like all hell broke loose in my business! In a period of seven months my consulting firm lost two thirds of its net worth, and our new sales dropped to only forty-five percent of normal; my business was in serious trouble. I was traveling all over the world and teaching other people biblical business success principles and my own business was in serious trouble. Several months later as I was attending a Christian meeting the speaker turned to me and began to prophesy, *"God has allowed you to go through painful experiences for the sake of the body of Christ, not because you have done anything wrong, but because you had to suffer this pain to acquire the level of depth in God...revelation and knowledge of God for the sake of the ecclesia (the body of Christ)... Opportunities will come upon your table but God says 'it is because I can trust you, it is because I can trust you that I am giving you this teaching. I declare your seed blest, I declare your seed blest, strong in authority."* If when you begin to apply the spiritual principles taught in *Business by the Spirit*, all hell breaks loose in your life, be encouraged! You are on the right track!

Rick Renner, in his book *Sparkling Gems from the Greek* (1), tells us that Hebrews 10:32 could be taken to mean "... *after you were illuminated, you endured a mega-sized ordeal that threw you into the biggest fight you ever faced in your life. But the most critical part of the struggle resulted from the un-remitting assaults that literally battered your mind..."*

Renner goes on to say, "You can be sure that if you take a stance of faith in response to a word you receive from God, every possible negative thought will come against your mind. Not only will the devil try to use people and circumstances to thwart the plan, but he will also affect your mind with all kinds of negative thoughts and accusations. He'll do everything he can to talk you out of doing what God has called you to do..." (1).

"If you've been in this place I'm talking about—or if this is exactly where you are right now—*be encouraged!* This is probably your clearest signal that you've received a real word from the Lord. You must be right on track, because the devil is terribly concerned about what will happen if you act on what God has revealed to you.

Don't back down. Don't surrender to the enemy's vicious lies in your mind, his attacks against your body, his challenges to your finances, or his assault on your relationships. Regardless of how much resistance he tries to bring against you, don't you dare backup on the word God gave you! ... *"The fight you face is the greatest evidence you're on the right track! Just hang on, and don't give up! you are clearly headed in the right direction!"* (1)
As you read the next chapter of *Business by the Spirit* you will see that Rick Renner's exhortation very clearly described the fight of faith I experienced when I began to obey the Word of the Lord. I wish I had been able to refer to Renner's exhortation from *Sparkling Gems from*

the Greek when I was in the test. It would have been a great encouragement to me, and I trust that by including it here it will be a great encouragement to you.

(1) *Sparkling Gems From the Greek*: Copyright © 2003 by Rick Renner P.O. Box 702040 Tulsa, OK 74170-2040, (pg. 49-50).

CHAPTER 18
FIGHTING THE GOOD FIGHT OF FAITH

"...The righteousness of faith speaks in this way...The word is near you, in your mouth and in your heart, that is the word of faith which we preach" (Romans 10:6 & 8).

On November 1 of 2002, which was the start of our 2003 fiscal year, I turned the operational management of my consulting firm over to a Christian man whom I had been training for several years; I will call him Joseph. It was my intention to allow Joseph to manage the company for a year, and then at the start of the following fiscal year sell the company to him. During the 2003 fiscal year, I still retained ownership of the firm, but I spent less time in the office, acting primarily in an advisory capacity to Joseph. For some thirty years it had been my habit to spend a considerable amount of my time doing Christian mission work in other nations, but after turning over my business to Joseph, I began to travel even more, making several trips within the country and mission trips to Italy, Wales, England, Germany, and Russia during the first seven months of the fiscal year.

During the seventh month of the company's fiscal, year I returned to my office to find that the firm's sales were extremely low; we had sold only forty-five percent of the work which was required to keep our staff busy. I also found that the company had lost some sixty to seventy percent of its net worth. (One month later this loss would increase to eighty-five percent of our net worth.) But the immediate problem was that our sales backlog was far below that which was required to keep our staff productively employed; we were in a desperate situation. Our situation was particularly alarming in that we routinely made eighty-five percent of our annual sales during the first eight months of the year, and this year we had sold less than half that amount. This meant that during the remaining four months of the fiscal year we had no reasonable hope of obtaining enough sales to meet our expenses, let alone to make a profit. In addition, it was clear that my wife Barbara and I would have to pledge our personal wealth to the bank in order to obtain the working capital required to keep the corporation in business.

It was apparent to me that if we didn't have a major increase in sales in the next several months, even with the new working capital, we would be out of business in ninety to one hundred twenty days. Joseph tried to put a happy face on the situation, assuring me that God would provide.

As I reviewed the desperate condition of my company, a spirit of the fear came upon me; from a human standpoint I saw no natural hope of our sales improving. One evening I told my wife Barbara "my faith isn't up to this situation." I knew I needed to increase my faith and I needed to increase it fast. I began to meditate (think upon and confess) the Word of God for several hours in the morning, and often I would spend several hours in the evening, sometimes even as many as five to six hours a day. Frankly the situation was so hopeless that I had nowhere to go but the Word of God. I went to Galatians 3:13&14 and began to confess that "Christ had redeemed me from the curse of poverty."

On the basis of Luke 6:38 and 2 Corinthians 9:6&8 and other similar scriptures, I began to confess: "I have given cheerfully. I have given abundantly and God will make all grace abound toward me so I always have enough to give to every good work. My companies are prosperous and successful." I went to Mark 11:23&24 began to confess the Word of God concerning His promises to prosper me. About a month later I sensed faith rising in my spirit. With this new found faith, I decided to not just believe God for the same sales volume as previous year, but to believe Him for 150 percent of the average monthly sales from the previous years.

The apostle Paul admonishes us to be imitators of God (Ephesians 5:1), and he also said that God calls those things which do not exist as though they did. (Romans 4:17). So I began to imitate God and call sales that did not exist as though they did. I confessed that my company was prosperous and successful while it was almost bankrupt. I confessed that we had sold more than 150 percent of last year's sales when we had sold less than 45 percent of last year's sales. I confessed that we had those contracts before they were ever manifested in the natural realm.

The first month after I began my confession (that we had sold more than 150 percent of last year's monthly sales), we sold 174 percent. The following month we sold 142 percent, and the month after that we sold 205 percent. It looked as if things had turned around, and then the devil counterattacked. You can always count on a counterattack from the devil because he won't give up easily. Suddenly our sales came to a halt. During the next four-month period, when we should have sold another 600 percent of last year's average monthly sales, we had only sold 124 percent. In the natural it looked like Mark 11:23 wasn't working. It is easy to rejoice when the sales report shows that you have sold 150 percent of your average monthly sales. But it's not so easy to rejoice when the sales report indicates that you have sold nothing.

More believers lose the good fight of faith during the devil's counterattack than at any other time. Things start to get better and it looks as if God is going to deliver you from your problem; then just when you thought the battle was won, the attack comes at you from another direction. If you lose the confession of your hope (Hebrew 10:23) and give up, the devil will defeat you soundly. I recently saw a billboard with a picture of Winston Churchill, the Prime Minister of Great Britain, during the Second World War. He was holding up his fingers to form his famous "V" for victory sign. On the billboard with the picture was the following quote: "Never, never, never give up." That's good advice when you are walking by faith.

By the beginning of the sixth month, our sales were far below that which I had been confessing were mine. But then I began to understand where I was missing it. I had in effect established a deadline for God to answer my prayer, and that is unscriptural. Time is the dimension of this earthly life that tests our faith, and by expecting God to meet my sales goal every month, I had unconsciously removed the time element from the fight of faith. If we always received an answer to our faith at the end of the month then there would be no fight to faith. Understanding this principle, my wife Barbara and I came into agreement and claimed the nearly 450 percent of sales that we were behind, but this time we did so without establishing a deadline to receive the answer. (See my discussion of this prayer of agreement in the chapter entitled "Spiritual Authority in the Area of Finances"). A month later we had received only a small portion of the sales we had claimed, but now we no longer had a deadline for God to answer our prayer.

Immediately the devil challenged my mind. He told me that there was no way we could possibly receive that amount of sales, particularly during the winter months when construction is slow. He continually tried to put the "fear of failure" into my mind and my heart. He tried to get me to think negative, fearful, defeat-filled thoughts. He tried to get my mind focused on the battle, and get my mind off the Word of God and the confession of my hope. He told me over and over that my company was too far gone and that it would never recover. He impressed his negative thoughts of defeat on my mind continually. He told me that my faith was too weak. And to my natural mind it looked like God's Word wasn't working because in the last few months we had received only twenty percent of the new sales which we had claimed. For the second time, I had to go to the bank and borrow additional working capital to keep the firm in business.

But now I understood where I had been missing it, and each month I simply claimed the additional sales that we required to reach my goal of 150 percent of last year's average monthly sales. At the beginning of March of 2004 we were more than five months behind our goal. In the natural things looked dismal, but I continued to confess that God's Word was true. I continued to confess, "My God supplies all my needs from His riches in glory" and "My Company is prosperous and successful." I confessed that my companies were successful even though my eyes could see deficits on the financial statements and my ears could hear the worried comments from my staff.

On March 8th of 2004, Joseph, the man that I had been training to take over the business, walked into my office and announced that he was leaving the company. He had become fearful that the company would fail.

Then two weeks after Joseph resigned, we received in one week thirteen new contracts totaling over five months of sales. And exactly one year after I began to believe God for 150 percent of last year's sales (a 50 percent increase over the previous year's sales), we ended the year with 155 percent of last year's sales and the largest profit the firm had ever experienced. *Joseph had missed his inheritance by two weeks.*

Keep in mind that during much of the time my company was in this test, I was not actively involved in the day-to-day operation of the business, so it was not my personal sales efforts that caused the increase. It was solely the fact that I had built up my faith so that I could believe God for a fifty percent increase over the previous year's sales. And I continued to confess what I believed even when it looked impossible. God's Word always works for the man or woman who will be strong in the lord and in His power and might. (Ephesians 6:10). It works for anyone who will take his stand on the Word of God in confession and prayer, and **"never, never, never give up."** If you will do these things, you will always win the fight of faith.

If you wait to confess and believe that you will have a fifty percent increase over last year's sales until after you actually receive them, you will never have them. You must confess your hope (that your company has the increased sales) with your mouth **before** you actually have them. By believing in my heart and by confessing with my mouth, my faith gave substance to my hope and it caused new sales to manifest in the physical world, the world in which I needed them.

THE FIGHT OF FAITH IS IN YOUR HEART AND IN YOUR MOUTH

The devil will try to get you to fight the fight of faith in your mind, but the Creator's Handbook tells us to fight the good fight of faith in your heart and in your mouth. *"The righteousness of faith speaks in this way..."The word is near you, in your mouth and in your heart" (that is the word of faith which we preach)."* (Romans 10:6 & 8).

The devil and his demons will pummel your mind with thoughts of defeat and failure; he will tell you it's no use to continue to fight because the battle is lost. He will attack you by trying to get you to doubt God's Word—he will try to get you to worry about your problems, he will remind you of your past failures, he will do everything in his power to keep the faith battle in the arena of your mind. He knows that if he can divert your attention from meditating on God's Word and get you to meditate on **his** thoughts of failure and defeat, then he will win the battle.

YOUR CONFESSION MUST BE CONSISTANT

Often we fail to maintain a consistent confession. *In times of crisis* we faithfully meditate on and maintain our confession of God's Word. But when things are going well, we get busy with other things, we neglect our time in the Creator's Handbook, and soon we are in trouble again. Don't wait until your business is in financial trouble before you begin to meditate upon the Word of God. When you are in trouble you can be making the right confession, but the negative circumstances that you see with your eyes, the negative reports that you hear with your ears, and the thoughts of failure that the devil and his demons will impress upon your mind, can cause fear to harden the soil of your heart and cause your faith to fail.

During the financial battle I faced in 2003, my eyes saw deficits on the financial statements, and my ears heard the negative remarks my employees were making concerning the condition of the company—my **senses** told me we were going bankrupt. And the devil was sitting on my shoulder, telling me, "*You are going bankrupt...see you had to borrow more money...you better just close this business down and see if you can cut your losses. You are going bankrupt, you are going, bankrupt, you are going bankrupt.* But I kept meditating on the Word of God and speaking to my mountain, and God brought the victory.

It's hard to develop faith in a storm. The development of your faith (the information you get from God to act on) is a process. You need to start confessing that your needs are met well in advance of the time that you face a need; this is especially true in the business and financial arena.

FAITH IS NOT BLIND

Faith is not blind to the reality or the severity of a situation, but it declares that the power of God will overcome the situation, and it makes that declaration right in the face of what appears to be a seemingly hopeless situation. Moses records a report given by twelve spies he had sent to spy out the Promised Land in Numbers 13:27-33 & 14:6-10. Ten of the spies gave the children of Israel a bad report (Numbers 13:32). But Caleb and Joshua gave them a good report, a faith-filled report. Caleb's declaration was in agreement with the promises that God had given to the

Israelites. He said, *"Let us go up at once and take possession, for we are well able to overcome it."* (Numbers 13:30). Caleb's faith, however, was not blind. He had surveyed the same land, and he had seen the same giants and the same walled cities that the other ten spies had seen. Faith confesses victory in the face of apparent defeat; it confesses abundance in the face of apparent lack. The unbelief of the other Israelites delayed Caleb's receipt of God's promise, but it did not prevent him from receiving it (Joshua 14: 6-14).

WE ARE TO BE IMITATORS OF GOD

The Creator's Handbook tells us to *"...be imitators of God as dear children."* (Ephesians 5:1). One of the God's attributes is that He *"...calls those things which do not exist as though they did,"* (Romans 4:17); this is the way God releases His faith. If we are to imitate God, then we must release our faith the same way that He does - we are to call conditions that do not exist **as though they do!**

CHAPTER 19
SPIRITUAL AUTHORITY IN THE AREA OF FINANCES

"...much more surely will those who receive [God's] overflowing grace (unmerited favor) and the free gift of righteousness[Putting them into right standing with Himself] reign as kings in life through the One Man, Jesus Christ (the Messiah, the Anointed One". (Romans 5:17 AMP).

UNDERSTANDING DELEGATED AUTHORITY

When my wife Barbara and I were young Christians, we hosted a small Bible study in our home. In one of the classes we were studying Kenneth Hagin's book *The Authority of the Believer,* and for many in the class it was difficult to believe that Christ had delegated His full power and authority to ordinary believers like them. But Tim Schlitzer, one of the men in our class, was a traffic policeman. He immediately caught the revelation of the believer's authority over the devil and his demons. He explained to the class that the city for which he worked had delegated its authority to him to direct traffic; therefore, he understood delegated authority. He further explained that while he had no personal power to make the people obey him, the delegated authority, which had been given to him to enforce the city laws, was backed by the full power and authority of the city. When he was directing traffic all he had to do was raise his hand and even the largest trucks would stop. It was not his personal power that caused the truck driver to stop; it was the "fear of" or the "respect for" the power of the city which was behind his delegated power that caused the trucker to stop. The same is true of the authority of the believer. It is not the believer's personal power that causes the devil to stop; it is the "fear of" the power of God that is in back of the believer's delegated authority that causes him to stop.

EXERCISING SPIRITUAL AUTHORITY IN YOUR BUSINESS

I related earlier in this book that in November of 2002, I turned the management of my architectural and engineering company over to an associate to whom I planned to sell the business the following year, and I began to travel more. During the 2003 fiscal year I spent considerable time traveling and teaching the "Business By The Spirit" principles contained in this book. From time to time, when I was home in Seattle I would review the company's financial records, and offer assistance and advice to my associate, but I was not actively involved in the daily management of the firm. When I returned from a trip to Siberia in the spring of 2003, I found that in the first seven months of the fiscal year the firm had lost nearly sixty-five percent of its net worth. We did not have enough work to keep our staff of engineers and architects busy, and we had only a few months before we would have to close the business.

Realizing that my faith was not up to the financial challenge, I began to spend three to five hours a day during the following month meditating on the Word of God, to increase the level of my faith. After a month of meditating on God's Word I sensed that my faith had grown to the place where I could believe God to not only provide the fifty-five percent of sales that we were behind, but to add an additional fifty percent increase over last year's sales as well. Over the next three months, our sales averaged 174 percent of last year's sales, and then just when I was sensing victory, conditions turned for the worse. Over the next four months sales dropped to a disparaging one third of our goal. We had once again fallen considerably behind in our sales, and for the second time it became necessary for me to put additional working capital into the firm. I knew that I was missing it somewhere; but I didn't know where. Therefore I began to spend considerable time in study and prayer asking the Lord to reveal to me the problem.

EXERCISING SPIRITUAL AUTHORITY MAKES YOU A "MARKED MAN"

It was during this intensified time of study that I was re-reading Kenneth E. Hagin's book entitled *The Believer's Authority* (2), and I came across the following admonition:

The Christian who puts on this armor and engages in spiritual warfare is marked. By spiritual warfare I simply mean doing the works of Jesus and taking our authority over the devil as we go about our daily lives. I am not talking about purposely trying to go head-to-head with Satan in some kind of prayer combat. The devil will do everything in his power to keep you from coming into this knowledge of authority over him. He'll fight you more over this than any other subject. Then, after you have come to the knowledge of this authority, he'll oppose you and try to steal it from you. There will be tests, and sometimes people fail those tests. The devil wants you to throw up your hands and say the authority of the believer won't work for you...

...The Enemy will resist your interference in his sphere, because he's exercising authority over the powers of the air, and he wants to continue to do so. When you interfere with Satan's kingdom by exercising your spiritual authority, he

will attack you in an attempt to get you to back down from using that authority.

If you successfully resist Satan's attacks in one area, he will come against you in another area. You may as well get ready for these attacks, because they're coming. In other words, your privileged spiritual position makes you an enemy to the devil.

You see the devil realizes he cannot hold in bondage a believer who knows his authority in Christ Jesus. Such a believer is aware that he is seated with Christ in heavenly places and that the devil is a defeated foe under his feet (Eph. 1:15-2:6). Furthermore this believer is convinced that no work of the enemy can prevail against him in carrying out the will of God on the earth (2).

Now I had read *The Authority of the Believer* (1) (the predecessor of *The Believer's Authority*), the first time in 1978, and I am certain that I had read this book and the expanded *Believer's Authority* or parts of it, some ten to fifteen times in the thirty years that I had been a Christian. But on this occasion, Hagin's admonition concerning the satanic opposition which will confront the man who dares to challenge Satan's authority came alive to me; it confirmed the very situation which I was experiencing. I was not only exercising authority over the devil concerning my own business, but I was traveling all over the world teaching others to exercise authority over him in their business activities as well. By doing so, I had become a major target for the devil. I knew I had to win this financial battle because it not only involved my financial future, but my ability to teach "Business By The Spirit" principles to other believers as well. The stakes were high, not only for me personally, but also for the kingdom of God.

TIME IS THE EARTHLY DIMENSION THAT TESTS OUR FAITH

As I read the aforementioned book, I began to see where I was missing it. At the end of each month I would check our sales report to see if we had sold the 150 percent increased monthly sales (fifty percent increase over the average monthly sales for the preceding year). During the first three months that I had believed God for this increase, we had actually exceeded that goal, and I found it easy to rejoice in the Lord. But then when the sales slowed, and we weren't making even a third of our goal, it was not so easy to rejoice. It was definitely not easy to confess victory and thank God for the answer to my prayers when I could see those negative figures on the sales report. Then I realized that by believing God would meet our sales goal every month, I had in effect established a deadline for God to answer my prayer, and that is unscriptural. The writer of Hebrews says, "And we desire that each one of you show the same diligence to the full assurance of hope until the end, that you do not become sluggish, but imitate those who through faith and patience inherit the promises" (Hebrews 6:11&12). Time is the dimension of this earthly life that tests our faith, and by expecting God to meet my sales goal every month, I had unconsciously removed the time element from the fight of faith. If we always received an answer to our faith at the end of the month then there would be no fight to the fight of faith.

Only weeks after I had reread The Believer's Authority, I also read how the Lord taught Kenneth Hagin to exercise spiritual authority in the area of finances. I describe that principle in the next chapter entitled "Activating the Angels." Now I had read this principle on several previous occasions; in fact, I had heard him relate it in his Bible seminars. But I guess I had dismissed it as being a little over the top - at least it was over the top of my understanding. But now my back was against the wall, and I had nowhere else to go. If something didn't change we would soon be out of business; it was only a matter of months. Our sales were now four months behind our goal, so my wife and I agreed on the following prayer: "I claim ___" (and I stated the amount of the four months of sales that we were behind).

Then I said, "Satan, in the name of Jesus, I command you to take your hands off our sales" and "Go ministering spirits and cause the sales to come into my company." Then every time we thought about the situation we simply thanked God that His ministering angels were bringing the required sales into the company. Thirty days later we had received only a small percentage of the monthly sales we had claimed. So we claimed an additional month of sales, and again said the exact same prayer that Barbara and I had spoken in faith just a month earlier. About half way through the following month, we received thirteen contracts totaling over 800 percent of our monthly goal, and we ended the year with 155 percent of the average sales for the three previous years.

There is a caveat to the above story. Unbeknown to me, Joseph, the man to whom I had promised to sell my company, had apparently became fearful when the devil's counterattack hit the company and it looked like the company was going to fail. His fear led him to search for work with other firms. Just two weeks before we experienced our breakthrough in sales, he announced he was leaving the firm. As I mentioned in the last chapter, Joseph's fear caused him to miss his inheritance by two weeks!

The following year I raised our sales goal and claimed 200 percent of the base year's sales, and when I sold my business, six months later, we had received sales contracts of just over 200 percent.

Jesus assures us of an answer to our petition, but He does not guarantee the time that the answer will manifest in the physical world. Jesus said *"For assuredly I say to you, whoever says to this mountain, 'Be removed and be cast into the sea,' and does not doubt in his heart, but believes that those things he says will be done, he will have whatever he says. Therefore I say to you, whatever things you ask when you pray, believe that you receive them and you will have them"* (Mark 11:23&24). We are to believe we receive the answer to our prayer at the time we pray, but the answer may not manifest in the physical world until sometime in the future. It is the very fact that we don't know the exact time that the answer will manifest that requires us to exercise faith. Faith is seeing things that are not visible, as clearly as if they were visible.

WE ARE TO REIGN AS KINGS IN LIFE

The Apostle Paul said that "those who receive an abundance of grace and the gift of righteousness will reign in life through the One, Jesus Christ." (Romans 5:17) The Amplified Version says they will "reign as a kings in life". A king reigns with authority over his kingdom; he does not allow his enemies to steal his land, his wealth, or to harass his subjects. The believer likewise is to exercise spiritual authority over his family, his property, his business, and his finances. He is to use the authority delegated to him to prevent the devil from stealing from and harassing him, his family and his business. But in order for you to effectively exercise your spiritual authority, you must know (in your spirit) that the full power and authority of the Godhead is back of the authority that Jesus has delegated to you. Sadly, most Christians are either ignorant of their delegated authority or are not fully convinced (in their spirit) that they may exercise that authority over the devil and his demons.

Paul concludes the book of Ephesians by saying, "Finally, my brethren, be strong in the Lord and in the power of His might" (Ephesians 6:10). Many Christians misread this scripture and try to be strong in "themselves" rather than in the Lord; then when the battle is long and difficult, they become tired and discouraged and are tempted to give up the fight. They don't understand that it is not their power and might, but the delegated power and might of the Godhead that is behind the authority which Jesus has given to the believer.

You are strong, because the Spirit of God Who is in you, is more powerful than the spirit that is in the world. "You are of God, little children, and have overcome them, because He who is in you is greater than he who is in the world." (I John 4:4) Satan is the god of this world and the world financial system, but he is not your god. He that dwells in you is Jesus Christ the anointed one, unto whom all authority in heaven and earth has been given (Matthew 28:18), and He has delegated that authority to you the believer. (Matthew 28:19).

SATAN DOESN'T HAVE AUTHORITY OVER YOU, THE BELIEVER

Satan has authority over the people in the world, but he doesn't have authority over you the believer, because God has delivered you, the believer, out of Satan's kingdom and conveyed you into the kingdom of God. "He has delivered us from the power of darkness and conveyed us into the kingdom of the Son of His love, in whom we have redemption through His blood, the forgiveness of sins" (Colossians 1:13&14). Spiritual authority over the devil and his demons is one of the spiritual rights and privileges that belong to the believer. But you cannot exercise the authority of the believer with your mind; you must exercise the authority of the believer by believing the Word with your spirit!

GOD'S POWER IS BEHIND THE BELIEVER'S AUTHORITY

The apostle Paul compares God's power toward us who believe with the mighty power that He used when He raised Christ from the dead (Ephesians 1:19-23). Satan and all of his demons opposed the resurrection of Christ, but God's power overcame those demonic hoards, raised Christ from the dead, and made Him to sit at His right hand in heavenly places—far above all principality and power and might and dominion, and every name that is named—and placed Him as head over all things for the church (Ephesians 1:19-23). Christ was made to be head over all things for the believer; that's you and I—we are the Church. Paul states further that when the believer accepts Christ, he is raised up together with Christ and seated together with Him in heavenly places (Ephesians 2:4-6). That statement means that the same authority that was conferred upon Christ was also conferred upon you, the believer.

JESUS HAS DELEGATED HIS AUTHORITY TO US

If you are to effectively exercise your authority over the devil, then you must get the scriptures listed at the end of this chapter into your spirit by meditating upon (thinking upon and confessing) them until they are thoroughly established in your spirit. Many believers know these truths in their head, but we cannot exercise spiritual authority with head knowledge; spiritual authority must be excised with your spirit.

WHATEVER WE ASK (DEMAND) IN HIS NAME HE WILL DO

Jesus has delegated the right to use His name to the believer, and He has given you and me specific instructions concerning the devil. Jesus said, "...I saw Satan fall like lightning from heaven. Behold, I give you the authority to trample on serpents and scorpions, and over all the power of the enemy, and nothing shall by any means hurt you" (Luke 10:17-19).

The word "authority" used in this scripture is a translation of the Greek word *dunamis* (doo'-nam-is); it means "miraculous power." You are to approach the devil as one having the delegated authority of Christ, and you are to demand that the devil obey you and stop his attack against you in the name of Jesus. To the natural eye, it may look like nothing has happened, but as you stand your ground the devil's attack will weaken and eventually retreat. I like to compare it with standing on the seashore and a wave is approaching you. It comes at you in a powerful intimidating way, but as it comes nearer and nearer it begins to slowly lose its power, and finally it stops and retreats back in the direction from which it came. That is the same way the devil tries to intimidate us when we use our God-given authority to rebuke him.

Since 2003, I have made it my habit to meditate upon (think upon and confess) the following scriptures in order to establish faith in these truths in my spirit. Not only has this meditation increased my authority in the area of finances, but also my authority in praying for healing and miracles. I trust that you will also make these scriptures and others like them a part of your daily meditation.

"All authority has been given to Me in heaven and on earth. Go therefore and make disciples of all nations, baptizing them in the name of the Father and of the Son and of the Holy Spirit, "teaching them to observe all things that I have commanded you; and lo, I am with you always, even to the end of the age" (Matthew 28:18-20).
"And these signs will follow those who believe; In My name they will cast out demons; they will speak with new tongues; they will take up serpents; and if they drink anything deadly, it will by no means hurt them; they will lay hands on the sick, and they will recover" (Mark 16:17&18).

"...I saw Satan fall like lightning from heaven. Behold, I give you the authority to trample on serpents and scorpions, and over all the power of the enemy, and nothing shall by any means hurt you (Luke 10:18-19).

"But you shall receive power when the Holy Spirit has come upon you; and you shall be witnesses to Me in Jerusalem, and in all Judea and Samaria, and to the end of the earth" (Acts 1:8).

The Apostles Paul, James, and Peter all gave instructions to the believer concerning the devil; I have included them below for your review. As I confess these scriptures, I sometimes personalize them as I have below with the Apostle Paul's prayer in the first chapter of Ephesians:

"God of our Lord Jesus Christ, the Father of Glory, give to me the spirit of wisdom and revelation in the knowledge of You, that the eyes of my understanding may be enlightened; that I may know what is the hope of Your calling, that I may know the riches of the glory of Your inheritance in the saints, and that I may know the exceeding greatness of Your power toward us who believe, according to the working of Your mighty power which You worked in Christ when You raised Him from the dead and seated Him at Your right hand in heavenly places, far above all principality and power and might and dominion, and every name that is named, not only in this age but also in that which is to come. And You put all things under His feet and gave Him to be head over all things for the church, which is his body, the fullness of Him who fills all in all (My personalization of Ephesians 1:17-23).

Paul went on to say in the second chapter of Ephesians, *"But God, who is rich in mercy, because of His great love with which You love me, even when I was dead in trespasses, You made me alive together with Christ, (for by grace I have been saved) and You raised me up together, and made me to set together in heavenly places in Christ Jesus" (My personalization of Ephesians 2:4-6).*

The Apostle James said, "...Resist the devil and he will flee from you" (James 4:7).

The Apostle Peter said, "Be sober, be vigilant; because your adversary the devil walks about like a roaring lion, seeking whom he may devour. Resist him, steadfast in the faith, knowing that the same sufferings are experienced by your brotherhood in the world" (1 Peter 5:8 & 9).

WE ARE TO DO BUSINESS UNTIL CHRIST RETURNS

I think it is also important for you to understand that as a Christian businessperson, you are engaged in spiritual warfare because the devil and his demon forces are arrayed against you. You must understand that even though Jesus has already fought the devil and won the victory, He has delegated to you the responsibility to enforce His victory. Therefore we are to take our stand on the Word of God, in prayer and confession, to enforce the victory that Jesus has won for us. His disciples thought that His kingdom would come immediately, but Jesus told them a parable and said, "...Do business until I come" (Luke 19:13).

(1) Reprinted by permission. *Authority of the Believer*, by Kenneth E. Hagin, © 1967, Rhema Bible Church/Kenneth Hagin Ministries, Tulsa, OK. All rights reserved.

(2) Reprinted by permission. *The Believers Authority*, by Kenneth E. Hagin, © 1984, Rhema Bible Church/Kenneth Hagin Ministries, Tulsa, OK. All rights reserved. [pg. 51-52]

CHAPTER 20
ACTIVATING THE ANGELS

In September of 1986, a Christian businessman by the name of Norvel Hayes was speaking in our Pacific Northwest Warm Beach Men's advance. One morning he said something I will never forget. He said that Jesus came to him (in a vision) and sat in the car with him and said, *"If my people would only worship me more, they could have whatever they asked."* Jesus went on to tell Norvel, *"Most churches advertise an 11:00 worship service, but nobody worships me. They just sing a few songs, take the offering and preach a sermon."* I don't remember anything else that Norvel said in that meeting, but I can still remember those words: *"...no one ever worships me."* For the next several weeks all I could think about was what Jesus had said to Norvel Hayes: *"If my people would only worship me more, they could have whatever they ask... but no one ever worships me."* Several weeks later I made a covenant with myself, not with God, but with myself, that whenever I would wake in the night, I would arise and worship the Lord just because He is God. Therefore, since September of 1986, it has been my habit that when I wake in the middle of the night, I rise and go into another room of our home where I worship the Lord and pray.

In February of 1994, my wife Barbara awoke to find my side of the bed empty. Suddenly the wall between our bedroom and the living room disappeared, and she saw me kneeling in prayer. Standing behind me were three large angels with their arms folded across their chests. The next morning, Barbara asked me where I had been praying the previous evening. When I told her, she said, "That's exactly where I saw you," and she went on to relate the vision she had experienced the night before. Barbara said that she had the distinct impression that the angels were waiting for orders. That vision caused me to focus my study of the Creator's Handbook on those scriptures concerning the ministry of angels as they relate to answered prayer. There are several hundred scriptures dealing with angels in the Bible, but let me share just three of these scriptures dealing with angels which I found particularly interesting.

1) The Psalmist said, "For He shall give His angels charge over you, to keep you in all your ways" (Psalm 91:11).
2) In another place the Psalmist writes, "Bless the Lord, you His angels, Who excel in strength, who do His word, Heeding the voice of His word. Bless the Lord, all you His hosts, You ministers of His, who do His pleasure" (Psalms 103:20 & 21).
3) The writer of Hebrews wrote of the angels, "Are they not all ministering spirits sent forth to minister for those who will inherit salvation?" (Hebrews 1:14).

A footnote to Psalm 103 included in my Thomas Nelson *Spirit-Filled Life Bible* entitled "Fivefold Ministry of Angels" shows God's purpose for angels and how they exist to serve God in five ways:

- "To "bless the Lord" (in worship and service).
- To "do His word" (concerning activity on earth).
- **To heed the voice of God's Word as it is spoken through the saints on the earth** *(emphasis mine)*.
- To minister on God's behalf (as described in Hebrews 1:14).
- To do God's good pleasure (as His hosts at His direction).

I began to ponder footnote number 3): "To heed the voice of God's Word as it is spoken by the saints on earth." Think about it! Whose voice speaks God's Word on the earth? Only the voices of God's people—that means you and I—speak God's Word on the earth. When you or I speak God's Word from our spirit, in faith, it penetrates into the spirit world, and the **angels of God** heed the words that we speak. God's Word (spoken in faith), activates the angels and causes them to bring that portion of God's Word to pass on the earth. "Forever, O Lord, Your Word is settled in heaven." (Psalms 119:89). But it is up to you and me to establish His Word on this earth. In February of 1994, when I first recognized this truth, I understood that it applied to prayer, and I wrote a small booklet entitled "Praying God's Word" because I understood that praying God's Word would cause the angels of God to bring the objects of our prayers to pass. But several years later God enlarged my understanding, and I understood that either praying God's Word or confessing God's Word would cause the angels to bring His word to pass.

We activate the angels of God to bring God's Word to pass when we speak the Word of God to the adverse circumstances that develop in our life. Speak the **Word of God** to your business and call your business prosperous and successful. Faith is the language of heaven, and when we pray or confess God's Word in faith, heaven is activated to bring His Word to pass in the earth. But to make sure that you do not misunderstand me, I want to make something very clear: the angels do not heed the voice of *your* word; they heed the voice of **God's** Word as it is spoken through you, in faith. You cannot order angels to do your will.

ACTIVATING THE ANGELS?

In November of 2003, I was a speaker at the Canadian National Convention of the Full Gospel Business Men's Fellowship, in Regina, Canada. Terry Law was also a speaker in that same convention. Terry is the author of an excellent book on angels entitled *The Truth about Angels* (1). As Terry and I were sitting together in one of the convention luncheons, I raised the subject of angels with him. Both of us had met individuals who thought they had the authority to command angels to do their bidding as if the angels were their personal servants. We agreed that such actions are just plain foolish, but regrettably there are a lot of foolish people in the world. Terry said that he had used the term "activating angels" rather than "commanding or ordering angels" in his book, in order to clarify and avoid the impression that people may order God's angels to do their will. I liked the term "activating the angels," and since our conversation in 2003, as I teach on this very important subject, I have used the phase often in order to avoid the wrong impression.

In his book *The Truth About Angels* (1) Terry Law teaches five principles that activate angels. One of those principles which we have discussed earlier is praying God's Word. Terry states "I have found that something special happens in the angelic kingdom when Christians speak God's Word in the midst of contrary circumstances. It somehow releases the angelic world to work alongside us"... "Problems do not activate angels. God's Word activates angels. Promises from God's Word brings provisions, including the assistance from angels if that is needed. Someone has said there are seven thousand promises in the Bible. God does not want to hear the problem. He wants to hear the promise that fixes the problem. He wants to hear us praise him in advance for that promise." (1)

AUTHORITY IN THE AREA OF FINANCES

Several months after speaking with Terry Law, I was reading Kenneth E. Hagin's book entitled *Biblical Keys to Financial Prosperity* (2). At the time I was experiencing the severe financial test in my business which I discussed in detail in an earlier chapter. It was, in fact, the most difficult problem I had ever had in the thirty-five years of being in business for myself. In the chapter entitled "Our Authority in the Area of Finances," the Reverend Hagin shares how the Lord taught him that angels were sent to minister "for" the believer. After pastoring churches for a number of years, the Lord had told him to leave his church and go into the field ministry. After traveling for a year, moving from church to church he had gotten considerably behind in his finances, so he began to fast and pray earnestly concerning his financial problems. One day as he was praying, the Holy Spirit said to him, *"The money you need is down there. It isn't up here in heaven. I don't have any American dollars up here. I'm not going to rain any money down from heaven because if I did it would be counterfeit. And I'm not a counterfeiter. The money that you need is down there. It's Satan who's keeping it from coming, not me."* Then the Lord said to brother Hagin, *"Don't pray about money like you have been. Whatever you need claim it in Jesus Name, and then you say, 'Satan, take your hands off my money.' And then say, 'Go, ministering spirits, and cause the money to come' "* (2).

It was 1950 when the Lord spoke this revelation to Brother Hagin, and it was all new to him. It was so new that he said to the Lord, *"What do You mean? I can* understand the part about how we can exercise authority over the enemy, claim the finances we need, and tell Satan, 'take your hands off my money.' But, what do you mean about the part, 'Go, ministering spirits, and cause the money to come?'"

The Lord said, "*Didn't you ever read in My Word where it says that angels are ministering spirits sent to minister for those who are heirs of salvation*'? (Hebrews 1:14). Kenneth Hagin said that he had read that scripture many times but he had thought it said that the angels are sent "*to minister to those who are heirs of salvation.*" But now for the first time in his life he saw that the ministering spirits (angels) mentioned in the first chapter of Hebrews are sent forth to "*minister for us*" (2).

PUTTING THE REVELATION TO WORK

Hagin went on to explain that after the Lord gave him this revelation; he put it work in the very next church in which he was holding a meeting, He relates: "You see, what the Lord had shown me was new to me, and my head was telling me, 'That's not going to work.' I just stood on the platform, and said privately, 'In Jesus' name, I claim ____" (he stated the amount of money that was required to meet his budget for the time he would be in that church). And then I said, 'Satan, take your hands off my money in Jesus' name. Go ministering spirits, and cause the money to come. ...' That's it; that's all I did."

He went on to tell the rest of the story: "Then I said to the pastor of the church 'Don't make any special appeal for money. When you get ready to take up my offering, just say as little about it as you can. Don't say a lot about it.' The pastor responded, 'If I just say that this is Brother

Hagin's offering and pass the plate, you won't get over a dime.' I said, 'If I just get a dime, you won't hear me say a word about it'".

Brother Hagin had preached in the same church the year before, and the church had given him only 40 percent of the amount he had just claimed, and the pastor had taken thirty or forty minutes to raise that offering! When he finished that meeting and counted the offering, he found that it was 120 percent of the amount he had claimed and nearly 300 percent of the amount that same church had given him the year before. Brother Hagin concluded by saying "...After that I didn't have to pray anymore about finances; I just said it **one time**. I put into practice what the Lord had taught me about faith for finances. *And in your own life, just say it once. And whenever you think about it, just praise God for the answer."*

Brother Hagin admonished the reader later in the chapter: "We're talking about claiming what the Word says is yours. We're not talking about claiming something that's off the wall. Somebody may say, 'Well, I'm going to claim ten million oil wells!' God didn't promise you ten million oil wells. You can only believe and confess in line with God's Word. Don't go off into left field". (2)

I had read the Reverend Hagin's revelation concerning the ministry of angels in the area of finances on several previous occasions, but I had not caught the significance of this very important principle. But now when my back was against the wall I saw clearly the ministry of angels in the area of finances. And more importantly, I saw that it would work for me in the business world. For more on how I applied this principal to my business problem see the chapter in this book entitled "Spiritual Authority in the Area of Finances".

DO MEN HAVE THE AUTHORITY TO COMMAND ANGELS?

Recently a friend gave me a book in which the author compared the Word of God to the standing orders that a military commander might issue to his command. The author suggested that men have the authority to command the angels to fulfill God's standing orders. While the author is correct in comparing God's Word with his standing orders, I am reluctant to imply that we humans have the authority to command angels. But when we put God's Word (His standing orders) in our heart and our mouth, the angels of God will bring those standing orders, the law of heaven, to pass in our lives, not because we command them to do so, but because our hearts and our mouths are in agreement with God's Word, His standing orders.

We are to meditate upon the **Word of God** day and night in order to establish faith in our hearts in that word which proclaims our agreement with the victory that Jesus has already won for us.

We are to take the **Word of God** before the throne of God in prayer and supplication, setting our case before him as an attorney would do before a judge (Isaiah 43:26).

We are to remind Satan of the **Word of God** as Jesus did when He proclaimed, "It is written" (Matthew 4:1-11).

We can either **say** God's Word, or we can **pray** God's Word, but we can't pray His Word without saying it.

As the **Word of God** becomes established in your heart, it becomes your faith. And your faith in God's Word will activate the angels of God to fulfill God's Word, to fulfill God's standing orders, to fulfill the law of Heaven on your behalf. Your faith in God's Word will produce victory in every circumstance of your life.

HOW DO THE ANGELS BRING NEW SALES?

Some time ago when I was teaching my "Business By The Spirit" principles in a church in the Midwest, I instructed the members of the class that after they had prayed for new sales, they were to confess that they had already received the new sales. I told them that as they confessed God's Word concerning the new sales, the angels of God would work day and night to bring them the increased sales. During the question and answer period following my teaching, the pastor asked, "How do the angels bring God's people new sales?" His question startled me for a moment; I had never thought about how they did it; it had been sufficient for me to just confess the Word of God and believe that the new sales would come. But immediately the Lord gave me the answer.

I asked the congregation "How many of you believe that evil spirits (evil angels) can influence people for evil?" They all raised their hands; then I asked then why can't we believe that good spirits (God's holy angels) can influence people for good? When you produce a good product or service, and believe God for increase, His angels will go before you to influence the people who buy your goods and services to give you new sales. Neither the pastor nor probably most of the congregation had ever considered that the angels of God can influence people for good. Quite frankly, I hadn't thought much about it myself.

(1) *The Truth About Angels*, by Terry Law, © 1994, Published by Charisma House, All rights reserved.

(2) Reprinted by permission. *Biblical Keys To Financial Prosperity*, by Kenneth E. Hagin, © 1995, Rhema Bible Church/Kenneth Hagin Ministries, Tulsa, OK. All rights reserved. [p. 57 - 67]

CHAPTER 21
BUSINESS AS THE SPIRIT WILLS

"But the manifestation of the Spirit is given to each one for the profit of all; for to one is given the word of wisdom through the 'Spirit', to another the word of knowledge through the same Spirit, to another faith by the same Spirit, to another gifts of healings by the same Spirit, to another the working of miracles, to another prophecy, to another discerning of spirits, to another different kinds of tongues, to another the interpretation of tongues. But one and the same Spirit works all these things, distributing to each one individually as He wills" (1 Cor. 12:7-11).

Bernard Burreson is a senior aerospace electronics engineer who is a consultant to the aerospace industry. Before he went into business for himself he worked for the Eldec Corporation, a Seattle area electronics firm. One morning just as Bernie arrived at work and was walking down the hallway toward his office, he passed by an office cubicle and noticed an engineer who was looking very ill. He had large black bags under his eyes, he had obviously not shaved for several days, and he looked very scruffy and discouraged. Bernie asked the engineer (who we will call John) if he was feeling okay and John began to blurt out a story concerning the failure one of the company's products that he himself had designed.

"Oh Bernie," he said, "We are in big trouble..." He told Bernie that he had just returned from Australia where he had been consulting with a submarine manufacturer whom we will call "Australian Sub." The Australian submarine company had just installed into the submarine a new product that John had designed, but it was not working. The new product controlled the submarines flood doors, and thus they could not launch the submarine until John's design was corrected. It was not a good situation for John or for Eldec Company because Australian Sub was threatening to sue Bernie's company for $1,000,000 per week for each week that their submarine could not be launched. John also had another problem: the representative from Australian Sub was scheduled to arrive in Seattle the next day, and John had no solution—he didn't know what to do. As they discussed the problem, John asked Bernie to help him. Bernie agreed to review the design to see if he could identify the problem. Let's let Bernie tell the rest of the story in his own words:

I had only spent about an hour looking at the design when John came into my office and asked me to attend a meeting with him which was being called by the vice president of our division. I agreed to sit in on the meeting. As the meeting was called to order I was asked what I was doing there. I replied that John had asked me to help him review the design and also accompany him to the meeting. Our Vice President who was also in on the meeting said that he thought it was an excellent idea, and told me to spend the rest of the day reviewing the design. At this time in my career, I had been promoted to the highest level of engineering. I had been doing a lot of research in magnetic sensing and had all the computers, programs and tools I needed to perform this type of engineering work. I was called the company's "guru."

I went back to my office and examined the design for the rest of the day, and I concluded that it was a bad design which would not work; I further concluded that we would likely need to completely redesign the sub's flood door electronic operating system. At the end of the day I reported my findings to the company executives, and they asked me to attend a meeting with the representative from Australian Sub early the following morning.

First thing the following day, I attended the meeting with the submarine company representative who was extremely upset, so much so that he would spit as he talked. His face was extremely red and he spoke quite loudly as he exclaimed with all the force he could muster, "Just get my electronics fixed!" Our vice president calmly told this man, as he pointed to me, that he had assigned the company's best engineer to the project, and then he introduced me to the Australian representative. I thought this was a little strange since I had reported to him only the evening before that our product would need to be completely re-designed. Then he told me to go back to my office and spend the remainder of the day looking over the design. He announced that we would meet again at the end of the day to discuss my findings.

At 5:00 P.M. the same day, we met again to review the results of my investigation, but this time it was in my building, and in a conference room that was just around the corner from my laboratory. Not only was our vice president there, but our company president as well. My immediate supervisor cornered me just before the meeting to get my feedback concerning the product, and again I told him that in my opinion the product needed to be totally re-designed.

As I sat down at the conference table, my supervisor sat across from me, and John the original product designer was sitting next to me. The man from Australian Sub was across from John, and the president and vice president sat at opposite ends of the table from each other. My supervisor called the meeting to order, and I expected him to tell the group that we needed to re-design our product, but instead he looked at me and said, "Bernie, get up on the whiteboard and show this man how you are going to fix his electronics." I could hardly believe what I was hearing, but I got up, went to the whiteboard, took out a marker and started to draw out the electronic schematic of the product. I had it memorized by now, having worked on it for the past two days. I was explaining how it worked as I was drawing it, stalling for time; I was trying to think of how I could best relate the bad news. But as I was pointing to a particular area of the circuit, all of a sudden, out of my mouth came these words: "I am going to put a capacitor right here and the circuit is going to work." There was a simultaneous slap of hands on the table as everyone pushed their chairs back from the table and said "great!" They all got up and left, leaving me standing there staring at the evil marker in my hand. A flood of thoughts was rushing through my head. Thoughts like, 'I have just taken full responsibility for this product working...I have just fired myself....what have I done?...how will I put my kids through college...how will my wife take this?'

I must have stood there for two or three minutes staring at the marker, when all of a sudden I realized that what I had just said did not come from my mind; it had come from my spirit and I had spoken it out of my mouth. It was the same way the Holy Spirit had spoken through me on other occasions. I thought, 'I wonder if that was God?' I rushed out of the room to the lab; all the technicians had left for the day. There lying on the technicians' bench was the submarine flood door systems circuitry all set up for testing. John must have been doing some experiments. I went over to the parts bins, and picked out a capacitor. I went back over to the flood door circuitry board, turned on the test equipment, attached it to the submarine flood door circuit board, and then turned on the system. It definitely did not operate properly. I then put the capacitor across the point that I had identified in the meeting, and – BOOM - the signals became totally functional. It worked!

I knew the technicians always came to work early, around 6:00 A.M., so I wrote them a note to get ten test boards modified like the one I had just worked with, and to begin a test program on all ten boards. The next morning I came to work at 8:00, and there was singing and dancing in the laboratory. Every board was working. I went back to my office, astounded at the grace of God.

At 10:00 P.M., John, the design engineer, came back into my office with his head hanging down and announced to me that when they put the flood door tests boards into temperature testing, the Build-In-Test-Equipment (BITE) stopped working. "What do we do now?" John asked. I told him to give me a minute, and he left my office and walked back down the hallway to the laboratory. I swung the chair away from my desk, bowed my head and said, "Father, that was You that gave me the solution yesterday, so please tell me what is wrong now." Instantly God said, "Change R10 to 47K and the circuit will work." I had the circuit memorized, but I did not know which resistor was R10, or did I know its value, but I jumped up and yelled down the hall to John, "Change the R10 to 47K and the circuit will work." He changed the circuit as God had directed and it worked perfectly. My asking God, His replying to me, and my yelling down the hall to John all took place in less than twenty seconds.

The circuits were all modified, and that flood door system is still working in the Australian submarines today. Later, I went back and reviewed the design again with the 47K resistor in place, but it still does not make sense to me as to why the change improved the products performance so much. The only thing I know for sure is that when I lacked wisdom and didn't know what to do, the Holy Spirit gave me wisdom and showed me what to do. Actually God gave me the answer to my problem without me ever asking Him for help. He just wanted to show me that he wanted to be involved in my business life.

This story describes the first time that the **gifts of the Spirit** operated in Bernie's business life to provide him with supernatural wisdom to solve a difficult engineering problem, but it was not the last. The Holy Spirit has given Bernie a number of other inventions, including the Non-Contacting Linear Transducer, a device used to measure and synchronize the position of the wing flaps on the Boeing 757 aircraft, and a GFI sensor among others. In some instances the Spirit gave Bernie a word of wisdom; in other instances it came as a dream or vision. But the important thing is that it came as a gift from the Holy Spirit to help him in the business world. If God did it for Bernie, He will certainly do it for you.

It might be an encouragement to you that the very first individual in the Manufacturer's Handbook to be filled with the Holy Spirit was an architect, a builder...a man by the name of Bezalel, the son of Uri. He was not filled with the Holy Spirit to do the work of the ministry, but was filled with the spirit to design and build Israel's first Tabernacle; he was filled with the Spirit in wisdom, in understanding, and in knowledge to work (Exodus 31:1-3).

"But the manifestation of the Spirit is given to each one for the profit of all; for to one is given the word of wisdom through the Spirit to another the word of knowledge through the same Spirit, to another faith by the same Spirit,... distributing to each one individually as He wills" (1 Corinthians. 12:7-11).

I have said a number of times in this book that faith is the only way you can receive anything from God, except through a manifestation of the *gifts of the Spirit*. Faith will work for you any time, but the gifts of the Spirit operate only as the Spirit wills them to work. Therefore it behooves each of us to understand what the gifts of the Spirit are, so that when the Lord manifests them in our lives, we will be prepared to act on them with our faith.

WHAT ARE THE GIFTS OF THE SPIRIT?

Paul describes nine gifts of the Spirit in the twelfth chapter of first Corinthians. Three of them are verbal gifts—they tell us something; three of them are revelation gifts—they reveal to us something; and three of them are power gifts - they do something for us. Below I have listed these nine gifts below under those three categories:

Verbal Gifts	**Revelation Gifts**	**Power Gifts**
Prophesy	Word of Wisdom	Faith
Tongues	Word of Knowledge	Gifts of Healing
Interpretation of Tongues	Discerning of Spirits	Miracles

Very often several of these gifts may operate together, but in order to better understand them, we will discuss them separately. While all of the gifts of the Spirit are important, I specifically want to discuss the **revelation gifts**. These are the gifts that reveal to us supernatural wisdom and knowledge. But they are not revealed when we want them to be revealed, they are only revealed as the Spirit of God wills them to be revealed. Operating in the gifts of the Spirit also requires faith on our part. In an earlier part of this chapter, Bernie Burreson received a word of wisdom concerning a solution to a flawed electronic design which was to open and close a submarine flood door. But even though Bernie received the design solution as a gift of the Spirit, he still had to exercise his faith to accept and act on that solution. You may not have all nine gifts of the Spirit manifest in your life, but you certainly should understand what all nine gifts are and desire them to operate in your life.

Word of Wisdom

Most of us would agree that God is omniscient—He knows everything. But He only reveals to us a **word of wisdom**, the part of His wisdom that we need to meet a particular need. God didn't reveal all of His entire wisdom concerning the design to Bernie; he only revealed the part Bernie needed. He revealed that if he would put a capacitor in a certain place in the submarine flood door circuit design that the system would work. But later, when the design failed in the heat test, the Holy Spirit (God) gave Bernie another small part of His wisdom: He told him to replace the R-10 resistor with a 47K resistor, and the problem was solved. When the system failed in the heat test, Bernie could have given up and thought *I guess I didn't hear from God after all.* But he exercised his faith and said, "God, you showed me what to do the first time, and you can show me what to do now."

Word of Knowledge

I believe that you would agree with me that while God also has all knowledge, he doesn't reveal to us all his knowledge. He only reveals to us the part of His knowledge we need at the time. One way to distinguish the difference between the **word of knowledge** and the **word of wisdom** is that a word of knowledge is always present tense while a word of wisdom is always future tense. Often a word of knowledge and a word of wisdom might work together. In the chapter entitled "Hearing the Holy Spirit in Business," I relate a story as to how God led my wife and me to buy an office building. One Sunday afternoon my wife Barbara said to me, "Bob, we need to buy an office building with a penthouse on top." The part of her statement about a penthouse on top was a word of knowledge; it was present tense, and it told us that the building we were to buy had a penthouse on top. The part about needing to buy an office building was a word of wisdom; it was future tense. It confirmed to me that the desire I had in my heart to buy an office building was from God.

The Discerning of Spirits

This gift gives us insight and understanding into the spirit world. It has to do with both good and bad spirits. My wife operates in the revelation gifts more than I do, and I operate in the power gifts more than she. In February of 1994, my wife Barbara saw into the spirit world and saw three huge angels standing behind me while I was praying, she related to me afterwards that it looked like the angels were waiting for orders. As a result of her discerning of the angels, I received a revelation from the word of God that angels do the word of God as it is spoken or prayed in faith by the saints in the earth, I share this revelation with you in the chapter entitled "Activating the Angels." Notice that the **Word** and the **Spirit** worked together to reveal this revelation to us.

Gift of Faith

The "gift of Faith" which is described as a gift of the Spirit is actually "special faith" given to us as the Holy Spirit wills for special situations where our own faith is insufficient for the job. On occasion when I am overseas and praying for people who are extremely ill or injured, I have sensed that gift of special faith. This gift of special faith allows you to believe things that you could not otherwise believe.

The Gifts of Healings

Notice that the Manufacturer's Handbook calls this gift "gifts" (plural) of "healings" (plural). Some men obtain more results in praying for hearing, others for eyes, but I have had great success in praying for muscular skeletal problems. These are gifts of healings given as the Spirit wills; they are given you to help others.

Gift of Working of Miracles

A miracle is an intervention of God in the ordinary course of nature. In the story related in chapter 16 in which Gunnar Olson (the Swedish industrialist) spoke to thousands of defective plastic bags—bags which had fused into a single sheet of plastic—to open, I believe Gunnar's faith caused the Holy Spirit to manifest the *gift of miracles* causing the bags to open. When he spoke the words *Listen heaven and earth! Who is Lord over Alfapac?*

His name is Jesus! In the name of Jesus, I command all those plastic molecules to come back into line, the Holy Spirit manifested the gift of miracles and the bags were transformed into useful merchandise.

The Verbal Gifts

The verbal gifts - **prophesy**, **tongues**, and **interpretation of tongues** - can confirm to us directions that the Holy Spirit has spoken previously to our spirits. As I will relate to you in the next chapter, Christians are to be led by the Spirit of God (Romans 8:14). They are not to be led by prophesy or tongues and interpretation of tongues.

ANSWERS IN THE NIGHT SEASON

In my own life, the Spirit often manifests immediately after I wake up—at a time when my mind is quiet, before it begins to think about other things. At this time of the day, it is much easier for the Spirit of God, who lives within my spirit, to contact my mind. Such was the case with Bernie Burreson when God gave him the design for the Boeing 757-300 wing flap skew project in a dream. Bernie had just completed the design of another Holy Spirit-inspired device called a "non-contacting linear transducer" which we will refer to as an NCL unit and his company had constructed a demonstration prototype of the NCL design.

THE GOD-ORDAINED PROGRAM

Bernie himself tells the amazing story about what came to be referred to as "The God-Ordained Program":
On a Friday morning we took the demonstration NCL unit to the Boeing Company to present its features to the Boeing engineers. At the end of the demonstration, four of the

Boeing engineers pulled me aside and said, "That was a neat demonstration but we have a very serious problem that needs attention. We need a new product on the 757-300. In fact, we need three new products, and we need them all completed in six months." The new products were needed to measure the wing flap position on the 757-300 aircraft to ensure that the flaps on both wings are deployed together. (This is extremely critical, because if the flaps do not deploy together, more lift will occur on one wing than the other and the airplane will roll and crash).

The Boeing engineers were trying to convince me that I needed to accept this challenge immediately. All of a sudden I realized that they wanted this product in a mere six months. I told them that this was an impossible project that it took our company two years to accomplish any new product design. We had never designed a product like this before, and since they really wanted three new products it would take at least two years. I told them "no thank you," and we packed up our demonstration NCL unit and left for our office at Eldec.

I arrived back at my office at 11:30AM, and at 2:00 P.M. the president of our company called and asked me to come over to his office. When I arrived, he told me that Boeing had called concerning three products for the wing flap position design. He explained that Boeing wanted us to design, manufacture, test, quality check, and deliver the three new products for the 757-300 aircraft in six months. I said, "Sir that is impossible." He said, "They are desperate; they need this design on that airplane, and they need to roll out that plane in six months. They will pay us whatever it cost and more." I said, "You are going to make me do this aren't you?" He told me that a program manager had already been selected to make a quick estimate of costs by that very *afternoon. By the end of the day, everything was in place—I was to begin the project the following Monday. I couldn't believe that they were asking me to do this! It had been agreed that since there were only six months to complete the entire project, we would divide the time three ways: two months for me to design and test, two months for manufacturing to build the products, and two months for the qualification testing and delivery of the product. This was crazy!*

On Sunday night the day before I was to start the project, I began to fret. My stomach was churning, and I couldn't go to sleep. The previous Wednesday, I had read Psalm 37 in my Bible study, and all I could remember from that study was that Psalms 37 said, "Do not fret…" And I was fretting! I prayed, "Father, you said not to fret, and I am fretting. If you don't want me to fret, then you need to help me." Immediately I felt the burden of the program lift, and I went to sleep.

At 2:00 A.M., I awoke with the complete design in my head. Now I could not go back to sleep as I was too excited. God had given me the design while I was asleep! I got up, but I was so excited that I could hardly wait until 6:00 o'clock when my technician arrived at the laboratory. I couldn't wait to show him the design. By 10:00 A.M., we had our first crude prototype, and it was working. I took the results of the prototype into the program manager and said, "Remember, the two months I said I needed? Well, here is our prototype complete. We are now two months ahead of schedule." He couldn't believe it. He asked me how I did it, and I began to witness to him of God's grace. From that time on the program manager called the program, "The God-Ordained Program."

We delivered our first products to Boeing two weeks ahead of schedule, and my company Eldec received many awards because of it.

The Holy Spirit Will Show You His Secrets

God is no respecter of persons! What He has done for Bernie Burreson, He will do for you…what He has done for Gunnar Olson, He will do for you…what He has done for me, He will do for you. If you fear the Lord and meditate on His promises day and night like these men do, He will show you His secrets and grant to you the blessings of Abraham—the blessings that He has promised to those who belong to Christ.

"Who is the man that fears the Lord? Him shall He teach in the way He chooses. He himself shall dwell in prosperity, and his descendants shall inherit the earth. The secret of the Lord is with those who fear Him, and He will show them His covenant (Psalms 25:12-14).

CHAPTER 22
HEARING THE HOLY SPIRIT IN BUSINESS

"For as many as are led by the Spirit of God, these are the sons of God" (Romans 8:14).

The twenty-first century world financial system is very interrelated and unstable; a massive terrorist attack, a war in the Middle East, a major earthquake, a hurricane, or Asian currency speculation can cause the world's stock markets to fluctuate wildly. The threat of inflation can change the national monetary policy and raise the long-term interest rates, which in turn depresses the housing market, which in turn depresses a myriad of building material suppliers and eventually the industries that supply them the raw materials. Then follows high unemployment, a series of bankruptcies among those companies and individuals that have over-extended themselves, and a reduction in consumer spending which initiates another round of economic reductions among those who manufacture and sell consumer goods.

The only way that a businessperson can be entirely confident in making good long term decisions is when they have received direction from the Holy Spirit. Only God, who knows the future, can guide us to buy property that will appreciate, even in an economic downturn. He can tell us when to increase production and when to reduce our staff; He can warn us of market fluctuations before they occur. The Holy Spirit will guide us in all the affairs of life if we will take the time to train our spirits to hear His voice. The hallmark of a son or daughter of God is "For as many as are led by the Spirit of God, these are the sons of

God" (Romans 8:14). But unfortunately, only a few of us are willing to take the time to meditate on His Word and to spend the time with Him in prayer—both of which are required to hear His voice.

Jesus is the revealed Word of God, (the Logos): "And the Word became flesh and dwelt among us…" (John 1:14). The Creator's Handbook, the Bible, is the written word of God (the logos). It is the sum of God's utterances; it is the expression of His thoughts. As we meditate upon (think upon and confess) the written Word of God, we are spending time with Jesus, the revealed word of God. We are getting to know his voice and establishing His Word in our spirit. Then when difficulties develop in our lives, the Holy Spirit is able to bring that Word, which we have stored in our spirit, to our remembrance to teach us and guide us as to the way we should go (John 14:26 & 16:13). The Apostle Paul exhorts the believer to take "…the sword of the Spirit, which is the word of God; praying always with all prayer and supplication in the Spirit…" (Ephesians 6:17). The "Word of God" in this verse is the Greek word *rhema*; it is a specific word which the Holy Spirit will bring to your remembrance to guide you when problems arise in your life. However, the Holy Spirit cannot bring to your remembrance a word which you have not first stored in your spirit.

GOD SPEAKS TO THE BELIEVER'S SPIRIT

When a man is born again, the Spirit of God moves into his spirit; and his inner man (his spirit) becomes a brand new creature (2 Corinthians 5:17). Therefore we do not hear the voice of God in our minds; we hear the voice of God on the inside of us, in our spirits. "The spirit of man is the lamp of the Lord, searching all the inner depths of his heart" (Proverbs 20:27). The writer of Proverbs is explaining that the Lord has sent His Spirit into our spirits to give us light, to give us direction. If God dwells in our spirits, then common sense tells us that is where He will speak to us.

THE PRIMARY WAY JESUS LEADS HIS PEOPLE

Years ago, when I was first baptized in the Holy Spirit, I found by experience that by praying in the Spirit (praying in tongues) for an hour or so, my spirit would became active and my mind and body would become inactive, thereby allowing me to get a leading or a sense of the direction as to the way I should go.

Several years later my wife Barbara and I attended a three-day faith seminar in Honolulu, Hawaii, the first such seminar we had ever attended. One of the speakers in that seminar was the Reverend Kenneth Hagin, founder of Rhema Bible training School. The subject on which he taught was "How to Hear the Voice of God." Subsequent to that seminar, he has published a book entitled *How You Can Be Led by the Spirit of God* (1). I would highly recommend that you obtain a copy and study this book.

In that seminar in Hawaii, Kenneth Hagin related a vision in which Jesus had appeared to him in February of 1959 in El Paso, Texas. During that vision, Jesus explained the ministry of the prophet to the Reverend Hagin. He explained that under the Old Covenant, only the prophet, priest and king were anointed by the Holy Spirit. The common people did not have the Spirit of God either on them or in them. Therefore, under the Old Covenant, the people would seek guidance through the prophet because he had the anointing of the Holy Spirit. But under the New

Covenant, all believers have the Holy Spirit in them; therefore, we should not seek guidance from a prophet, but from the Holy Spirit who dwells within our spirits. It is okay to receive guidance from a prophet, but that guidance should be used to only confirm what God has already revealed to us in our spirits. In the vision Jesus said to Hagin, "Under the New Covenant, it does not say, 'As many as are led by prophets, they are the sons of God.' The New Testament says, 'For as many as are led by the Spirit of God, they are sons of God'" (Romans 8:14).

Then Jesus said, *"The number one way, the primary way, that I lead all My children is by the inner witness."* The inner witness is a sense that you have in your spirit concerning a matter. Perhaps you sense that you should move ahead on a situation; you feel good about it—you have a green light, so to speak, concerning the matter. On the other hand, you may sense that you shouldn't move ahead; you have a check in your spirit about it—you may have a red light, so to speak. Perhaps you have had an occasion to sit down write a letter or make a phone call, but you had a check in your spirit concerning the matter. For instance, there have been times when making a proposal on a project that I have had a check in my spirit. I would sense that it would be a problematic job and that we shouldn't pursue it.

When I first heard these principles in Hagin's seminar, my spirit jumped because it confirmed my own experience, and it explained why I seemed to get a leading—an inner witness—when I would pray in the Spirit about a decision and get quiet before the Lord. Hearing Brother Hagin share these principles gave me greater confidence in my ability to hear the Holy Spirit guide me in the way that I should go. Now we are not to accept any vision unless it lines up with the Word of God; therefore, I suggest that you should check out this revelation against the following scriptures: Romans 8:14, 16; Proverbs 20:27; John 14:23, 26, 16:13; 1 Corinthians 3:16; and 2 Corinthians 6:16. In his Hawaii convention, Kenneth Hagin used the Paul's experience when sailing for Rome by way of Crete (Acts 27) to verify the biblical accuracy of the vision. Paul said, *"Men, I perceive that this voyage will end in disaster and much loss...."* Paul perceived in his spirit that they shouldn't sail for Crete. You might say he had a check—a red light in his spirit; he had a caution that they would be in danger if they sailed for Crete. The primary way that God leads us is the inner witness; it is a gentle inner leading.

In the above vision, Jesus made the following statement to Kenneth Hagin; it is a statement that is particularly important for a business person!

"If you will learn to follow that inward witness, I will make you rich. I will guide you in all the affairs of life, financial as well as spiritual. I am not opposed to My children being rich; I am opposed to their being covetous". (1)

I am so glad that my wife Barbara and I heard this teaching early in our Christian walk, for as we have followed the inner witness, the Lord has prospered us abundantly.

HOW THE INNER WITNESS LED US TO BUY AN OFFICE BUILDING

In the winter of 1989, the lease for my consulting firm's office space was coming up for renewal. For ten or more years I had wanted to own my own office building. In fact I had looked at a number of buildings in the south end of our city, but I had never found a building that really met all our requirements. They were either too old, too large, too small, wrong location, etc. But with the decision to sign another five-year lease, I determined that I would once again look for an office building that I could purchase. Actually I hadn't even shared with my wife Barbara that I was looking for a building, but she was aware that the lease on our office building was coming up for renewal. One Sunday afternoon in February of 1999, Barbara blurted out a **word of wisdom** from the Lord.

At the time, neither Barbara nor I recognized it as a word from the Lord. She said, "Bob, we should purchase an office building with a penthouse on top!" I laughed and shook my head. I thought, *Penthouse on top? That is really ridiculous! How many office buildings have a penthouse on top?* Early Monday morning of the following week, I drove to Portland, Oregon, on business. As I was returning to my office on Wednesday, I decided to drive through Tukwila, a city near my office, to look at an office building on which I had received a mail advertisement the previous week. After searching for that building for nearly a half hour and not being able to find it, I decided to return to my office by a different route than I normally take. As I drove toward my office I saw a three-story office building that was for sale. My spirit jumped. I had an inner witness that this was our building. Actually I had seen this building being constructed several years earlier. At the time I remember saying to myself, "That's the kind of office building I would like to own." It had an attractive design, was in a good location, and was about the right size.

When I got back to my office, I immediately called the real estate agent. He said that it would be a great building for an architectural and engineering firm, as it had been designed and constructed for use by an engineering firm. He pointed out that it had a concrete (fire resistant) basement for storage of our drawings, and it had a penthouse apartment on top. When he said there was a penthouse apartment on the fourth floor of the building my spirit jumped again - now I **knew** that this was our building. At the time I spoke with the realtor, approximately half of the building was vacant. (There was an office building vacancy rate of nearly forty percent in the area where this particular building was located.) This made the building very unattractive to other buyers, but it was great for my company, because when we moved into the building it would bring the building's occupancy to one hundred percent.

Because Barbara and I have always given a large percentage of our income to missions, we didn't have the surplus cash required for the twenty percent down payment. In addition, the banks had lost considerable money on commercial office building loans early in the 80's, and they would only offer a five-year mortgage on the building. From the natural financial standpoint, everything was against our buying that office building, but nine months later we moved in! And better yet, God has blessed us with stable renters which have given us a very low vacancy rate for nearly two decades.

THE SECOND WAY GOD LEADS US

Have you ever had your conscience convict you when you said or did something that was wrong? Have you ever had what we refer to as a "hunch" concerning a decision you had to make? Even a natural man, because he is a spiritual being, can know things in his spirit, his inner man. This inner man has a voice; we call it our conscience or intuition. We have all experienced that small inner voice, our conscience, attempting to give guidance to our minds. Your conscience is the "voice of your spirit." Before a person is born again, his conscience will let him do many things that it won't let him do after he is born again. But when one becomes born again, the Holy Spirit moves into his spirit and begins to guide him according to the will of God. Paul said he always obeyed his conscience (Acts 23:1 and 2 Timothy 1:3). Often as I get quiet and seek the Holy Spirit concerning a business problem or a decision that I must make, He will bring a word or a scripture to my spirit to guide and direct me. My spirit man then attempts to pass the information he receives from the Holy Spirit on to my mind. Your spirit man speaks to you by a still small voice within you (your conscience), but you have to get your mind quiet in order to hear him. I have found that the best time for me to hear my spirit is right after I awake from sleep, while my mind is still quiet.

HOW GOD LED ME TO SELECT A BUSINESS ASSOCIATE

In 1995, I decided to sell my business to a long time employee. This employee had been with our firm for some twenty-one years and I had promised her on several occasions that I would give her the first option to purchase the company. Frankly, when it came time to sell the business I didn't feel very comfortable with the above arrangement—you might say I had a check in my spirit. But because I had given her my word, I knew that I had to keep my promise. This is an important principle: God's Word cautions us that "He honors those who keep their promises, even a promise that turns into a deficit (Psalms 16:4). I hired a business-consulting firm to value the business, handle the negotiations with the employee, prepare the ownership transfer contracts, and administer the ownership transfer. As the deal was about to be consummated, the firm who was handling the transfer called me and warned me that something was not right with the employee. They had discovered that the employee was double-crossing me. She apparently had been collecting information on our clients and past projects. She was planning on going into partnership with a former employee and starting her own business. That way, she reasoned, she would not have to pay me for the business. I obviously did not end up selling the business to her, and her new business partnership lasted for about one and a half years before going out of business. I subsequently learned that either the woman or her partner had threatened a lawsuit against the other in some kind of a business disagreement. You see, if we belong to Christ, we are Abraham's seed and therefore heirs, according to the promise that God made to Abraham (Galatians 3:29). And one of those promises is "I will bless those who bless you, and I will curse him who curses you." (Genesis 12:3).

The business consulting firm, which I had hired to develop the ownership transfer, wanted me to sell the business to another firm, but I didn't feel right about doing that. I sensed in my spirit that God said He would "bring me a Joseph." This "Joseph" would be an individual who was skilled at my profession and would take over the business and purchase it from me. You might wonder how I knew that. I just had a "knowing" in my spirit; I had no natural evidence.

Well, I waited a year, but there was no Joseph! One Sunday afternoon I got down on my knees in my living room and prayed, "Father, are you going to bring me a Joseph or not?" Immediately the Holy Spirit spoke a scripture into my spirit. On the inside of me, I heard the words "Genesis 48:2." I did not hear it with my physical ears; it was just, as best that I can describe it, a strong knowing on the inside of me. I grabbed my Bible and turned to Genesis 48:2 and read "...*and Jacob was told, 'Look, your son Joseph is coming to you.'* " What an answer!! That word from God became my faith. It told me what would happen in advance. I, of course, wanted a Joseph now, but it was a good thing I received such a direct word from God, because it was another four years before "Joseph" arrived at my business. Through that experience, I learned that it is through "faith and patience" that we inherit the promises (Hebrews 6:12).

Now you have already read in the chapter entitled "Fighting the Good Fight of Faith" that Joseph did not work out, and when it looked like the company was going to go bankrupt he found another job and left the company. He left just two weeks before the financial breakthrough came. You may be wondering, "If God told you to wait five years for this man to come to your company, then why didn't he work out? Didn't God know what would happen?" Of course He did! Now let me ask you a question: when God told Samuel to anoint Saul king over Israel (1 Samuel 9 &10), didn't God know that Saul wouldn't work out? Yes! God knows the beginning from the end, but He gives each of us the opportunity to succeed or fail because he has given us a free will. Because Saul was disobedient to the Word of the Lord, he failed (1 Samuel 15). It is the same with you or me. God has plans to prosper us, but if we are not willing and obedient, we can nullify His plans.

God gave the biblical Joseph a dream concerning a future time when his father and his brothers would bow down and be subservient to him. But Joseph was willing and obedient; and even though he went through a number of trials and tests in his life before the dream came to pass, God eventually promoted him to the second highest office in Egypt. The only evidence that he had that his dream would come to pass was the information that he received from God in the dream. The psalmist says, "Until the time that his word came to pass, the Word of the Lord tested him" (Psalm 105:19).

The only evidence I had that God would bring me a "Joseph" was the word of Genesis 48:2, which God had spoken into my spirit. Walking with God requires that we exercise faith in His Word, until the Word He has given us has come to pass. Even though the first man that God brought to me did not work out, He had another man waiting in the wings, and within a month of Joseph leaving the firm, he brought me a man who bought my firm at the price which I named.

If you are born again, you can trust the voice of your spirit because the Spirit of God dwells in your spirit. Therefore your spirit is a safe guide. Let me give you an example. Before I was born again, I would curse habitually as a normal part of my daily vocabulary. I would curse to express anger or just to make a strong point. My conscience never once convicted me. As soon as I became born again, I don't believe a curse word has come out of my mouth more than half a dozen times, and each time my conscience immediately convicted me.

Paul says that "…in latter times some will depart from the faith…having their own conscience seared with a hot iron"

(1 Timothy 4:1-2). If you immediately obey the voice of your spirit (your conscience), it will keep your spirit tender toward the Spirit of God. But if you ignore your spirit (your conscience), it will become hardened and cease to speak to you.

A THIRD WAY GOD LEADS US

God also leads us by the voice of the Holy Spirit. You might ask, "How can I determine the difference between my spirit and the Holy Spirit?" When the Holy Spirit within you speaks, it is with a more authoritative voice. It is so real that it might sound like someone said it to you in a human voice.

Young Samuel heard the Holy Spirit speak and thought that it was the priest Eli calling him. He ran to Eli and said, "Here I am." But Eli said, "No, I didn't call you; go back to bed." After the voice spoke to Samuel a third time, Eli counseled young Samuel to answer and say, "Speak, your servant is listening" (1 Samuel 3: 1-20). Samuel could hear an audible voice but Eli couldn't. Why? Because the Holy Spirit on the **inside** of Samuel spoke to him, there was no audible voice; therefore, Eli couldn't hear the voice.

HEARING THE VOICE OF GOD

To my knowledge I have personally heard the authoritative voice of the Holy Spirit on only two or three occasions. One occasion was in April of 2000, as I was about to make a sizable investment in the stock market. On Sunday afternoon, I made a list of stocks that I intended to buy the following morning. I woke up on Monday morning and was just lying in bed, only about half awake, when suddenly the Holy Spirit spoke the following words to me very authoritatively: *"STAY OUT OF THE MARKET."* Frankly, it startled me, but I followed His advice and stayed out of the market. Several days later, the market (the NASDAC composite) dropped thirty-five percent. Praise the Lord! God will help you in the business world if you will be open to Him. Unfortunately, however, I must confess that I have often made decisions without seeking the Lord!

Three months after the Lord told me to stay out of the market, the market appeared to stabilize and started to rise, so without seeking God, I invested in the very market that the Holy Spirit had told me to stay out of. Several months later, I went to Russia on a mission trip and while I was out of the country the market fell again. As I write this some eight years later, I have still not recovered the money I lost. Needless to say, I lost a substantial amount of money, but I gained some very expensive understanding: *don't make major financial decisions without seeking a green light from the Holy Spirit.*

WE ARE NOT TO SEEK VISIONS OR ANGELS

The Creator's Handbook reveals that on certain occasions God would lead His people through visions or angels. But such supernatural guidance did not occur every day in the lives of these individuals. Supernatural guidance, if it occurred at all, occurred only once or twice in their lifetimes. And in most instances, it occurred to give direction to these believers either when they were in great danger or if God's purpose for them would be foiled if they did not receive supernatural help. Knowing this, we may not be quite so anxious to receive such supernatural guidance, as it might indicate that we have a difficult road ahead.

God may or may not give you a vision or dream. He may or may not send an angel to guide you. But we are not to seek visions or angels or voices; we are to seek the Holy Spirit.

WE DO NOT TAKE TIME TO ASK GOD

In my own experience, I have found that praying in tongues is one of the best ways to get my body quiet and my mind in "neutral," so I can hear what my spirit is saying. You see, if your mind is constantly bombarding you with a problem concerning a family difficulty, your job, or a payment which is due at the bank then you are not going to hear what the Holy Spirit is saying. That's why it's easier to hear from God when you first wake up in the morning; your mind is usually quiet, and it hasn't yet started to think about the problems of the day.

As I have sought God's guidance about major decisions in my life, sometimes I have had to pray night after night over a period of several days or weeks before I get an answer. Many times God speaks to me just as I wake up, while my mind is quiet. The problem with most of us, including myself sometimes, is that we are simply not willing to take the time or pay the price to hear God's direction for our lives, our businesses, or our families. If we want God's plan, we must be willing to spend time with Him to obtain it.

(1) Reprinted by permission. *How You Can Be Led By The Spirit Of God*, by Kenneth E. Hagin, © 1978, Rhema Bible Church/Kenneth Hagin Ministries, Tulsa, OK. All rights reserved. [p.33]

INTRODUCTION TO PART V: DEVELOPING WISDOM FOR WEALTH

I, wisdom, dwell with prudence, and find out knowledge and discretion …That I may cause those who love me to inherit wealth, That I may fill their treasuries. (Proverbs 8:12&21).

I grew up on a farm, and as a young boy I learned the basics of farming by observing the older, experienced men as they went about their daily duties. As I grew older and started to attend public school, I was given a few simple farm chores to perform. Later I began to drive the farm trucks and tractors during the planting and harvesting of the crops. By the time I was sixteen years old, I could accomplish most of the tasks required to operate the farm with some degree of competence.

Unlike the farmer who teaches his son or daughter how to plant and harvest a crop in the agricultural environment, most urban fathers have failed to teach their sons and daughters how to plant and harvest a financial crop in the urban environment. Your father didn't teach you, because his father didn't teach him. For the most part, we have turned the job of teaching our children over to the public school system, and they have done little to prepare this generation for the realities of the urban financial environment.

The prosperity message taught in many churches is good; but it doesn't go far enough. In fact, it leaves many with the impression that the giving of tithes and offerings is some type of magic, get-rich scheme which replaces the need to study, develop skill and work hard. Have you ever heard a sermon on saving a portion of the harvest (the paycheck) for seed? Have you ever heard a sermon on the necessity of sowing seed (investing) in order that God might have something to bless, something He can cause to increase? Perhaps most importantly, have you ever heard a sermon which taught that it is just as important for a Christian man or woman to become financially literate and develop the business skills necessary to compete in the twenty-first century market place as it was for the Jewish farmer of the Old Testament to learn how to plant and harvest his crop or tend to his herd in biblical times?

The creation of wealth in the free enterprise system requires some startup capital (the seed) and the knowledge of how to use that capital to bring increase (understanding how to plant the seed and harvest the crop); but the elixir which turns these ingredients into wealth is ***faith!***

In Part V of *Business by the Spirit,* you will be exposed to some basic financial principles such as the reading and development of a financial statement; the importance of sacrificing present pleasures in order to obtain the seed required to produce a future financial harvest; the negative effect that consumer debt has on the creation of wealth; a no-risk investment that pays 18-20 percent interest; and the two basic types of investments that are available to you to build wealth and bring increase in your life. In addition, you will learn that traditionally investors have built wealth by being **owners,** not lenders; you will learn how to avoid investments that sound too good to be true, as well as the importance of doing your financial homework before you invest your hard earned money in the marketplace.

CHAPTER 23
KNOW THE CONDITION OF YOUR FINANCES

WE ARE ADMONISHED TO KNOW THE CONDITION OF OUR FLOCKS

"Riches can disappear fast. And the king's crown doesn't stay in the family forever—so watch your business interests closely. Know the state of your flocks and your herds; then there will be lambs wool enough for clothing, and goats milk enough for food for all your household..." (Proverbs 27:23-27 LB).

"Any enterprise is built by wise planning, becomes strong through common sense, and profits wonderfully by keeping abreast of the facts" (Proverbs 24:3 & 4 LB).

HOW DO PEOPLE BECOME WEALTHY?

If I were to ask, "How do people become millionaires?" many would suggest they inherit it. Others might say they get a college education; still others might advocate that millionaires got a lucky break in life. But the truth is that most people became millionaires by a lifetime of hard work, perseverance, saving, investing and perhaps most importantly, self-discipline.

In the mid 1980's two university professors, Dr. Thomas J. Stanley and Dr. William D. Danko, began investigating how people become wealthy. They attempted to do so by surveying people who lived in upscale neighborhoods and drove expensive cars. Amazingly they found that many of those people did not have much wealth. Even more amazing, they found that many of the people who have a great deal of wealth do not live in expensive homes or drive luxury cars. They reported the findings of their study in a book entitled *The Millionaire Next Door* (1) which was first published in 1996. They found that "usually the wealthy individual is a businessman who has lived in the same town all his adult life. This person owns a small factory, a chain of stores, or a service company. He has married once and remains married. He lives next door to a person with a fraction of his wealth. He is a compulsive saver and investor. And he has made his money on his own. *Eighty percent of America's millionaires are first-generation rich.*" They went on to say, "Affluent people typically live well below their means; they allocate their time, energy, and money efficiently, in ways conducive to building wealth, and they believe that financial independence is more important than displaying high social status" (1).

THERE IS A DIFFERENCE BETWEEN WEALTH AND INCOME

You should understand that wealth is not the same as income. You may make a good annual income and still not be wealthy. Wealth is what you accumulate, not what you spend. Unfortunately, because most people don't understand the difference between the two, their economics tend to be debt based and consumption oriented. They allow the desire for things to influence their purchasing decisions; they want instant gratification to their desires. To fulfill those desires they pile up debt and relegate the payments to the future, and by their example, they teach their children to do the same and to live in the same way they do.

LEARNING A NEW VOCABULARY

I've written this book as a guide to the small businessperson or the young men or women who are desirous of establishing enough wealth to accomplish what God has called them to do in this life and to allow them to live comfortably in their retirement years. But before we go further, I would like to make sure that we all understand some basic financial vocabulary.

When you were attending school, your report card told you how well you were doing academically. If you received a low or failing grade in a particular subject, the report card warned that you were in trouble and that you that you needed to make a correction in your study habits concerning that subject. Since you received your report card every three months, you generally understood where you stood academically. Once you graduate from school, your ***financial statement*** takes the place of your report card; it is designed to tell you how you are doing financially and to warn you of problems that may be developing in your personal or business financial life.

Unfortunately, most people have never learned how to prepare or even read a simple financial statement. They don't understand how to borrow money, how to calculate interest on a loan or for that matter the difference between simple and compound interest. They simply don't understand the basic realities of personal finance. Therefore, they never prepare a personal financial statement; they buy most of their possessions on credit and think as long as they're making their monthly payments to the finance company, they are succeeding in life. They may have a good paying job, a nice home and drive a late model car and yet receive a failing grade on their financial report card.

THE NEED FOR UNIFORM ACCOUNTING PRINCIPLES

Imagine for a moment that every school could develop its own grading standards. You go to a school where the teachers give an "A" for an excellent semester of work, and I go to a school where they give an "E" for excellent work? Comparing our academic performances would be quite difficult without a recognized standard of grading. The same would be true if every business could invent its own accounting methods and terminology for measuring profit and preparing their financial statements. Common sense tells us that financial statements like report cards should follow a uniform reporting standard. For this reason the accounting industry has developed uniform set of financial reporting standards. In America, these standards are called "Generally Accepted Accounting Principles" (GAAP). In the following paragraphs, I want to familiarize you with the standard financial reports maintained by most individuals and businesses.

When most people graduate from high school or college, their "financial I.Q." is quite low. Sadly, the same is true of many small-business owners; they don't understand how to read or interpret their company's financial statement. To them it is just something they have to prepare to keep the government off their backs; but there are at least five other groups of people who have a vested interest in the accuracy of your financial statements: your **customers**, who buy the products and service you sell; your **employees**, who provide services to your business and are paid wages and provided with benefits; your **suppliers** and **sub-contractors**, who sell you a wide range of goods and services; your **sources of capital**, who loan money to the business and have to be repaid at definite dates in the future; and your **equity sources of capital**, the individuals or institutions who may invest money in your business.

When you were going to school in order to get good grades, you probably had to do some homework. It's the same in business. Most people, whether they are working for themselves or others, do not become wealthy by just working—although working is important; they become wealthy by doing their financial homework.

PROFIT IS NOT A DIRTY WORD

Go anywhere in the world and you will find that the primary way by which anyone evaluates management is the management's ability to produce a profit. Even if you were the manager of a collective farm or industrial plant in the former Soviet Union, your superiors would measure your success or failure by the profit you were able to produce. They wouldn't use a capitalistic term like *profit*; they would probably call it a *production quota*. But that quota would measure the amount of surplus that was left after all expenses had been paid. In capitalistic terms, they would judge you on your ability to make a profit.

Many small business owners shrug off the importance of generating a profit. I have observed a number of immature Christian businesspeople start a business with great fanfare, often emphasizing that they are going to operate their business on Christian principles. Many announce that they will donate a large percentage of the profits to God's work, apparently hoping that such a declaration will entreat God's favor. They understand reasonably well the product or service they plan to provide, but know little or nothing about the financial side of the managing a business. These individuals operate their business for a short time and find that instead of making a profit, they are going deeper and deeper into debt. They eventually end up owing a great deal of money, and some even find it necessary to file bankruptcy.

YOU MUST BE ABLE TO READ A FINANCIAL STATEMENT

Now that we understand the importance of the financial statement in living a prosperous and successful life, your first homework assignment is to learn how to prepare and read a financial statement. In fact, if you are in business you should know more about the operating side of your financial statement than your bookkeeper or your accountant. You simply cannot delegate the financial management of your company to others. If you delegate such responsibilities, it is very possible that one day one of your employees will give you the bad news that there is no money to make the payroll. Or worse yet, they may inform you that they have not paid the payroll taxes for the last three months because there was not enough money in the bank account.

If you understand how your financial statement works, you will have more confidence in your personal and business financial position, more control over your company's operations, and you will be able to make the corrections to your business that are necessary when you underbid a project or lose a big client.

Now let's take a look at the basic elements of the financial statement:

Income Statement Diagram

Income
Expense
Profit or loss

Balance Sheet Diagram

Assets	Liabilities
	Owners' Equity

There are two basic elements to a financial statement: they are the income statement (sometimes referred to as the profit and the loss statement) and the balance sheet. A third element, which is a part of the financial statement in large companies, is called a cash flow statement.

Cash flow is very important in the operation of a business. It is important because cash needs to flow smoothly if your business is to operate in a trouble-free manner.

The cash flow statement allows the business owner to track where the money came from, where it is currently being used, and how often it is turning over.

Now let's take a more detailed look at the income statement and the balance sheet.

Income Statement

The income statement summarizes the profit- making activities of a business. In its simplest form, it is the revenue derived from the sale of goods and services, less the cost of producing the goods and services, which equals the net income, often referred to as profit or loss. The income statement should generally be developed monthly.

Revenue − Expense = Profit or Loss

IMPORTANT
In the operation of your business, the income statement should get most of your attention, as it will reveal the areas of your business or personal life that must be changed in order to maintain a healthy, financial condition.

Balance Sheet

The balance sheet summarizes the business or individual's assets, liabilities and equity accounts at the close of a particular accounting period. The balance sheet is also generally developed monthly.

The balance sheet derives its name from the fact that the business or individual's assets always balance their liabilities plus their equity.

Assets = Liabilities + Equity

Equity is sometimes referred to as the net worth. In the case of individual wealth, "net worth" is an accurate description. However, in the case of a company, net worth is not an accurate description as it rarely represents the company's actual value, which is generally based on a multiple of a company's annual profit.

The **Balance Sheet** is made up of the following sub-parts:

Assets = Cash in the bank + non-cash assets, such as the current value of computers, automobiles, and/or buildings owned by the business or individual.

Liabilities = Operating liabilities such as the telephone bill or the office rent + debt such as money you have borrowed from the bank to purchase the computers, equipment and/or buildings you listed as assets.

Equity = Invested capital, (money the owner invests to get the company started) + retained earnings (earnings from previous years that the owner allows to remain in the company for use as working capital).

Cash Flow Statement

Cash Flow Statement summarizes the sources and uses of cash during the accounting period. In a small business this statement may not be necessary as it is generally apparent to the small business owner where his cash has gone. In a larger business, however, it is a good idea to utilize this statement regularly. For instance, in my business, on a monthly basis, I would review a list of all major expenses before the checks were written. This gave me a good overview of where the money was being spent.

One thing about cash flow that the small business owner must watch carefully is the time it takes to collect the money once the invoice is sent to the customer. This is referred to as cash turnover. If the payment time gets too long, it can radically affect the amount of working capital it takes to operate your business. Cash turnover is defined as the number of days it takes to collect your money after you have billed the customer. As a rule of thumb, cash turnover in most businesses should not be allowed to exceed ninety days. A cash turnover of ninety days means you would need more than four times your monthly billings in working capital—the money you spend during the month in which you produce your product or service plus the three months (ninety days) it will take you to receive payment for your product or service—to operate your business comfortably.

Cash turnover can be calculated by dividing your total accounts receivable by your average daily income.

Cash turnover =
Accounts Receivable
Average Daily Income

RELATING THE INCOME STATEMENT TO THE BALANCE SHEET

Income
Revenue causes an influx of money into the asset accounts.

Expense
Expense causes an outflow of money from the asset accounts.

CASH BASIS ACCOUNTING

Generally speaking, a business uses either *cash basis* or the *accrual basis* of accounting. The cash basis of accounting, as the name implies, is limited to recording only cash inflows and outflows. Under the cash basis, profit equals cash receipts from sales and other income less cash payments for expenses. But in the twenty-first century, we no longer operate in a cash basis world. Most businesses sell their products and services on credit rather than cash, and they usually don't collect all their sales revenue and pay all their expenses by the end of each accounting period. Under the cash basis of accounting, a manager might receive an extremely skewed view of a company's actual financial position, because items purchased on credit and work billed to customers are not accounted for until the cash is actually received.

ACCRUAL BASIS ACCOUNTING

Accrual basis accounting, which is the most accepted basis of accounting, goes way beyond recording only cash inflow and cash outflow transactions. Under the accrual method, purchases made on credit are recorded as soon as the purchase takes place, and revenue is recorded as soon as it is earned, even though the cash may not actually be received from the customer until several months later. Under the accrual basis of accounting, the manager always knows the profitability of his company at the close of each accounting period.

HOW DO WE DEFINE WEALTH?

The Old Testament patriarchs would have used a cash basis accounting system to define a man's wealth. They defined his wealth by the size of his herd or the bushels of grain that he had in his barns. For instance the Bible describes Job as follows —"He was also very wealthy-seven thousand head of sheep, three thousand camels, five hundred yoke of oxen, five hundred donkeys, and a huge staff of servants, the most influential man in all the East!" (Job 1:3 MSG).

During the time that Job lived on the earth, buying and selling transactions were cash deals. As soon as Job purchased a team of oxen, it belonged to Job; there was no mortgage on the oxen. But in the twenty-first century world, a man's team of oxen might be purchased in January of 2008, but the purchase price might be paid in twenty-four payments over the next two years. And we would never describe a man's wealth by listing the number of sheep, camels, oxen and donkeys or real estate that he owns. We would convert the value of his livestock and real estate into dollars (or the currency of the nation in which the individual lives) and enter that value into the asset section of his financial statement. Then we would subtract the debt that He owed to his creditors to determine his net worth. In the twenty-first century, in order to determine Job's wealth, we would determine his net worth.

Job's wealth (or his net worth) = Job's Assets – Jobs Liabilities

If Job's possessions were worth $10,000,000, and he owed his debtors $2,000,000...

...Then his net worth would be: $10,000,000 - $2,000,000 = $8,000,000

YOUR FINANCIAL STATEMENT DESCRIBES THE CONDITION OF YOUR BUSINESS

The writer of Proverbs admonishes us to know the condition of our business or personal finances, and the most efficient way to truly know the condition of your business or personal finances is to understand your financial statement. This is true because every element of your business or personal wealth may be translated into its dollar equivalent (the standard unit of the nation's currency) and accounted for on your financial statement. Materials, labor, equipment, cattle, corn, taxes and other elements of business and personal wealth may all be expressed in dollars. Units of measure such as pounds, tons, bushels, lineal feet, or cubic feet of materials and products may also be expressed in dollars. Thus the single controlling element by which you can know and understand the condition of your business or your personal financial standing is the financial statement.

Financial statements however, have many numbers in them, and the significance of many of these numbers will not be clear unless they are compared with other numbers. For instance you should:

1) Compare them to other numbers in your financial statement to determine the relative size of one number to another;
2) Compare them to the past financial history of your firm from previous months or years to understand how you are doing this month verses last month or this year versus last year;
3) And finally compare them to the performance of other firms in your industry or service sector by comparing them to key financial indicators and ratios reported for your industry or service sector. (These are available from financial consultants who accomplish financial surveys of industry of service sector groups; or they are often available from your own industry of service sector association).

PROFIT IS THE LIFEBLOOD OF A BUSINESS

Profit is the main financial goal of a business. You have to understand the way the business operates and its strategies to account for its profit. At first glance, making profit may seem fairly simple – sell stuff and control expenses. Bring in more dollars from sales revenue than the dollars paid out for expenses. The excess of revenue over expenses is profit. What's the big deal?

But making a profit isn't nearly as simple as you may think. Business owners and managers must not only make sales and control expenses. They must understand which products or projects are making a profit or causing a loss, as well as determine where the profit went if the cash account doesn't increase by the same amount as your profit (and it usually doesn't).

Your financial reports should provide enough detail that you can put your finger on a problem without even leaving your office. You have to depend on your financial statements and other internal accounting reports to know how much profit you are making, how much loss you have suffered, and which projects or which products are producing that profit or loss. Therefore, it is important that you design your financial reports so that they will provide you with the information you need to properly manage your business.

IT'S EVEN MORE IMPORTANT TO UNDERSTAND THE DYNAMICS OF YOUR BUSINESS

Every type of industry or service business is different, but every business has overhead expenses that are relatively fixed (they do not change, at least not in the short run), and direct expenses which are generally proportional to the quantity of products or services provided. Overhead expenses are the personnel and physical resources that are necessary to make your sales, design your product or service, house your staff and equipment, prepare your payrolls, bill your clients and prepare your financial records. They are generally fixed; they do not change with the volume of your production. Direct expenses are the personnel, equipment and raw materials necessary to actually produce your product or service; they are generally proportional to the quantity of products or services you accomplish.

Now let's say that last year your total annual sales were $1,100,000, your fixed overhead expenses were $600,000, your direct expenses were $400,000, and your profit was $100,000 (approximately 9 percent of your annual sales). If you were to increase your sales by 10 percent or by $110,000 over last year's sales, your profits would increase at a much greater rate than the 10 percent increase in sales. The converse is also true; if your sales were to decrease by 10 percent or by $110,000 under last year's sales, your profits would decrease at a much greater rate than the 10 percent decrease in sales. For example with a 10 percent increase in sales, your new sales total would become $1,210,000, and since your overhead expenses are fixed, they would remain at $600,000. Your direct expenses, however, will increase by 10 percent to $440,000, and your total expenses will increase to $1,040,000. Your new sales of $1,210,000 less your new expenses of $1,040,000 would leave you a new profit of $170,000 (14 percent of annual sales). You can see that a 10 percent increase in your sales actually resulted in a much larger 70 percent increase in profit.

But on the other hand, if your sales were to decrease by 10 percent to $990,000, your overhead expenses will not decrease; since they are fixed, they will remain at $600,000. Your direct costs to produce less products or services will decrease by 10 percent to $360,000 and your total expenses will decrease to $960,000. Your new sales of $990,000 less your new expenses of $960,000 would leave you a new profit of only $30,000 (3 percent of annual sales). You can see from the above example that a 10 percent decrease in sales actually resulted in a decrease in profit of 70 percent. Understanding the dynamics of your business can make the difference in your company becoming successful or for it to file for bankruptcy!

THE NEED FOR A COST ACCOUNTING SYSTEM

Let's say your company works on ten different projects or manufactures ten different products during the year. Reviewing a conventional income statement like the one presented earlier in this chapter will not tell you which project or product is making a profit or losing money. You will need a cost accounting system that can track your income and expense for each product or project in order to identify the profit or loss for each product or project.

Some expenses (costs) are easily identified as being directly required in the production of a product or the providing of a service. For instance, a company producing ten different products can easily segregate the direct labor and material components used on each product's assembly line. By collecting the direct cost for each assembly line and dividing by the number of units produced, we can calculate the direct cost to manufacture each unit. Similarly, a company providing a service can easily separate the direct labor, material and subcontract cost by a customer or a project. Company-wide costs, however, such as accounting, legal, office supplies, rent, and new business development cannot be easily distributed to the specific products or service. These costs are generally collected under the heading of *indirect* or *overhead* costs. They are then prorated to each product or project on some predetermined basis. For instance in my consulting firm we generally distributed overhead costs as a percent of direct labor. A manufacturing company on the other hand may distribute overhead as a percentage of direct product cost, each industry has their own unique method of distributing overhead costs.

One of the biggest mistakes that small business owners make is the failure to establish a cost accounting system; without this they are flying by the seat of their pants...they are flying blind, and it is only a matter of time until they crash. They may know that they are losing money, but they don't know which product or projects are causing the loss. Or on the other hand, they may be making money, but if they had the knowledge of which products or projects are making money and which are losing money, they could become even more profitable.

(1) *Millionaire Next Door*–Copyright © 1996 by Thomas J. Stanley and William D. Danko
(Pg. 1, 4) Published by Longstreet Press, Inc.

CHAPTER 24
GETTING STARTED RIGHT IN LIFE AND BUSINESS

This is what the LORD of Heaven's Armies says: Look at what's happening to you! You have planted much but harvest little. You eat but are not satisfied. You drink but are still thirsty. You put on clothes but cannot keep warm. Your wages disappear as though you were putting them in pockets filled with holes! Haggai 1:5-6 (NLT)

Western society seems to be a consumed with debt, and here in America we have come to accept living with significant consumer, corporate, and national debt as a normal way of life. Consider this it took 200 years for our national debt, (the amount of debt owed by our National Government) to grow to $1 trillion Dollars (1980). But it only took another five years for it to grow to $2 Trillion Dollars (1985), and another twenty years for it to grow to $8 Trillion Dollars. (2005) [1] U.S. National Debt Clock

Consider also that consumer savings dropped from 10% of income in 1980 to just 0.01% in the second quarter of 2005 and consumer debt which includes mortgage payments and personal debt (including credit cards), as a percentage of income, increased from 11% in 1980 14% in 2005. [1] By 2003 lower to middle income families carried a credit card balance of from 9% to nearly 12% of their family income. [2]

During the same twenty-five year period (1980 to 2005) personal bankruptcy filings in the United States increased, per capita nearly 350%; Bankruptcy has risen from 1.2 persons per thousand persons in 1982 to nearly 5.4

persons per thousand in 2005. Predicatively it is lower to middle income individuals that are more likely to file bankruptcy in response to an insolvency event, given their relatively limited access to financial counseling and fewer and less diversified financial resources. (2)

(1) Federal Reserve Bank of St. Louis "The Rise of Personal Bankruptcy's" Thomas A. Garrett.

LET'S TALK ABOUT DEBT

"Train up a child in the way he should go. And when he is old he will not depart from it."(Proverbs 22:6)

This is a familiar scripture, but notice the next verse seven, "The rich rules over the poor, and the borrower is servant to the lender." (Proverbs 22:7) Unfortunately, most of us have never correlated verse 6 with verse 7.

Not only do we not teach our children that the borrower is servant to the lender, but by our actions we have trained them to use debt to gratify their desires, rather than trusting God and waiting for His timing and provision for what they need.

Many Christians are influenced by the world and the things in the world, and live their lives like their neighbors in the world. They are in debt up to their eyeballs, because they have yielded to the lust of the flesh, the lust of the eyes, and the pride of life. (1 John 2:15-16) So they use debt to buy a bigger house, a better car or a bigger boat than their neighbor, and then they spend the rest of their life trying to get out of debt. If you want to be financially successful then you must know the difference between good and bad debt.

DON'T FOLLOW THE CROWD

When the average individual graduates from high school or college they lack the experience, the money or other types of assets that are required to go into business, thus the only way that they can earn a living is to sell their personal service, or a creative idea. Having neither assets nor creative ideas most people go to work for money.

They search the help wanted advertisements of the newspaper or on an internet employment website until they find a position that meets their skill level or their area of interest. Then they submit their employment application and resume to the company for the position. If they are selected for an interview, they go to that interview without any special preparation, hoping to be hired. They give little thought as to how they can best present their skills or their interest in the position; their primary concern is "how much money will I make". Once hired, they pace their output against what others in their department or company produce.

Having established what they consider a good income, they allow their desire for things to influence their purchasing decisions; they want instant gratification to their desires. To fulfill those desires they pile up debt and relegate the payments to the future. They never stop to consider the total cost of an item purchased on credit; and by their example they teach their children to do the same, and to live in the same way they do.

Forty years later if they are lucky, they retire with a small retirement fund and a social security check and are inwardly envious of rich people. You often hear these same people saying things like "I heard that piece of land sold for $2,000,000.00 I could have bought that property for $50,000.00". They sit around talking about what they could have done when they were younger but didn't, because they didn't do their financial planning homework.

Because they didn't do their financial homework when they were young they often continue to make poor financial decisions when they retire. I personally know a number of retired people who have invested their retirement funds into what they believed to be a secure investment. Nearly always; however, these investments promised returns that were considerably higher than conventional established and generally secure investments. Every one of the individuals who invested their retirement funds into non-conventional, high return investments lost their badly needed retirement nest egg because they didn't do their homework.

MAKE MONEY YOUR SERVANT, MAKE IT WORK FOR YOU!

These people are a servant to money; they buy a new house, a new car, new boat and other consumer toys and they struggle continuously to meet their financial responsibilities. They think "if I could just get a raise or a better job I wouldn't have any more financial problems". But it is not the size of their paycheck that makes them the servant of money; it is what they do with their paycheck that makes money their master. The reality is that the more money most people make the further in debt they become. They are a servant to money; therefore they are constantly working for money. But if you want to go into business for yourself, if you want to become financially secure, you need to change the way you think about money, you need to stop working for money, and make money work for you.

HOW CAN I MAKE MONEY WORK FOR ME, I DON'T HAVE ANY?

"Develop your business first before building your house." (Proverbs 24:27 LB)

The writer of proverbs admonishes us to invest our time and money in developing our business before we invest our time and money in improving our living standards.

SACRIFICE PRESENT PLEASURES FOR FUTURE BENEFITS

Elsewhere in "Business by the Spirit" I point out that the Jewish Americans are disproportionately more successful than the American population as a whole. One of the maxims of the Jewish culture is to "sacrifice present pleasures for future benefits". ("Thou Shalt Prosper" page 11) But this maxim seems to have been lost on the average American family who uses credit to fulfill their every desire and to provide them with instant gratification.

You may be wandering "how can I go into business? How can I invest in real estate or the stock market if I don't have any capital?" Let me suggest that you break away from the crowd, adopt this Jewish maxim and sacrifice some of your present pleasures for the benefits that you will gain by saving a portion of your salary and investing it in your future". Live your lives simply, forgo many of the non-essential things and pleasures that your friends may be experiencing until you have saved enough capital to start and operate your dream business or invest in income producing assets. If you are currently heavily in debt, make it your number one goal to get out of debt. If you are not in debt make it your number one goal to stay out of debt, and put aside the money you will need for the working capital when you actually start your business.

While you are busy working for someone else, saving your working capital, begin to do your homework by acquiring the knowledge and skills that are required to be successful in your future business. At the same time spend time in the word of God changing the way you think about yourself, and developing faith in the creator's ability to guide and prosper you, in successfully operating a business or investing your savings.

IS BORROWING MONEY SCRIPTURAL?

Several well-known Christian leaders teach that borrowing money is unscriptural; they quote "Owe nothing to anyone except to love one another; for he who loves his neighbor has fulfilled the law" (Romans 13:8) as support for their view. But I can't agree that this verse means we are never to borrow money. In the Old Testament the Law provided a year of remission (every 7 years) and a year of Jubilee (every 50 years), when all debts were forgiven.

Thus it is obvious that borrowing money was not forbidden in the Old Testament.

Therefore, if Paul was saying in the above scripture that borrowing money was contrary to the New Testament scriptures, He would have been teaching a new doctrine and he would have made a special point of explaining that doctrine, the same that he did when he introduced other New Testament doctrines.

These leaders are correct, however when they point out the dangers of borrowing. Below are some of the disastrous results of borrowing.

- Strife in the marriage leading to divorce.
- Stress in business and personal lives leading to bankruptcy.
- The destruction of millions of lives.
- The undermining of a nation's economy.

Most of us borrow money on the presumption that the economic future is predictable. But we do not know the future, only God knows the future. That is why it is so important that we learn to seek God in our personal and business decisions particularly with regard to long term borrowing.

One Christian financial planner offers the following three principles to guide the Christian borrower.

- Don't borrow needlessly.
- Don't sign surety (don't guarantee another person's debt).
- Don't take long term debt*.

*I would add a caveat, "Don't take on long term debt unless you have gotten a green light from the Holy Spirit."

CONSUMER DEBT

There are four basic types of debt; consumer debt, mortgage debt, business debt, and investment debt, but of these, consumer debt is far more insidious than the other three, chiefly because it is so readily available.

Consumer debt is generated to buy food, clothing, jewelry, boats, cars etcetera satisfying people's needs or desires, rather than for producing goods and services.

CONSUMER CAR DEBT

Let's look at one of the most frequent types of debt among young people, car loans; I recently read where the average American family will spend some $300,000.00 on car loans during their lifetimes. More than half of that amount or $150,000.00 will be spent on interest. If they had simply driven their old car a few years longer, saved their money and paid cash for each of their new cars, they would have saved $150,000.00 which could have been invested in a business, income property, the stock market or a number of other income producing ventures. Have you ever noticed the exceptionally high first year depreciation on a new car? Have you ever thought about saving your money and buying a quality used car?

Over the years automobile prices have risen much faster than income, the average new car now costs in the area of $30,000. Therefore, automakers and dealers have developed new ways to entice the consumer to buy their expensive cars. Loan terms have been stretched from three years to as many as seven to eight years. Have you noticed that the automobile ads on television, radio, and in newspapers rarely mention the sticker price; instead they focus the buyer's attention on the monthly payment or lease amount (i.e. $299, $399, $499)? Or perhaps you have read that the manufacturer is offering zero interest rates on new car purchases. Don't be fooled by the advertised low interest or low monthly lease rates; be aware that automakers often make more money from their financing divisions than they do from making and selling cars.

Consider this, the prototypical American millionaire drives an American made car, only a minority of them drives a current-model-year automobile, and only a minority of them ever leases a motor vehicle. (1) Millionaire Next Door

NO RISK INVESTMENT THAT PAYS 18-20 PERCENT INTEREST!

If I were to tell you that I have a surefire no-risk investment that would pay you 18-20% interest, would you be willing to sell your boat, take out a second mortgage on your home, or cut back on your discretionary spending to invest? Well, all you have to do to get that type of return on your investment is to pay off your credit cards!

CONSUMER CREDIT CARDS DEBT

One day one of my daughters came to me to discuss the purchase of a new car. When I asked her how much interest the bank would charge she said 1.9 percent. I was not familiar with the interest that a bank charged for a car loan, but I told her that I thought that bank interest on a car purchase would be much higher than 1.9 percent. She told me that she had just gotten a credit card from her bank and the interest was only 1.9%. She, like most people, saw only the large print "**1.9% INTRODUCTORY OFFER**", they never read the small print which indicates that after six months the interest rate will increase to 18 percent or more.

Many people, having received a new low interest credit card, can't resist the urge to charge an extra tank of gas or buy a new dress. The tragedy is that they never even notice when six months later the interest is raised to 18% or higher. They don't notice because all they ever look at is the minimum monthly payment. Recently I received a credit card offer with zero percent interest for the first six months. How could one go wrong purchasing consumer items with zero percent interest?

Would you consider making payments on a tank of gas or a new dress that you purchased twenty years ago? That is exactly what you are doing if you make the minimum monthly payment on a credit card charging 18-20% interest. One in six families with credit cards pays only the minimum due every month. (Sources: American Bankers Association, Federal Reserve).

Banks are quite sophisticated in identifying those middle and lower income consumers who are likely to borrow extensively on their credit cards. Not surprisingly, it is often the lower-income individuals, those just getting started in life that carry the heaviest credit card debt in relationship to their income. And credit card providers, even those who advertise low interest rates really sock it to you when you make a late payment. Interest rates on late payments can rise as high as 30 percent or more. And many companies even add a $25-$35 late fee which raises the effective interest rate even further.

I have used credit cards for more than forty years because they make purchases easy and they don't require me to carry large amounts of cash.

However, I have never used credit cards for consumer credit; I pay them off at the end of each month.

Credit cards are dangerous credit traps because 1) they are easy to get, 2) the advertised six month introductory interest is deceptive, 3) most people don't understand how the interest and penalties are computed, and 4) making the minimum payment would take a person twenty years or more to pay off the owed balance.

HOW ABOUT MORTAGE DEBT ON REAL ESTATE?

Borrowing money to invest in real estate is reasonable if you do your homework before you buy. Generally economic growth will increase the value of real estate if you purchase it at the right price, and in the right area. Interest costs associated with borrowing for the purchase of real estate are also tax deductible and compared with consumer credit for cars and credit cards is available at much lower rates. If the property is used for your business or for rental to others, the operating expenses associated with the property are also deductible.

Financing your home can also make good financial sense as long as select a reasonably priced home, in a good neighborhood. As a home owner your monthly mortgage payment are fixed and are not exposed to inflation and the interest and property taxes are tax deductible. But keep in mind the additional expense of insurance, utilities, and maintenance that are associated with home ownership when selecting the price you intend to pay for your new home. The price of your home will generally escalate and the equity (the difference between the market value of your home and the amount that you owe the bank) will build and become a significant part of your net worth.

Since I have written this book to guide young people desiring to become an affluent business person, I suggest that as a part of your home buying homework, you consider the following example which considers the total cost of a thirty year mortgage, rather than just the monthly cost. For instance, If you purchase a $200,000 house on a typical thirty year mortgage, at seven percent interest, making a $15,000 down payment and paying $6,000 closing cost, the total cost of that home over thirty years would be $449,000, which includes 228,000 paid in interest.. But when you consider the income taxes you would have to pay on the $449,000 you made in house payments you would have to earn nearly $600,000 in order to pay for a $200,000 house. This is not counting the cost of insurance, property taxes, repair, and maintenance, etc., which add further to the cost of homeownership.

The average American will work and earn between $1,000,000.00 and $5,000,000.00 between the ages of twenty and sixty-five. It is calculated that most of these people will spend between one half to two thirds of their lifetime income servicing their debt. Imagine the amount of income producing property, such as apartments, office buildings, and other commercial property that these individuals could own if they had saved only half of the interest that they will pay over their lifetime to banks, mortgage and credit card companies. Imagine what would happen to the furtherance of the great commission if only ten percent of the money saved on interest were invested in the Kingdom of God.

WHAT ABOUT BANKRUPTCY?

Inflation was at an all-time high in 1980, but there were only 240,000 personal bankruptcies in America but by 2005, that number had exploded to 1,605,000. Is bankruptcy wrong? The Bible calls the person who doesn't pay his debts "wicked." "The wicked borrows and does not repay, but the righteous shows mercy and gives." (Psalms 37:21). It is my personal view that bankruptcy is wrong. Christians are to be the light to the world. Unfortunately, many Christians have bought into the world's financial system. They have allowed the lust of the flesh, the lust of the eyes, and the pride of life to purchase the highest lifestyle they can finance. Some allow the pride of life to motivate them to make large donations to charity and even give elaborate gifts into church or Para-church organizations. Then when they lose their job or when the business cycle dips, they turn to bankruptcy as a way out of their financial problems.

BANKRUPTCY AND CREDIT CARDS

Jay Westbrook, a law professor, and one of Americas most distinguished scholars in the field of bankruptcy, conducted an extensive study of people who filed personal bankruptcy and found that they were most often well-educated, middle-class individuals who over-consumed with credit cards.

Several years ago I counseled a man who was in deep financial trouble. He had mortgaged his house to the hilt, had used his credit cards to finance his business transactions and at the time I was counseling him, he could no longer make all the payments. I encouraged him that God could bring in the needed sales and pull him out of his financial problems, if he would only apply the principles that are taught in this book. He said that he believed that God could do it. I prayed the prayer of agreement with him; we claimed the amount of sales that he needed each month to pull him out of the debt. We bound the devil and told him to take his hands off the man's sales and we released the ministering angels to go forth and bring in the required sales. We agreed together that whenever we thought about his financial problem that we wouldn't pray again, we would just thank God that his ministering angels were bringing in the agreed upon sales. I left him a copy of the material included in this book and encouraged him to study and apply the success principals, included in it. From time to time when I thought about my friend's financial problem, and I would thank God that his angels were bringing in the sales that we had agreed upon in prayer.

He promised that he would meditate on the promises of God contained in the book and apply them to his financial problem. A month and a half later I called him to encourage him. I was shocked when he told me that he had decided that his company was just too far gone for God to help him. He said that if he had begun to apply the principals earlier, they might have worked, but he decided that he was just too far in debt, So he had filed bankruptcy. After I got off the telephone I thought "What if Jairus, when he heard his daughter was dead, had thought that she was too far gone for Jesus to raise her from the dead? (Mark 5:35-43)

By contrast, another friend of mine who is a homebuilder got caught with a number of unsold homes in the early 1980's when home mortgage interest hit 13% and sales dropped to zero. Interest rates at that time on his construction loans were over 20%. He was in an impossible situation. He owed the bank five million dollars. His attorneys counseled bankruptcy, but he and his wife decided to honor their debt. They moved themselves and their five children out of their large home in an affluent neighborhood and into a small house in the country. They cut back on expenses and toughed it through the market turndown. After ten long hard years the debt was paid in full. Today, this couple is still in the homebuilding business, their company is building 200 homes a year and their company is worth over $20,000,000. They are Godly people who live and share their faith wherever they go. They are able to support the work of the Gospel as God leads them to give to ministries all over the world. Thank heaven they didn't believe that they were so far in debt that God couldn't help them.

CHAPTER 25
INVESTING FOR A BOUNTIFUL HARVEST

"Any enterprise is built by wise planning, becomes strong through common sense, and profits wonderfully by keeping abreast of the facts" (Proverbs 24:3&4 LB).

"A faithful man will abound with blessings, but he who hastens to be rich will not go unpunished" (Proverbs 28:20).

"...Well done, good and faithful servant; you have been faithful over a few things, I will make you ruler over many things. Enter into the joy of your lord.' (Matthew 25:23)

WE ARE TO BE GOOD STEWARDS

In the parable of the unjust steward (Luke 16:1-13), Jesus amazingly commended an unjust manager because he had dealt prudently—he exercised sound judgment concerning his own interests. Then Jesus said something even more startling, "For the sons of the world are wiser in their generation than the sons of light." He was not commending the unjust manager's fraudulent business activities, but his prudence in using present opportunities for his future welfare. Then He said, "If you are not faithful in unrighteous mammon, who will commit to your trust the true riches." (For a definition of true riches review the definition of **salvation** - Strong's # 4991 - under the earlier chapter entitled "The Law of Faith.") In this parable, Jesus equates the "love for money" with the service of mammon (Luke 16:13). (Mammon is generally considered to be the name of the demonic principality, which dominates the world's financial system.) Paul says that the "...the **love** of money" is a root of all kinds of evil..." (1 Timothy 6:10). Notice that Paul did not say, "Money is the root of all evil"; he said the "love of money...." Money must be handled carefully and used wisely in order that the desire for it doesn't seduce us from true devotion to God. The Manufacturer's Handbook says, "The blessing of the Lord makes one rich, and He adds no sorrow with it" (Proverbs 10:22).

Stewardship is the careful and responsible management of the wealth entrusted to one's care. God has entrusted a certain amount of resources (time, possessions, and wealth) to each of us and we are to manage those resources to cause them to increase, so that we may provide for our family, support the spreading of the Good News to the nations, and leave an inheritance for our children's children.

HOW WOULD YOU DEFINE A WEALTHY INDIVIDUAL?

If we were to ask the average American to define a wealthy individual, most would say "a person who has abundance of material possessions." But many people who have an abundance of material goods live a high-consumption life style and actually have a very little actual wealth. The most appropriate way to define wealth is based on an individual's "net worth." Net worth is the current value of one's assets less his liabilities. Therefore wealth is built by accumulating assets. A millionaire is an individual whose current assets exceed his liabilities by $1,000,000 or more.

YOUR FIRST DECISION ON THE ROAD TO CREATING WEALTH

Many people who receive high annual salaries and possess an abundance of material goods appear wealthy, but are not. They consume most or all of their income buying expensive homes, driving expensive foreign cars, wearing expensive clothes, and purchasing a number of other expensive consumer goods and services on credit. It is their extensive use of credit which makes them appear to be wealthy, but in reality their net worth is very low. If they were to lose their high paying jobs, they could only survive for two to three months. The prototypical American millionaire, on the other hand, lives in a modest home, drives an American made car (only a minority of them drive a current model year car), wears inexpensive suits...and if he left his job he could live comfortably for more than twelve years (1). Therefore it is important for you to decide early in your working career whether you want to appear wealthy or whether you want to be a good steward by managing the resources God had entrusted into your care "to become wealthy."

HOW DOES ONE ACCUMULATE WEALTH?

As we have pointed out in an earlier chapter, more of the nation's millionaires have built their wealth by investing in small businesses than through any other investment vehicle. The prototypical American millionaire is self-employed; he owns a small factory, a chain of stores, a service business, or is a self-employed professional. Only about one third of American millionaires are employed by others. (1)

HONOR THE LORD WITH YOUR POSSESSIONS

"Honor the Lord with your possessions, And with the first fruits of all your increase; So your barns will be filled with plenty, And your vats will overflow with new wine" (Proverbs 3:9-10).

If this proverb was written in the vernacular of the twenty-first century, I believe it would read something like this:
"Honor the Lord with your assets (your possessions), and give Him the first portion of your income, (your increase), so that your income statement will be filled with profit, and your balance sheet will overflow with new assets."

The Jewish farmer, to whom this proverb was first written, was trained from childhood by his father to farm the family's land. By the time he inherited the land from his parents, he was a seasoned farmer. He understood that after he had given his tithe to the Lord, the rest of the increase was available for him and his family to use - everything, that is, except a portion of the newly harvested seed (usually the best seed) which would be required to plant the next year's crop. But he didn't expect the Lord to pour grain, or herds of cattle, or wine out of heaven; he expected Him to bless his produce and herds with increase (Deuteronomy 28:4) and to give rain to the seed he had planted and fertility to the herds he tended (Deuteronomy 28:11&12). He expected God to rebuke the devourer so as to protect his crops and herds from insects and disease (Malachi 3:11).

The problem with most twenty-first century Christians is that their fathers never taught them how to plant and reap in the twenty-first century financial fields. Therefore, they have never saved and invested (planted) a portion of their income (their increase), and they have therefore never accumulated any assets (lands and herds) which the Lord could increase and protect from inflation, natural disasters and evil men as he did for the Jewish farmer.

HARVESTING IN THE 21st CENTURY REQUIRES EXPERIENCE & CAPITAL

In order to successfully invest in the financial or real estate marketplace, start a successful business, or buy a stake in an existing one, an individual must have both experience and capital. But when most people graduate from high school or college, they have neither capital nor experience, so they go to work for others. Yet just because a person works for someone else, doesn't mean he has to give up his dream of becoming a wealthy investor or starting and owning a small business. Working for someone else is an excellent opportunity to save and invest a portion of your earnings to obtain the capital you will need to enter the financial markets; it is an excellent way to start or buy a stake in an existing business. It is also the perfect time to do your financial homework.

OKAY, HOW SHOULD I INVEST MY MONEY?

Recently a young couple I know was planning a rather large and expensive wedding. They asked where they should invest their savings from their future earnings. I asked them if they had any short term consumer debt. As I recall they said they had $15,000 in credit card debt, and a car that they were buying on credit; but they were otherwise fairly debt free. I mentally estimated that the wedding would probably cost them another $10,000 to $20,000. I gave them the following advice:

1. **Reconsider their plans** for the large expensive wedding in favor of a smaller wedding attended only by their close friends and relatives.
2. **Establish a firm financial foundation** by paying off their credit card debt and automobile loans before they begin to invest. (Interest on consumer debt is usually much higher than they could reasonably earn from investments in stocks, bonds or real estate.)
3. **Do their financial homework** while paying off debt by beginning immediately to educate themselves concerning the various types of investments (i.e. stocks, bonds, mutual funds, exchange traded funds, real estate, etc., and the various risks and potential returns associated with each.
4. **Set up a tax-sheltered retirement account** in which to do their investing. (Tax sheltered retirement accounts are discussed later in this chapter.)
5. **Establish a financial goal** and determine how much they would need to save and invest to reach that goal.

WHERE SHOULD I INVEST MY MONEY?

It is not my purpose throughout this chapter to advise you as to where to invest your money; it is my purpose to familiarize you with the types of investments that are available to you and give you an understanding of some of the issues that can affect each type of investment. Basically there are only two types of investment options available to you: the first is lending investments, and the second is ownership investments.

LENDING INVESTMENTS

A lending investment is an investment in which you lend money to an individual or an organization. For example you might deposit your money into a bank savings account or a bank "Certificate of Deposit" at an agreed-upon interest rate. Another common option might be to purchase a government or corporate bond. Bonds are basically IOU's issued by a government or private company. Lending investments are generally fixed investments, and they normally protect your principal. For example, if you purchase a five-year bond issued by the General Motors Corporation at seven percent interest, you are in essence lending your money to General Motors Corporation for a period of five years at seven percent interest. General Motors Corporation agrees to pay you seven percent interest each year for a period of five years, and at the end of five years, to return your original investment (your principal).

The Most Common Lending Investments Are:

- Bank certificates of deposit (CD's) available at any private bank.
- U.S. Treasury obligations, such as Treasury bills, bonds, and notes offered by the U.S. Government. These investments are considered one of the safest because they are backed by the U. S. Government.
- Municipal bonds are similar to U.S. government bonds, except they are issued by states and municipalities. The interest paid by municipal bonds is free from federal taxation. Municipal bonds are also considered to be reasonably safe because they are backed by the state or municipality that issued the bonds.
- Corporate bonds, fixed-income investments issued by corporations. Several agencies rate corporate bonds from the safest to the least safe based on the corporation's ability to pay the agreed interest on the

bonds, and repay the principle (your original investment) at the end of the purchase term. Investment grade bonds are as follows. AAA, AA, A, BBB; however, anything below BBB is considered junk bonds because they carry a higher risk even though they also usually pay a higher interest.

OWNERSHIP INVESTMENTS

An ownership investment is an investment by which you own a piece or all of a particular asset or company which has a potential to produce earnings. The most time-tested way to build wealth with ownership investments is to invest in three areas: publically traded stocks, real estate, or a small business. When you purchase a share of stock of General Motors Corporation, you are purchasing a piece of the ownership of General Motors Corporation. When you purchase a piece of land or a building, you are making an ownership investment in real estate. When you invest your money to start or purchase a business, you are making an ownership investment in a small business.

The Most Common Ownership Investments:

- **Stocks** are probably one of the most common ownership investments. Publicly traded companies issue shares of stock that an individual can purchase on one of the major stock exchanges such as the New York Stock Exchange or the NASDAQ exchange. When you purchase a share of stock, you purchase a part of the company (a part of the equity of the company). That is why stocks are often referred to as "equities." The value of a stock fluctuates constantly, depending on what people consider it to be worth. When more people think the stock will rise in value than think the stock will fall, the stock price will rise, and conversely when more people think the price of the stock will fall than think it will rise, the price will fall. Owning an equity share of a business is similar to owning your own business—the upside increase is limitless, while the downside loss is limited to the money that you invest in it. In the case of starting a new business, the downside loss may also include many hours of your personal time away from your family.

> **Investing in real estate rental property** is another way that you can build wealth. Rental property, whether it is an apartment building or a small office building, can be a particularly good investment for the individual who has personal construction skills. Such an individual can purchase property which is in a good location but has been allowed to deteriorate, and use their personal construction skills to improve the property and place it back on the market at a higher price. But real estate, like any business, requires that the buyer does his or her homework. It is particularly important to know the vacancy rate for the type of real estate they are considering, as well as the income and expense possibilities of the property. But the keystone of success in real estate investing is location, location, location; its importance cannot be over emphasized. If you don't have a lot of personal time to spend with your real estate and you don't want to be a landlord, you might consider investing in a real estate investment trust (REIT). A REIT is a diversified investment company that provides advantages similar to those of a mutual fund or ETF in that it offers a diversified portfolio of real estate and is

managed by professional managers. You may invest in a REIT by purchasing it directly or by purchasing it on a major stock exchange.

➢ **Ownership of a small business** is one of the best ways to become wealthy. In fact, more of the nation's wealthiest individuals have built their wealth by investing in a small business than through any other investment vehicle. This shouldn't be surprising because more new jobs are created annually by small business than from any other source, and small businesses are the economic engine that drives much of our nation's economic growth. While it is possible to become wealthy by purchasing stock in businesses owned by others, the most common way is to become a self-employed small business owner.

WE BUILD WEALTH BY BEING OWNERS NOT LENDERS

Traditionally investors build wealth by being owners not by being lenders. Over the last two hundred years, those investing in the U.S. stock market have earned an average of about 10 percent per year, while those investing in the U.S. bond market over the same period have earned an average of only 5 percent per year. But small (owner-owned) companies often earn returns that are far superior to the average stock or bonds earnings. Although my consulting business struggled financially during its formative years (the first six or seven years) and at times faced some financial challenges, it was not uncommon for me to earn 20 to 30 percent or more return on my investment in the business. Those returns were after I had also received a salary for managing the business.

CONSIDER THE FOLLOWING WHEN DOING YOUR FINANCIAL HOMEWORK

Taxes

Federal, state and local income taxes can take a large bite out of your income. So don't forget to study the tax structure when you are doing your financial homework. The first thing you need to do is to determine your current tax rate, particularly your marginal tax rate. (Marginal tax rate is the rate you pay on the last dollars of your income). Since tax rates are structured, you pay a lower tax rate on the first dollars you earn, and as your income increases you pay higher and higher rates. For instance, in 2007 a married couple would pay the federal government only 10 percent on the first $15,650 of taxable income, but they would pay 15 percent on the portion of their taxable income between $15,650 and $63,700. The tax rate increases at various intervals until your taxable income exceeds $349,700 at which time you pay 35 percent. Taxable income is your income from employment and investment less various deductions allowed by the government. Taxes have a major impact on financial decisions such as investing, purchasing real estate, and retirement planning. One of the best ways for you to reduce your taxable income is to invest a portion of your funds in a tax-deferred retirement account.

Investing in a Tax-Deferred Retirement Account

If you are investing money in a tax-deferred retirement account, the earnings from your investment are not taxable until you withdraw your funds from the plan. However, if you withdraw funds from these types of accounts before you reach retirement age, you will not only have to pay taxes on the earnings, but you will have to pay a penalty as well. There are a number of tax deferred retirement accounts available, such as 401(K), Keoghs, Simplified Employment Plan, Individual Retirement Plan (SEP-IRA's), and Individual Retirement Accounts (IRA's). One of the benefits of being a self-employed individual is that you may set up a "SEP-IRA" or a "Keogh Plan" which allows you to save more than if you were saving as an employee under an employer plan. But here are the two most popular tax-deferred retirement plans:

➢ The 401(K), which must be established by an employer for the employee. In 2007, a 401(K) plan allowed an employee to shelter up to $15,500 plus their employer's matching funds
➢ The Individual Retirement Accounts (IRA), which an employee may establish for himself. In 2007, an IRA plan allowed an employee to shelter up to $4,000; this increases to $5,000 per year if the individual is over fifty years of age.

Investing outside of a Tax-Deferred Fund

Now, if you are investing dollars outside of a "tax-sheltered" retirement fund, taxes could eat up a large part of the annual interest and dividends earned by your investment. The profits earned by selling an asset, such as a stock or real estate (outside of a tax-sheltered retirement fund), are taxable in the year the asset is sold. We call the profits earned by the sale of assets "capital gains."

Fees Paid an Investment Manager

If you're investing through a personal investment advisor or a mutual fund or exchange traded fund manager, the amount of the fee is very important. If you were to invest a $1000 a year for twenty-five years, your earnings would be reduced by approximately $4,800 for every 1 percent in annual management fees you pay. Mutual funds and exchange traded funds are required by the Securities Exchange Commission (SEC) to clearly identify their annual expense ratio in their prospectus. Make sure you understand these costs when investing in such funds.

Inflation

Some types of investments are more susceptible to the ravages of inflation than others. For instance, if you were to invest your money in a five-year bond that pays a fixed 5 percent interest, your interest income would be radically reduced by the 4.5 percent annual inflation experienced in the United States in 2007. On the other hand, investments such as real estate or gold and other precious metals may actually benefit and increase in value due to inflation.

International Investments

International investments are susceptible to currency value fluctuations relative to the U.S. dollar. For instance, if you were to invest in international stocks and the U.S. dollar becomes less valuable in relation to the currency in which international stocks are valued, your investment would gain value. On the other hand, if the U.S. dollar becomes more valuable in relation to the currency in which international stocks are valued, your investment would lose value. Keep currency fluctuations in mind when investing in international stocks.

IF IT SOUNDS TOO GOOD TO BE TRUE, IT PROBABLY IS!

"But people who long to be rich fall into temptation and are trapped by many foolish and harmful desires that plunge them into ruin and destruction. For the love of money is a root of all kinds of evil. And some people, craving money, have wandered from the true faith and pierced themselves with many sorrows" (1 Timothy 6:9-10 NLT).

In October of 2003, I was attending a meeting of Christian businessmen in Brussels, Belgium. I was sitting in the lobby of the hotel when a man from Germany, a man whom I had known for a number of years, sat down beside me and began talk to me about a sure-fire investment in which he and his charitable organization had become involved. According to this man, a company called International Product Investment Corporation (IPIC) which was owned operated by an American business man named Greg Setser, was returning huge profits to the investors—20 to 30 percent in four to six months. He explained that Setser would allow Christian businessmen like me to partner with IPIC in the purchase and sale of surplus goods which it had acquired from other companies, and these investments were returning huge profits. He pointed out that a number of large worldwide Christian ministries were investing in and endorsing Setser's company, and he went on to name the ministries. My acquaintance assured me that he had spoken with the head of several of these ministries and they had verified that IPIC was a legitimate company from which they had received huge profits. He pointed out that Setser was actually on the board of directors of one of the best known of these Christian ministries. Then my German acquaintance offered me an opportunity to invest with IPIC through his charitable organization. As he explained the huge short-term profits to be earned, I sensed an overwhelming urge to invest with IPIC. After all, most of my stock and real estate investments were earning only 5 to 10 percent per year, and here was an assured opportunity for me to earn 25 percent every four months. In addition my friend's charitable organizations would receive an additional 20 percent. That overwhelming urge I experienced in Brussels was a satanic "spirit of greed" which was trying to impress itself on my mind. (If you don't understand what I mean, review the chapter 5 in this book entitled "Overcoming Fear.") Frankly, I found it difficult to say no, but I had experienced this spirit before. It had come upon me previously when I had been offered investments in gold mines, oil wells, and other similar "can't lose" investments. I have watched others become involved in these types of investments and every one of them lost their money. When investing your money, stay with what you understand.

In November of 2003, just one month after that meeting in Brussels in which I was offered the opportunity to invest in IPIC, Greg Setser was arrested by the United States Security Exchange Commission and charged with fraud. He was subsequently convicted of twenty-two counts of fraud, conspiracy and money laundering, and was sentenced to forty years in prison. Nearly everyone who invested in IPIC lost his money.

Several years ago, Dave Soliem and I (Dave's story is highlighted in Chapter 2) counseled a mutual Christian friend concerning a similar investment he had made which purported to provide a 25 percent return on investment every three months. We told him very forcefully that there was no way a legitimate business enterprise could continue to pay those types of returns, but he wouldn't listen. For several months he received the promised 25 percent return. Based on this initial success, he involved many of his friends and acquaintances in the same investment. Suddenly the earnings checks stopped coming, however, and he and his friends lost not only their personal money, but money that they had borrowed from other sources to invest in what turned out to be just another "Ponzi scheme." They lost their money because they didn't do their homework.

BEWARE OF WHERE YOU GIVE YOUR MONEY

I have also sensed the same spirit of greed trying to impress itself upon my mind when certain charismatic preachers take an offering. These preachers are in great demand as convention and television fund raisers because they are very adept at raising money by manipulating the scriptures to support their fund-raising efforts. In a convention several years ago, a well-known prosperity preacher proclaimed that God would pay off the home mortgage of anyone in the audience who would give one month's house payment into the offering. As he made this challenge, I sensed that same familiar spirit of greed described in the previous paragraphs. As this man presented the mortgage cancellation challenge, it was all I could do to stay in my seat, as some 500 to 600 people rushed to the front of the ballroom to give a month's house payment into the offering. When you hear someone promise a one hundred fold return, when you hear someone promise a supernatural debt cancelation - keep your money in your pocket. Last week my wife and I were looking over the programming on the Christian television stations, when we saw an evangelist offering "green anointing oil" which he called "prosperity oil." Certainly God wants us to be prosperous, but it is your obedience to Him and His Word that will make you prosperous—not your obedience to a man, even an anointed man, or anointing yourself with green prosperity oil.

CHRISTIANS ARE PARTICULARLY SUSCEPTIBLE TO THESE INVESTMENTS

If it sounds too good to be true, it probably is! Christians seem to be particularly vulnerable to such investments for two reasons: first they trust others who claim to be Christians and share the same Christian-Judeo values that they do (this was the case with those who became involved with Greg Setser); and second, they have often been taught that if they give to God's work, He will literally open up the windows of heaven and pour out a such a blessing that they cannot contain it. Therefore, when an investment appears to provide an investment so large that they cannot contain it, they immediately suppose that is must be provided from God, and they fail to take the time to do their homework and to seek God for guidance and direction concerning their investment decision.

INVESTING IN THE STOCK AND BOND MARKET

Individual Stocks

There are potential rewards from investing in stock or bond markets, but there are also significant risks. Investing in individual stocks and bonds requires a great deal of time—time that most investors, particularly young investors, do not have. Therefore, many investors have turned to mutual funds and exchange-traded funds rather than picking and choosing individual stocks on their own.

Mutual Funds

Mutual funds are investment companies managed by professional managers who purchase and manage the stock of a large number of companies, thus eliminating some of the risks of picking individual stocks. Mutual fund investors make money by receiving dividends and interest and by the rise in value of the securities owned by the fund. While mutual fund shareholders may buy or sell their shares at any time, their purchase and sale price is not determined until the market closes at the end of the day. In a rapidly rising or falling market, considerable value may be lost between the times that the buy or sell order is placed at 9:00 AM(EST) and the market closes at 4:00 PM(EST).

Exchange-Traded Funds (ETFs)

Exchange-traded funds (ETFs) are similar to mutual funds in that they are an investment company managed by professional managers. They also allow investors a convenient way to purchase a broad basket of securities in a single transaction. But ETFs differ from mutual funds in that they can be bought and sold during the day just like common stocks. Essentially, ETFs offer the convenience of a stock along with the diversification of a mutual fund

Mutual Funds and ETFs Provide Diversity

Because both mutual funds and exchange-traded funds are managed by professional managers who purchase and manage the stock of a large number of companies, they also provide diversity and eliminate some of the risks of picking individual stocks. But many mutual funds and ETFs fail to beat their relevant market indexes; therefore an investor should investigate the historic rate of return and annual expense ratio of a fund before buying. You should also look at a fund's management efficiency by selecting funds that maintain low operating costs and no-load (sales charges).

Managing Individual Stocks

I personally have not invested in the stock or bond market outside of my tax-deferred retirement accounts. Over the years I have subscribed to several investment newsletters to guide me in my stock market investment decisions regarding those retirement accounts, but frankly I have not had the time to pick and manage individual stocks. However, I have found ETF stocks to be a better way for me to invest in the market. Exchange-traded funds have the advantage of being able to establish preset "stop loss orders" similar to individual stocks, which allows you to automatically sell at a predetermined price in real market time. Years ago when I was on a mission trip to Russia, I learned the importance of "stop loss orders." While I was out of the country, the NASDAC exchange took a huge drop, and since I had not established a preset "stop loss order," I lost a large portion of my investment in that market. (I discussed this loss in an earlier chapter of this book).

If you chose to invest in individual stocks or to time the markets (move in and out of the market), remember that you are competing with professionals. Discussions with many of my friends and associates have revealed that those who have tried to pick individual stocks or have invested in stock tips from their friends and associates have often lost considerable amounts of money. It has been said that there are just two emotions in the investment markets—fear and greed. Warren Buffet, one of the wealthiest business men in America, warns, "Sell when others are greedy and buy when others are fearful."

DON'T INVEST YOUR MONEY UNTIL YOU DO YOUR HOMEWORK

In the preceding paragraphs, I have familiarized you with some of the more common vehicles that are available to you to make your money work for you, yet you are not yet ready to lend or invest your money. There is still a lot of homework for you to do! Financial literacy is absolutely necessary before you lay your hard-earned money on the table.

Don't invest in the stock market until you know something about the stock market. Learn the language of the market. Open a small account with one of the discount brokerage firms—there are a number of them available. Place your money in the brokerage firm's money market and begin to familiarize yourself with the firm's website. Practice getting a quote on various stocks, mutual funds or ETFs by typing the applicable stock symbol into the quote box. Practice accessing and reading the available stock summary information. Study how the stock has performed over the last day, the last week, six months, or year, and even five years—it should all be available on your brokerage firm's website. Understand the stock's price earnings ratio (earnings per share), whether the stock routinely pays a dividend, and if it does, how much it pays. Familiarize yourself with how to buy or sell shares. Gain an understanding of a market order, a limit order, how to establish a stop loss order and how long a stop loss order is in effect before it expires. It's important to understand these and a host of other routine market tasks. It would be good for you to subscribe to one or more investment newsletters. Two investment newsletters that I have used for years for ETFs are the Fabian Newsletter, which may be reviewed at www.fabian.com; and Richard Young's Intelligence Report which may be viewed at www.intelligencereport.com. I would also recommend the book *A Christian's Guide to Investing* by Danny Fortana. Fontana, a stockbroker and the founder and CEO of Triune Capital Advisors, tends to write about the market with a Christian world view.

Similarly, don't buy property until you understand the basic essentials of real estate. There are literally hundreds of books available in your local bookstore to guide you in the purchase, management and ownership of real estate investment property. As a starter I would recommend *Rich Dad, Poor Dad* by Robert Kiyosaki and Sharon L. Lechter.

Before you start your own business, I suggest you work for someone else in the same industry or service business. Keep your eyes and ears open and learn all you can about the business. Depending on the type of business or industry you are interested in becoming involved in, there may be also be university or community college courses available to educate you in the basic issues of the business, but there is nothing like hands-on experience. While the major book stores have instructional books dealing with the operation of the more popular industries, it may be difficult to find instructional books on specialty businesses. Don't overlook going to work for an older owner (one who has no children working in the business) who will be ready to retire about the time you have obtained the experience that is required to run the business. Work hard; make yourself indispensable to the owner. You may be able to negotiate a buyout of the business from the owner; get him to mentor you in the management of the business and even help you finance the ownership transfer.

ONE FINAL ADMONITION CONCERNING THE DEVELOPMENT OF WEALTH

In opening paragraph of this chapter, we discussed the parable of the unjust steward (Luke 16:1-13) in which Jesus amazingly commended the unjust manager because he had dealt prudently (he had exercised sound judgment concerning his own interests). Then Jesus said something even more startling: "For the sons of the world are wiser in their generation than the sons of light." Jesus was not commending the unjust manager's fraudulent business activities but his wisdom in using his present opportunities to provide for his future welfare. He was simply pointing out that worldly men are often wiser than spiritual men in using their skill and wisdom to store up wealth for their future. Then He proclaimed that men ought to use their money to make friends for themselves both in this world and in the next. The irony, as we pointed out in an earlier chapter, is that many of the principles which the world uses to succeed in life have been in the Word of God all the time. It is time that God's people wake up and begin to use these same principles to make themselves successful. In this book we have endeavored to teach you both spiritual and earthly wisdom concerning the development wealth and success in your life. Now it is time for you to apply these principles to manage your resources and cause them to increase so that you may provide abundantly for your family in this life...and so that you may prepare for the life to come by funding the spread of the Good News of Jesus Christ to the nations and by leaving an inheritance for our children's children.

(1) *Millionaire Next Door* –Copyright © 1996 by Thomas J. Stanley and William D. Danko
(Pg. 8,9,10, &11).

INTRODUCTION TO PART VI: LIFE'S MOST IMPORTANT ISSUE LIFE AFTER DEATH

One day a rich young businessman came to Jesus and asked Him, "… what good thing shall I do that I may have eternal life?" Jesus answered him "… if you want to enter into life, keep the commandments." The young man asked "Which ones?" After Jesus had related the applicable commandments, the young man was still not satisfied and replied, "All these things I have kept from my youth. What do I still lack?"

Jesus said to him, "If you want to be perfect, go, sell what you have and give to the poor, and you will have treasure in heaven; and come, follow me.: But when the young man heard Jesus' answer, he went away sorrowful, for he had great possessions. Then Jesus turned to His disciples, and said, "Assuredly, I say to you that it is hard for a rich man to enter the kingdom of heaven. And again I say to you; it is easier for a camel to go through the eye of a needle than for a rich man to enter the kingdom of God" (Matthew 19:16-24).

When His disciples heard what Jesus said this to the young man, they were astonished. Wealth was considered by the Jews as evidence of God's favor; it is still considered a sign of God's blessings in some churches today. But if wealth alone were a sign of God's blessings, then crime bosses and drug lords would be spiritual giants. When the rich young man opened his conversation with Jesus, he asked: "…what good thing shall I do that I may have eternal life?" Like most people, he thought that he had to earn eternal life.

I used to think like that myself; I knew I wasn't living right, to I thought I had to do something good to find favor with God if there was a God. Just before talking to the rich young man, Jesus had told his disciples that to enter the kingdom of God; one must be converted and become as a little child (Matthew 18:3). Children are trusting and teachable; they always want to learn from their father.

It's particularly hard for those who trust in their wealth and are proud of their possessions to humble themselves and put their trust in a Savior and yield to His plan for their lives. But you can't remain neutral toward Jesus. You are either for Him or against Him; there is no middle ground.

In the next chapter I share how my father, because his wife had prayed for the salvation of his soul for more than fifty years, accepted Jesus as his Savior just days before he died, and how I, also being the recipient of more than forty years of my mother's prayers, accepted Jesus and was baptized in the Holy Spirit quite late in life, (I was forty-three years old).

As I shared earlier in this book, that decision radically changed my life and had caused me, an ordinary businessman, to travel to the four corners of the earth sharing and demonstrating the Good News of Jesus Christ. The good news is that Jesus has redeemed you and me from the curse of poverty, sickness, and spiritual death. He will not only give you eternal life and baptize you in His Holy Spirit, but He will heal you of sickness and cause you to have success in your life and your business.

If you have not yet received Christ as your Savior or have not yet been baptized in the Holy Spirit, then for you, the next chapter is the most important chapter in this book.

CHAPTER 26
DEALING WITH THE MOST
IMPORTANT ISSUE OF LIFE

"For bodily exercise profits a little, but godliness is profitable for all things, having promise of the life that now is and of that which is to come" (1 Timothy 4:8).

My father was a typical hard working, small business man—he was honest to a fault, he was forceful in the business world but quiet in a social setting, and he had a great love for his family and a strong loyalty toward those who worked for him. Actually it was a miracle that he was successful at all since he grew up without a father, as his mother and father divorced when he was quite young. I don't remember my father ever saying he loved me, but I knew he did; he just didn't know how to say it. He was thoughtful and industrious in many ways, but he never dealt with the most important issue of life—that is, not until he came face to face with open heart surgery.

In his early sixties my father was diagnosed with a number of blocked arteries, and his doctor recommended that he have open heart surgery. As was typical of my dad, he ignored the bad news; he simply didn't have time for open heart surgery. Actually he was able to work for another fifteen years before the chest pain became so unbearable that he could wait no longer. When it came time for the operation, I could tell that he was nervous. My mother had prayed for many years that dad would accept Jesus as his Lord and Savior, but she had seen little change in his attitude toward Jesus and the health of his soul. One evening shortly before his heart operation, I decided to drive to my father's home located an hour south of Seattle to talk with him about getting right with God before the operation. When I arrived at my folk's home, my mother shared with me that dad had prayed with her to accept Jesus as his Lord and Savior the night before. I knew, however, that even though dad had prayed and asked Jesus into his heart, he didn't really understand the born-again experience as well as why it was necessary for Him to accept Christ as his Lord and Savior. So I related to him an incident that a friend of mine Harald Bredesen had shared several weeks before in a breakfast meeting of Full Gospel Business Men's Fellowship.

Harald Bredesen was a Lutheran minister whom my father had met in our home several months earlier—giving me an opportunity to relate the story as part of the evening conversation. Harald had been driving on the New Jersey turnpike at a time when the turnpike was still under construction. His gas tank was running on empty, but the gas stations on his side of the turnpike had not yet opened as they were still under construction. The gas stations on the other side of the freeway, however, had been completed earlier and they were open for business. Finally, in desperation, Harald made a U-turn across the median strip to the opposite lanes of the turnpike in order to obtain the gas he required to complete his trip. Just as he pulled into the gas station, a police officer pulled in behind him and wrote him a traffic citation for making an unlawful U-turn. Because Harald lived out of state, the arresting officer required Harald to accompany him to the local judge. The judge, also a Lutheran, saw Harald's white ecclesiastical collar and did not want to prosecute him. The judge said, *"Officer, this Lutheran minister is a man of the cloth. I really don't want to fine him; would you consider dismissing the charge?"* However, the officer, who was a staunch Roman Catholic, exclaimed, *"I wouldn't dismiss the charge even if he were a Catholic Priest!"* The judge told Harald that even though he didn't want to do so, the law required that he find him guilty as charged; and he fined Harald $15.00 for the offense. (This incident occurred in the 1960's, when traffic fines were much less than they are today.) You see, because the judge was just and fair, he had to uphold the law.

Likewise, God is absolute justice—mankind has broken the law of heaven; he has committed treason. Even though God's "loving nature" wants to forgive mankind, He cannot violate His "just" nature, which requires that He find mankind guilty of violating the law. Like the New Jersey judge, justice requires that God find mankind guilty, and man must pay the penalty for violating God's law.

Several days after Harald arrived home, he received a letter from the New Jersey judge. It went something like this:
"Dear Pastor Bredesen,
I am sorry that I had to find you guilty of the traffic violation yesterday; but justice demanded that I do my duty, and it required that you pay the penalty for your violation of the law. However, I have enclosed a check for $15.00; I want to pay the fine for you. God bless you in your ministry. You see, I too am a Lutheran."

The letter was signed by the judge that had heard Harald's case.

I shared with my father that this incident in Harald's life reveals so clearly the reason that God has to hold mankind responsible for their sin; and it also reveals God's plan for the redemption of mankind. While God had to find the human race guilty of their sin, He paid man's penalty Himself. He sent His only Son, Jesus Christ, to die for mankind's sin and to redeem mankind from hell. Anyone who believes in what God's Son has done and accepts Him as his Savior (his Redeemer) is justified (declared righteous) and receives eternal life (the nature of God).

As I finished the story I could see by the sparkle in my father's eyes that he understood God's plan of salvation, and why it was necessary for him to ask Jesus to be his Lord and Savior. Because my mother prayed for my father for more than fifty years, he had the opportunity to deal with the most important issue of his life, "life after death." And he dealt with it just in time because two days later, my father died on the operating table. Will you have the same opportunity that my father did? It's possible that any one of us might be killed unexpectedly, like the young soldiers in Korea who all died when the military airplane crashed in the Han River, a story I related earlier in the book.

WHAT IS THE BORN AGAIN EXPERIENCE?

Most non-believers and even many Christians, though they have accepted Christ as their Savior, don't understand the incredible rights and privileges that belong to the born again believer. They think that being a Christian means that they have to go to church every Sunday, put their hard-earned money into the offering plate and try hard all week to live a good moral life. For the first forty-three years of my life, that is what I thought being a Christian was. I didn't understand that when we accept Christ, the Spirit of God moves into our spirit to empower us to live a victorious life.

My view of Christianity began to change when I came in contact with a book entitled Power in Praise written by Merlin Carothers (1), a retired Lt. Colonel in the United States Army. Initially I thought that it was a secular success motivation book, so I eagerly began to read it. After reading several chapters of *Power* in Praise, I realized that Carothers was not talking about business success; he was talking about spiritual success and God's gift of eternal life. He explained that God has given us many wonderful gifts, and they are free for the asking; but most of us only know them as ten-cent gifts, and therefore we never get very excited about them. Carothers said,

"Many church-going people think of God's plan of eternal life as a ten-cent gift. They believe they have to struggle to live a good life to keep their "free gift." Trying hard to live a good life puts them under such a continual strain that they often wonder if trying hard to be a Christian is worth it. To them it just means going to church on Sunday, staying away from things that might be a lot of fun, and giving their hard-earned cash into the offering plate" (1).

I didn't classify myself as a church person, but frankly that's exactly what I thought being a Christian was - I thought it meant leading a boring life.

In chapter seven of this book, I related a story in which my brother was seriously injured in a car accident. While he was in the hospital, my father promised God that he would build Him a new church if He healed my brother. Like my father, most of us have been conditioned to believe that we only get what we deserve or what we are willing to pay for. But God doesn't give eternal life to people who meet some minimum standard of behavior by being good or by giving a large amount of money into the offering plate. God says, "I will destroy all human plans of salvation no matter how wise they seem to be, and ignore the best ideas of men, even the most brilliant of them" (1Corinthians 1:19 TLB). As I read *Power in Praise*, Carothers shared several scriptures from a modern translation of the Bible:

"This Good News tells us that God makes us ready for heaven- makes us right in God's sight – when we put our faith and trust in Christ to save us" (Romans 1:17) (1)

"...No one can ever find God's favor by being good enough. For the more we know of God's laws, the clearer it becomes that we don't obey them" (Romans 3:20). (1)

"Then what can we boast about doing, to earn our salvation? Nothing at all. Why? Because our acquittal is not based on our good deeds; it is based on what Christ has done and our faith in him. So it is that we are saved by faith in Christ and not by good things we do" (Romans 3:27-28). (1)

I, like many of you, knew that I was not living right and that there were many things in my life that were not acceptable to God. Therefore in my mind, I saw no way that I could ever be acceptable to God. But someday, I reasoned, maybe when I get older, I would begin to live a better life and then I could approach God. But reading the above verses began to change my thinking. They proclaimed that there was no way that I could get good enough to receive "eternal life"; I had to believe that Jesus Christ had already paid the penalty for my sin. I read this chapter on eternal life over and over for nearly two months before I had the faith to act on it. I remember the occasion vividly. I was at home in the bathtub with a Jacuzzi unit, massaging a chronic spasm in the muscles of my lower back.

It was about 2:00 in the afternoon of March 8, 1976. I prayed "Jesus, I believe that you are the Son of God. I believe that you died and paid the price for my sins, and I believe that you have risen from the dead. Now I ask you to come into my heart and be my Lord and Savior." Then I continued, "Lord, help me to change the way I live." When my prayer was finished, I got out of the Jacuzzi and lay down on my bed and fell asleep, the most peaceful sleep that I had ever experienced. I no longer had the fear of death; I knew that if I died I would be in heaven with Jesus.

"It is from God alone that you have your life through Christ Jesus, He showed God's plan of salvation; He was the one who made us acceptable to God; He made us pure and holy and gave himself to purchase our salvation" (I Corinthians 1:30).

I continued to read *Power in Praise* for another seven months, particularly the third chapter of the book which was entitled "Power Unlimited." That chapter talked about the baptism in the Holy Spirit. Carothers explained that because we belong to Christ, we are children of God. We have entered His kingdom, and now the power, privileges, and rights that belong to that kingdom belong to us (Ephesians 1:3).

Then he went on to describe the baptism in the Holy Spirit, saying, "The very first free gift God wants His new children to ask for is the baptism in the Holy Spirit. That's right. The baptism in the Holy Spirit was provided as a 'first feeding' for newborn believers. They need it to grow."

He explained that the Holy Spirit comes to dwell in the new believer the moment he accepts Christ as his Savior. Then he pointed out that Jesus had told His disciples that they were to wait in Jerusalem until they were baptized in the Holy Spirit, at which time they would receive the power to be His witnesses and tell others about Him (Acts 1:8).

Well, I could see from reading *Power in Praise* and reading these scriptures that the baptism in the Holy Spirit was an important gift. After all, the early disciples had received it just days after Jesus was raised from the dead and received into heaven, where He was seated at the right hand of the Father. But somehow I had the idea that this gift was only for spiritual people like a priest or pastor. I didn't understand that it was for everyone. But as I read and reread about the baptism in the Holy Spirit, faith was developing in my spirit. The scriptures have a lot to say about the benefits of praying in tongues. (The term *tongues* used in the Manufacturer's Handbook refers to a personal prayer language that the Holy Spirit gives to you when you are baptized in the Holy Spirit.)

Finally, one evening in mid-September of 1976, in the living room of my home, I knelt down by our sofa and I asked Jesus to baptize me in the Holy Spirit. Realizing that I needed to receive it by faith, I thanked Jesus for baptizing me, and then I began to speak some syllables by faith—not complete words, just syllables—and the Holy Spirit took those syllables and formed them into words. They were words I didn't understand, but I could tell they were words. Praying with these new words seemed to energize my spirit, my inner man; it felt good. The next day, indeed the next several weeks, I prayed in the spirit whenever I got the opportunity to do so. Jesus became real to me; the Word of God came alive. I didn't tell my wife Barbara that I had received the baptism of the Holy Spirit right away because I wanted to make sure I understood it before I explained it to her. When I told Barbara about my experience, I thought she would be thrilled. After all, when we were married she had told the pastor who married us that she wanted to have a true Christian marriage.

However, I must tell you that Barbara was not very happy about me receiving the baptism in the Holy Spirit and praying in the Spirit. She had been raised in a denominational church, which had taught that anyone who spoke in tongues was a "Holy Roller," a sect of Christians who were considered out of the mainstream of Christianity. But after watching the dramatic changes that took place in my life over the next several months, she too asked Jesus to baptize her in the Holy Spirit. The very afternoon that she was baptized, she was singing in the kitchen, and she realized that she was not singing in English but in a new Holy Spirit prayer language. As I related in the chapters entitled "Business as the Spirit Wills," and "Hearing the Voice of the Spirit in Business," the baptism in the Holy Spirit is very important to the manifestation of the "the gifts of the Spirit" and your ability to be led by the Spirit of God in your life and business.

Let me give you some information from the Manufacturer's Handbook which I believe will encourage and help you to receive and exercise your new prayer language. Actually, the Trinity; the Father, the Son, and the Holy Spirit, all agree with the baptism in the Holy Spirit. The Father is the one who promised the baptism in the Holy Spirit (Acts 1:4 & Joel 2:28-29); Jesus is the one who actually baptizes us in the Holy Spirit (Matthew

3:11, Luke 3:16, John 7:38); and the Holy Spirit is the one who gives us the utterance, or the words (Acts 2:4). The "initial sign" of the baptism in the Holy Spirit is speaking in other tongues (Acts 2:4, Acts 10:44-46, Acts 19:2-6).

Because this gift has been such a blessing to me, I want you to become aware of some of the benefits which will accrue to you when you are baptized in the Holy Spirit and are able to pray to God in your own private prayer language. First, you will receive ability or power when the Holy Spirit comes upon you (Acts 1:8); second, you build up your most holy faith when you pray in the Holy Spirit (Jude 1:20); third, you edify yourself—a spiritual "battery charge" of sorts—when you pray in tongues (I Corinthians 14:4); fourth, when you don't know how to pray about a situation, or an individual, the Holy Spirit will pray through you (in words that cannot be articulated in English) the perfect will of God (Romans 8:26-28); and fifth, when you pray in tongues, you speak mysteries to God (1 Corinthians 14:2).

Because the individual praying in the Spirit doesn't understand what he is praying, some begin to wonder *what good is it doing to pray in tongues?* You see, when you pray in tongues, you are not speaking to men; you are speaking to God who understands everything you say. It is your private, coded prayer language to the Father; it is a language that the devil doesn't understand.

Believe it or not, some denominations actually teach that speaking in tongues is from the devil. When we ask Jesus to baptize us in the Holy Spirit, our heavenly Father is not going to give us something evil, He will give good gifts to whosoever asks (Luke 11:9-13).

Years ago I was in the vestry of St. Luke's Episcopal Church in the city of Renton, a suburb of the city of Seattle, when the telephone rang. I answered the telephone, and the man on the other end of the line who was calling from Gloucester, Virginia, asked for Father Dennis Bennett, a well-known Episcopal priest who had written several books concerning the baptism in the Holy Spirit. Father Bennett was the priest in another Episcopal church in the city of Seattle by the same name; the information operator had given this man the wrong church. The man said that he had just read Father Bennett's book entitled *Nine O'clock in the Morning* and he wanted to know if he needed someone to lay hands on him and to pray in order that he might receive the baptism in the Holy Spirit. Because of my experience of having been baptized in the Holy Spirit while reading a book, I told him that he did not have to have hands laid on him in order for him to receive the baptism in the Holy Spirit.

I assured him that if he would follow my instructions all he had to do is to act in faith and receive. I told him if he was ready, I could lead him into the baptism in the Holy Spirit over the telephone. He said he was ready, so I used a method which I have used many times over the years to lead people into the baptism in the Holy Spirit. It worked for the man in Gloucester, and it will work for you if you will simply follow my instructions and act on them in faith.

I generally share a few of the scriptures which I mentioned on the previous page, then I ask the candidate to listen very carefully as I read Acts 2:4, because I will give them a test on the content of the scripture. I read, "And they were all filled with the Holy Spirit and began to speak with other tongues, as the Spirit gave them utterance" (Acts 2:4). I generally read this scripture several times, and then I ask, *"Who spoke in other tongues?"* Most answer, *"The people spoke with other tongues,"* but occasionally some will answer that the Holy Spirit spoke in other tongues (because they believe that the Holy Spirit will supernaturally move their lips to make them speak in other tongues).

Then I ask them, *"What does the Holy Spirit do?"* The answer of course is that He gives them the utterance or the words! I then generally explain to the candidates that words are made up of syllables. If they believe that Jesus has baptized them in the Holy Spirit, then after we pray, by faith they must speak some syllables and allow the Holy Spirit to have their tongue so that He can form the syllables into a new language or a new tongue. Like everything we receive from God, we must act on His word in faith to receive. Then I lead them in the following prayer: *"Father, the Word says that You have promised to send the Holy Spirit"* (Acts 1:4&5, Joel 2:28). *Jesus, the Word says that You are the baptizer* (Mark1:7&8); *baptize me now in the Holy Spirit. Holy Spirit, the Word says you will give me the utterance* (Acts 2:4). *I thank you now for filling me and giving me a new language, and I will now speak in other tongues. I seal my request in the name of Jesus."*

After they have prayed this prayer, I encourage them to confess to me that they have just received the baptism in the Holy Spirit. This is an important step, because we are to receive the answer to our prayer when we pray (Mark 11:24). Once they have confessed that they have received the baptism of the Holy Spirit, I simply tell them to speak out some syllables and let the Holy Spirit within them have their tongue. After they have prayed in their new language for a minute or so, I ask them to stop, but then I ask them to start again. I want them to understand that they may pray in the spirit at will, that they may pray loudly or softly, and that they may pray in a monotone or with emotion. I want them to understand that it is up to them. The prophet controls his own spirit and his own tongue. The Holy Spirit will not make you do anything; He is a gentleman (I Corinthians 14:32).

Now that you have received the Holy Spirit, I encourage you to pray in your new language as often as possible. I do so at every opportunity because it gives me a spiritual battery charge and it builds up and strengthens my spirit. I have never known anyone who does not pray much in the Holy Spirit to flow in the gifts and power of the Holy Spirit.

IF YOU ACCEPTED CHRIST AS A RESULT OF READING THIS BOOK

If you have accepted Christ while reading this book, it is important for you to find a church that teaches the Word of God, continually reaches out to the community; to get people born again and baptized in the Holy Spirit, to help the poor and needy, and that has made it their primary mission to take the Good News of Jesus Christ to the nations of the world. Living your life by the Spirit of God is not only important in this life but in the life to come.

(1) *Power in Praise*, by Merlin Carothers, © 1972 by Logos International, (Pg. 20,21,22 & 41)

I Remember Bob

Letter to the Fellowship: Barbara Bignold

Following this message, Barbara shares a personal conversation she had with the Lord after the last Convention, where Bob announced that he would be standing down in 2017 as FGBMFA President.

There is much to be said about dedicated men who put God's call first in their life and have a passion to see people saved, healed and delivered. The Full Gospel Business Men's Fellowship in America has been such a ministry continuing to set men free to follow God's call and instilling the courage to walk in the Gifting's of the Holy Spirit in the Marketplace ministry.

Bob Bignold was one of these men. In 1976 his life was touched by the Holy Spirit which set him on a search to find like-minded men, (after reading many books on FGBMFI that carried God's VISION given to Demos Shakarian). Now we know these were all divine appointments for a searching heart.

Bob was a successful businessman with his own Architectural and Engineering firm serving cities and towns, and included a lot of military work. With other financial investments, he was truly in the Marketplace and pursued success as many individuals who walk that path. However, after giving his heart and soul to Jesus Christ, with the baptism of the Holy Spirit, his 'passion' for building wealth grew dim, however the fire he carried was for God's VISION. God revealed that His treasures were more effective and precious when the Word and the Spirit flowed in a person's life than all the trade secrets of the world.

As Bob applied these truths, he was being transformed into a 'brand new man'; to his employees, his friends and especially to his family and throughout his home life. This process was in action until his last day on earth – each day and year surrendering his will for the will of God whether it brought appreciation or conflict.

I have had the joy and blessing of knowing him up close and personal, so my testimony is true even though it is biased with much love for him and God. His passion to see the Vision accomplished took dedication, compassion, sacrifice, integrity and endless effort. These were the building blocks for the foundation of his new life in Christ and the call on his life. These traits advanced him up the ladder of leadership where he truly fell in love with the "Airlift ministry to the nations" - seeing lives transformed, leaders raised up in their calling, and whole families united in love. In the ensuing years, he saw the same thing happening to men working with the prison ministry, the Godmobile calling, the chapters to the military outreaches, conventions and conferences, (plus many more). Sometimes, he/we were packing bags for up to two weeks of travel, flying to nations three to four times a year – commitment has a cost no matter how happy one may be.

After being elected as the first President of Full Gospel America, his passion was to see the VISION INTENSIFIED, for there is nothing as grand as seeing men's lives transformed into strong warriors for Christ Jesus, families coming back together, God centered - not self-centered; the works of Jesus being done, as well as husbands and wives walking in the *strength of unity* in this day to His Glory.

As many of you know, the last eight years God had touched Bob's heart to pursue the Joshua Generation (ages 18-40) for Christ; to become mighty warriors like Joshua, Barak, Samson, David, Joseph, Samuel, and Gideon – mighty men of valor! He had such love for these young men that he invested this part of his life to them; mentoring and building relationships that included his personal finances for taking them to the nations.

It also gave Bob a great thrill seeing the older men (Moses) taking these younger ones under their wings to invest in their calling so that both sides could take the fire of the Spirit to a hurting world. The Fellowship opened their hearts and made available a platform for them to minister. Special thanks go out to Jerry DeFlorio (Holy Smoke Hangout), John Tolo, Doug Raine, and Chris Burge (VP Director of Joshua Ministry), plus so many more. Bob's passion and drive was to continue on with strong leaders led by the Spirit, *rather than* just word speakers, so that signs and wonders will follow all.

Bob so loved all the men of the Fellowship [his band of brothers] and he poured out his life for God in this ministry. I saw up close & personal his sacrifices, and there were many he made that were behind closed doors where just he and God spent time. Often it was his family who missed time with him, but as his partner in the Fellowship, I gladly did the extra things to set him free to spend hours writing articles, letters, and tending to the many details of his responsibilities. We all loved who he had become in Christ, so all that was given was given freely and with love for God.

Now you are the ones to carry on, so seek the Lord daily and only move as He directs. Thank you for your prayers –

they have been so needed and deeply appreciated as the days turn into months. Sometimes I feel like I am only half here, but only by God's grace comes healing; I know He is enough and I know with Him I am complete!

Loving you all,
Barbara Bignold
Wife and partner of the President, fulfilling the call.

Words from the Lord in July 2016

By Barbara Bignold

This was just three weeks before my world shifted dramatically!

"Now *we* are about to go to a new work in Your kingdom on earth – may *WE* bring You Glory in whatever *we* set our hands upon in Your Name. Lord, may *we* have a little talk? Seems like it has been too long since our last one due to stuff."

What is it you want to know?

At first, I thought of the future and then again I don't want to know that because the world seems to be filling with darkness… however, You are still the Light of this world that will never go out – so what is there to fear?

"You are right – the TIMES are changing fast by My people will walk in new strength, light wisdom to confound the world: This is the TIME of the manifestation of ALL My Glory as My Son will soon return for His Bride.

The task of the church/the Saints is to be:

- Hungry for ALL there is of My presence and to walk boldly in My power and wisdom as truth will be revealed and the rebirth of signs and wonders the world has yet to see.
- This will be accomplished by My people from the smallest child to the oldest saint. NEW! I say New

revelation is coming to those who are hungry and thirsty for TRUTH and will seek My presence.

You may think this is the end times, but I tell you it is the beginning of My kingdom coming to earth for the world to see! I have loved this world so much that I sent My Son for the lost and hurting, that LOVE has not ceased nor grown cold!

But sin is not tolerated nor deception or ungodliness in Any Form! However, I want everyone to be saved and in MY Family which only comes through repentance and obedience to the living Word/Jesus.

Keep your candles lit – walk in My Word; call forth the lost to know and accept My ways; to SEE the "greatest harvest" ever known. Call to those who have allowed their hunger and light to dim – for they are in danger of losing as they ride the fence between My WORD and this world's values.

This "time" will be wonderful, beautiful, fun, exciting, gifted times. But, they are also devastating, fearful, perilous, deceptive times and even the elect/contented believers can fall from GRACE!

SO, be alert, watching, discerning, and listening only to My Voice, Who leads the people back to the TRUTH. For I said it's better to be hot or cold *than lukewarm* that will be vomited out of My mouth!!

"Lord, You know we desire to walk fully in Your word and Your will! May Bob and I always walk out Your perfect plan for our lives and that You be clearly seen by the world so everyone will desire ALL of You too. Amen."

Thursday, July 28, 2016
A day that changed my life as no other… 5:00 a.m.
During prayer time, I was asking the Lord WHY… [reflecting on the move to Colville WA]…

> ➢ We are here. What is *our* purpose? How can we serve? [My question, Father, WHY is it taking so long to get plugged into Your purpose here? I know You brought us here, *I feel like* one without a clear VISION, because what came earlier has grown dim by distractions of all the responsibilities of daily chores.

"Have you forgotten?
I AM more than enough.
My ways are not your ways!
Be at PEACE in the middle of the *storms of life*.
So the world will know you are MINE!
The 'answer' *IS* on its way – have your hands open to receive it.
The last month of challenges was day by day,
And *still I provided what was needed*. [yes!]
This is the walk of FAITH that pleases Me!
One day at a time – from our fellowship,
To see My Glory manifested.
You will SOON have your (ministry/calling) future revealed."

8:00 – 10:00 a.m. – Bob went HOME.

Made in the USA
Columbia, SC
11 February 2024